GREEK MYTHOLOGY

AN INTRODUCTION

D0111428

ALEXIS AQUINO PEREZ

THE JOHNS HOPKINS UNIVERSITY PRESS

Baltimore and London

GREEK AN INTRODUCTION
MYTHOLOGY

FRITZ GRAF

TRANSLATED BY THOMAS MARIER

This book has been brought to publication with the generous assistance of the David M. Robinson Fund

Originally published as *Griechische Mythologie.*
Copyright © 1987 by Artemis Verlag, München und Zürich

Johns Hopkins Paperbacks edition, 1996
9 8 7 6 5 4

The Johns Hopkins University Press
2715 North Charles Street
Baltimore, Maryland 21218-4363
www. press.jhu.edu

LIBRARY OF CONGRESS CATALOGING-IN-PUBLICATION DATA

Graf, Fritz.
   [Griechische Mythologie. English]
   Greek mythology : an introduction / Fritz Graf ; translated by Thomas Marier.
      p.   cm.
   Translation of: Griechische Mythologie. 1987.
   Includes bibliographical references and index.
   ISBN 0-8018-4657-9 (hc : alk. paper)
   ISBN 0-8018-5395-8 (pbk. : alk. paper)
      1. Mythology, Greek.   I. Title.
BL782.G6713   1933
292.1'3—dc20   93-10774

A catalog record for this book is available from the British Library.

CONTENTS

Translator's Note ix
Preface to the English-Language Edition xi
Introduction: A Provisional Definition 1

I. THE RISE OF THE SCIENTIFIC STUDY OF MYTH 9
    The Beginnings of Modern Mythology 9
    The Eighteenth-Century Forerunners of Heyne and
        Herder 13
    The Romantics 19
    The Science of Myth in the Nineteenth Century 22
    The New Romantics 31
    Mythology from Fontenelle to Frazer 32

II. NEW APPROACHES TO THE INTERPRETATION OF
   MYTH IN THE TWENTIETH CENTURY 35
    Myth and Psychoanalysis 36
    Myth and Society: From Myth-and-Ritual Theory to
        Functionalism 39
    The Structures of Myth and of Mythical Narrative 43
    The Myth-and-Ritual Theory Revised 50
    The Semiotic Approach 53

III. MYTH AND EPIC POETRY 57
  Myth and Homer 57
  The Origins of Greek Myth 68

IV. THE ORIGIN OF THE WORLD AND THE GODS 80
  Hesiod's *Theogony* 80
  The Eastern Background 86
  Theogony and Cosmogony after Hesiod 96

V. MYTH, SANCTUARY, AND FESTIVAL 101
  Delian Etiologies 102
  Understanding Mythical Etiology 110
  Myth, Sanctuary, and Festival 118

VI. MYTH AS HISTORY 121
  Myth and Historiography 121
  Genealogies 125
  Mythical Constructions of History 131
  Theseus and Athens 136
  Myth as History 140

VII. MYTH, CHORAL SONG, AND TRAGEDY 142
  Athenian Tragedy 142
  Tragedy and Choral Poetry 145
  The *Oresteia* 157
  Euripides, Myth, and the Gods 168

VIII. PHILOSOPHERS, ALLEGORISTS, AND
    MYTHOLOGISTS 176
  Myth after the Fifth Century B.C. 176
  Philosophical *Mythologia* and *Mythopoeia* 1: The
    Sophists 178
  Philosophical *Mythologia* and *Mythopoeia* 2: Plato 183
  Euhemerus 191
  Mythographers 193
  Allegorists 194

Abbreviations and Sources 199
    Abbreviations 199
    Literary Sources 200
    Visual Sources 200
Notes 203
Suggestions for Further Reading 223
Index 231

Illustrations follow p. 120.

TRANSLATOR'S NOTE

I wish to thank Christopher Bonanos, Wendy Closterman, George Davis, Barry Goldfarb, and Velvet Yates for their comments on the final draft of this translation. I also thank Jerrold Cooper, who kindly reviewed the section on Near Eastern influences, and Georg Luck, who offered valuable advice on problem spots. I am indebted to David Diamond, who greatly improved my rendition of the introduction and the theoretical chapters, and Nicholas Gal, who gave meticulous attention to two whole drafts. My greatest debts are to Adrianne Pierce for untold hours of assistance in the revision of early drafts and in the checking of references, and to my wife Susanne for sustaining, advising, and encouraging me from beginning to end. Finally, I am grateful to Brian MacDonald for his careful copy editing of the manuscript.

PREFACE TO THE ENGLISH-LANGUAGE EDITION

This book is a revision of the second German edition, *Griechische Mythologie: Eine Einführung* (Munich, 1987). I have corrected obvious mistakes and altered the text to reflect changes in my thinking on certain points. The German original lacked notes; these were added to the Italian translation (1987) and have been added to the present translation as well, with numerous omissions and augmentations, again to reflect progress in research in mythology since 1987. Exhaustive documentation was precluded not only by the vast quantity of current research but also by the scope of the book; however, I have included Suggestions for Further Reading, a section that I have also brought up to date.

With its publication in English, this book returns, as it were, to its place of origin, for it was the Society for the Humanities of Cornell University and its Fellows that made it possible for me to write the German version nearly a decade ago. With gratitude I here record my debt to the society. I also wish to thank Manfred Fuhrmann, who suggested that I write the book; Sir Hugh Lloyd-Jones, who read the manuscript before the publication of the first edition in 1985; Walter Burkert, who introduced me to the study of myth and whose work continues to be an immense source of inspiration. Finally, I wish to thank Eric Halpern and Thomas Marier for the dedication and scrupulousness with which they have helped bring this version into existence.

GREEK MYTHOLOGY

AN INTRODUCTION

INTRODUCTION

A PROVISIONAL DEFINITION

> *Poets have learned us their myths,*
> *but just how did they take them?*
> *That's a stumper.*
>
> W. H. Auden, *Archaeology*

Stories such as those of Orpheus, Oedipus, and Helen of Troy are generally recognized as myths—stories that belong to the cultural heritage of the West but that may have analogues in the mythical corpora of the Egyptians, Teutons, Indians, or Bushmen. That the term *myth* is of Greek origin is also generally known. It is easily forgotten, however, how deeply rooted in the Greek corpus our notion of myth is. Before the rise of ethnology, myth was studied mostly by classical scholars, and in particular by Hellenists.

It is still difficult to define myth satisfactorily, for all the intense scholarly attention that the problem of definition has received in the course of two and a half centuries. Many solutions have been proposed, only to be rejected. The most banal and least controversial of these may serve as a starting point: myths are traditional tales.[1] That a myth is a tale is indicated by the etymology of the word: for the early Greeks, a *mythos* was a "word" or "story," synonymous with *logos* and *epos*; a *mytho-*

logos was a "storyteller." Only when the traditional tales were called into question did the meaning of the word begin to be restricted. Herodotus, writing during the sophistic enlightenment, was the first to use the word in the sense of "implausible story" (2.23.1, 2.45.1). Thucydides distinguished his history, with its new claim to veracity, from "the fabulous" (*to mythōdes*), that is, mere storytelling (1.22.4). Plato set his new art of dialectic apart by using more sharply defined concepts, opposing *logoi*, propositions demonstrable with the aid of dialectic, to *mythoi*, which, for him, were often lies.[2] To Plato we may trace back the meaning that myth often has today: a thing widely believed but false (as the statement "love at first sight is a myth").

A myth is a peculiar kind of story. It does not coincide with a particular text or literary genre. For example, in all three major genres of Greek poetry the story of Agamemnon's murder and of Orestes' subsequent revenge is told: in epic (at the beginning of the *Odyssey*), in choral lyric (e.g., in Stesichorus's *Oresteia*), and in the works of all three tragedians. A myth is not a specific poetic text. It transcends the text: it is the subject matter, a plot fixed in broad outline and with characters no less fixed, which the individual poet is free to alter only within limits. Whereas a single variant, a single poetic work has an author, a myth does not. Myths are transmitted from one generation to another, without anyone knowing who created them: this is what is meant by *traditional*. (The same can be said of oral poetry in preliterate societies. The mythical variant in the oral poem, like the mythical variant in the written poem, has an identifiable author, and certain bards are more proficient or more popular than others. But this variant generally goes unrecorded; it vanishes along with the oral performance. An oral composition, it should be added, is no less "poetic" than a written one, for the language of oral poetry is no less artificial than that of the written poems that have come down to us from ancient Greece.) Those who record myths are fully aware of their traditional nature. Plato, for example, claims to have heard the tale of Atlantis, which he himself invented, from Critias, his uncle, who heard it from his grandfather, who heard it from his father, who heard it from Solon, who heard it in Egypt and intended to use it as subject matter for a poem. Thus, the origins of the tale are so far removed in time and space as to be irretrievable (*Timaeus* 20e–21e).

One obvious consequence of this definition is that a myth can be translated without loss from one language to another (Lévi-Strauss has taken this to indicate that it is the structure of the myth alone that matters). Every plot summary is in this respect translatable, unlike a work of literature, which can never be adequately translated. In works written for a Western readership the myths of preliterate peoples are usually paraphrased. Recently, however, scholars have begun to record directly present-day African mythical narratives, and they have shown that it is hardly possible to record them without loss, let alone to translate them into a Western language, because they are syntheses of musical, dramatic, and narrative art forms.

The reason for the continuous mutation of myth—the motor of the tradition, so to speak (that which ensures that it will continue to be handed down from one generation to the next)—is its cultural relevance. A myth makes a valid statement about the origins of the world, of society and of its institutions, about the gods and their relationship with mortals, in short, about everything on which human existence depends. If conditions change, a myth, if it is to survive, must change with them. Its capacity to adapt to changing circumstances is a measure of its vitality. In preliterate, oral cultures such adaptations are amply documented.[3] The myths of ancient Greece also exhibit this adaptability. The crisis of Greek myth came at the moment when the cultural relevance of its narration was called into question by the critical advocates of the new rationalism—the moment when the fluid tradition, in which myths were told over and over again and, with each retelling, were adapted to the conditions of the present, was being replaced increasingly by the poetic version composed once and for all time. The notion that myth was veridical, however, survived this crisis. Rhetoricians still defined a myth as a "fictitious story that illustrates the truth" (Theon, *Progymnasmata* 3),[4] and allegorists attempted, down to the end of antiquity and beyond, to find philosophical truths and truths about the physical universe beneath the surface of myth and in this way to uphold its cultural relevance. Even Plato, who resolutely excluded myths from the realm of truth, believed that, in the realm that could not be reached through dialectical reasoning, myths had at least some expressive power (see Chapter 8).

To be sure, the cultural relevance of a myth is quite different from the validity of a philosophical proposition. A proposition is considered valid by anyone who can either prove or disprove its veracity through the use of reason. The proof or disproof of a proposition is a logical operation; it is at all times and in all places possible for an individual to determine the validity of a philosophical proposition. A myth, by contrast, is considered valid only by the community in whose tradition it has taken shape—a community, it should be emphasized, that exists at a particular time and in a particular place. The cultural relevance of a myth varies with the social context in which it is narrated. Plato drew a distinction between "greater" and "lesser" myths. The lesser were told by mothers, grandmothers, and nurses, the greater by poets (*Republic* 377c). The difference between the two kinds lay above all in the occasion of the telling. Nurses and grandmothers told stories privately, whenever the opportunity presented itself, and were free to adapt them as they wished, whereas the truly relevant narration of myth, until the time of Euripides, was public and took place at times prescribed by the religious calendar: thus, only the "greater myths" were subject to group control. Originally, tragedies were performed only at the Dionysia, a city festival held in honor of Dionysus. Choral songs, too, were sung at festivals of the gods and victory celebrations. The Greek victory celebration was held not privately but by the clan (*genos*), tribe (*phylē*), or polis. Similarly, epic recitation usually took place, at least in post-Homeric times, on set occasions. The Homeric poems were recited in Athens at the Panathenaea. Hesiod performed at the obsequies of a Euboean aristocrat. Even lyric monody was composed for special occasions. Archilochus and Alcaeus composed for symposia, which bore the marks of a religious event. Sappho's poems were recited at the rites of a *thiasos* (religious society) of maidens.[5] Often the performance took the form of a contest, such as the tragic or rhapsodic competition. In public settings such as these, the discrete, poetic variant of the traditional myth was liable to the scrutiny of the collective. It was the judgment of the group that limited the flexibility of the mythical subject matter. Euripides, who deviated farthest from the tradition, also gained the fewest victories. The prose book of Hecataeus of Miletus (active ca. 500 B.C.) marks, so far as we can tell, the beginning of the practice of retelling myths so as to historicize and rationalize them, and thereby to purge them of all implausibilities. Hecataeus's book was not subject to the direct censorship of the polis or group. The philosophers and postclassical poets similarly removed themselves from public scrutiny.

To clarify: what is being suggested here is not a revival of the old thesis, which has had its advocates even in the twentieth century, that myth is poetry, "an aesthetic creation of the human imagination."[6] It is true that among the Greeks, as among other peoples, an oral or written representation of mythical subject matter may be called an aesthetic creation in deliberately stylized language and form, so far as the representation lays claim to general validity (i.e., purports to reflect the beliefs of the listening or reading public). But this thesis tells us nothing about the origins of myths (as opposed to mythical narratives). It is just possible that myths were passed along in nonpoetic forms—in prosaic, quotidian narratives not bound to set institutions, as were the tales told by Plato's nurses and grandmothers. But these tales were told for private entertainment and occasional instruction and never had the social impact or cultural reverberation of

the poetic narration of myth. Admittedly, we can scarcely imagine in what form the mythical narratives of the archaic period
were transmitted, except that they were, for the most part, oral.
Still, a stray piece of information about Arcadia, the most archaic
region in ancient Greece, offers a clue to the mystery. Polybius
reports that even in his day Arcadian children "were accus-
tomed, from an early age, to sing hymns and paeans in which
they celebrated their local gods and heroes in accordance with
ancestral custom" (4.20.8). Here the form in which the mythical
subject matter was passed on from one generation to the next
was a poetic one, and one that had institutional ties. For the
youths did not just learn the hymns; presumably they also sang
them within the context of the communal festivals of their gods
and heroes.

Scholars have often found it difficult to distinguish between
myth and other kinds of traditional tale: saga, legend, folktale,
and fable. It is not always necessary or even possible to draw
such distinctions. For speakers of German the term *saga* (*Sage*)
is more or less synonymous with myth (*Mythos*): the best
known collection of Greek myths is Gustav Schwab's *Die schöns-
ten Sagen des klassischen Altertums*, and the most influential
treatment of Germanic sagas is Jacob Grimm's *Germanische
Mythologie*. In Grimm's usage the two terms are sometimes
synonymous, though occasionally he seems to want to restrict
myth (*Mythus*, as he writes it) to antiquity. If distinctions are
drawn, they usually have to do with the cultural context in
which the tale was generated. Thus, local tales are called sagas
("Valaisan sagas," "Tyrolean sagas"), foreign ones myths. The
same is true of the term *legend* (*Legende*). In the broad sense,
legend is synonymous with myth; in the narrow sense, a legend
is a tale about a Christian saint. Once again, what is local and
Christian is opposed to what is foreign and heathen.

It is somewhat easier to distinguish myth from fairy tale or
folktale (*Märchen*). At first glance the categories seem to be so
elastic as to be interchangeable. Most of the volumes of the col-

lection *Märchen der Weltliteratur* contain stories that elsewhere are called myths; classical myths turn up later in postclassical folktales and are even told as folktales in their own right. One such myth is that of the wandering and homeless "Swellfoot" (Oedi-pus, a speaking name that is typical of such stories), who liberates a kingdom from a monster, the Sphinx, thereby winning for himself throne and queen. The plot is in perfect accord with the structural schema developed for the Russian folktale by Vladimir Propp.[7] When modern scholars speak of folktale motifs in myth, however, they are simply skirting the problem of definition. The difference lies in the cultural centrality of myth. The folktale carries no pretense to cultural relevance, and that is why it is set outside the bounds of space and time. "Once upon a time there was a princess who went into the forest . . .": thus begins the well-known collection by the Grimm brothers. Myth, by contrast, tells of a particular place (Thebes, in the myth of Oedipus) and, at least among the Greeks, of a particular time as well (two generations before the Trojan War). The folktale is not bound to a collective and is not performed; we may call Plato's "lesser myths" folktales, if we like, but since no such folktales have survived in written form, we cannot say with certainty whether they were what we would call folktales. Apuleius's tale of Cupid and Psyche (*Metamorphoses* 4.28–6.24), although it does conform to the folktale type of the "animal husband," is nevertheless markedly different from what is usually meant by "folktale." Cupid, Psyche, and Psyche's daughter Voluptas stand for the Platonizing ideas of Hellenistic philosophers (these figures personify love, the soul, and pleasure, respectively), and yet the tale, like many myths, has a divine apparatus.[8] In speaking of ancient and non-European cultures, it is perhaps better not to use the category folktale at all, and to regard it, in its peculiar form and social function, as a product of later European social and intellectual history.[9]

The animal fable is a special case. The Greeks had a special term for it: *ainos*. Aristotle, however, speaks of *Aisōpou mythoi*, the myths of Aesop; Philostratus (*Life of Apollonius of Tyana* 5.14) asked whether the Aesopic fable, with its simple moral lesson, was the best kind of myth or not.[10] A fable that does not offer such a lesson is difficult to distinguish from a myth. Ibycus (fr. 342 *PMG*) and Sophocles (*TrGF* vol. 4, F 362) told how Zeus once instructed a donkey to bring to mortals the herb of eternal youth as a reward for their assistance in his struggle with Prometheus. Along the way the donkey became thirsty and wished to drink from a spring, which was guarded by a snake. As payment for the water the snake demanded the load that the donkey was carrying. The donkey gave him the herb; hence mortals grow old, whereas snakes do not (they merely slough off their old skin). Although this tale, with a donkey and a snake as its main characters, looks like an animal fable, it has no simple moral. It does, however, explain a basic fact of human nature. It is not surprising, then, that the motif is found in a text as early as the *Epic of Gilgamesh*. After a long search, Gilgamesh finds the herb of immortality, but loses it to the snake on his return (*ANET* 96). What sets fables apart from myths is not their use of animals but their immediate aim, which is to convey a moral lesson. Accordingly, fables are much easier to invent, as Lessing, among others, demonstrated. In addition, fables were not performed publicly, on set occasions, as mythical narratives characteristically were. There was no such thing as a fabular competition, a contest for reciters of fables—which indicates that the fable was not classified as a kind of myth until the old myths had lost their social function and were being moralized by most ancient interpreters.

CHAPTER I

THE RISE OF THE SCIENTIFIC STUDY OF MYTH

The Beginnings of Modern Mythology

The modern concept of myth, along with the scholarly term *myth*, goes back to the German philologist Christian Gottlob Heyne (1729–1812), a pioneer in the scientific study of antiquity in all its facets.[1] Heyne laid the foundations for mythological research both in Germany and elsewhere. In his early years he worked with Johann Joachim Winckelmann in the library of Count Heinrich von Bruehl in Dresden; Winckelmann, with his newfound enthusiasm for antiquities, left a lasting impression on him. In 1763 he was appointed professor of Greek at Göttingen. His ideas shaped the educated German's conception of antiquity for nearly half a century, during which ancient Greece exerted an influence of unprecedented intensity on intellectual life in Germany. Myth was of primary interest to Heyne; indeed, it remained so throughout his life, from his first speech before the Göttingen Academy, in which he presented his views on the subject in programmatic terms,[2] to one of his last treatises, in which he summarized his interpretive method.[3]

Heyne approached myth as a philologist, an expositor of texts, just as he approached geography, astronomy, or ancient history. Ancient texts abound in allusions to myth, and some even take myth as their subject matter. Therefore, to understand these texts, Heyne supposed, one had to understand myth. That meant taking myth seriously. To set himself apart from those of his predecessors and contemporaries who had used the Latin *fabula* or French *fable*—terms that had always borne a hint of fiction and absurdity—Heyne coined the term *mythus*.

For Heyne, understanding myth meant ascertaining its origin. He believed that myth arose in prehistoric times, during the childhood of mankind. To gain some sense of this childhood, he turned to the "savages" of his day (he made use of ethnological material in lectures on the "ancients" delivered in 1779).[4] Heyne did not suppose that myth was a bizarre invention of primitive man; instead, he thought that it came into being naturally and inevitably at the moment when early man, overawed or frightened by some natural phenomenon, first sought to explain it, or when, moved by a feeling of gratitude toward some exceptional person, he wished to recount and extol that person's deeds. Thus, in Heyne's view, myth served primarily to explain natural phenomena and secondarily to memorialize events of the past. The first human beings, as Heyne imagined them, were by nature emotional and not given to reflection; their environment was inhospitable; most important, their language was so rudimentary and awkward that it could convey only the sensuous and the concrete. When myth arose, its form was naturally sensuous and concrete as well. Later, from the archaic period to the time of Pindar and Aeschylus, poets deliberately took over this form and cultivated a language derived from it, along with the mythical content.

Heyne was not reducing myth to a manner of expression, to a mode of knowledge; myth, he believed, was also bound to man's religious development. He did not, however, equate myth with religion. In fact, he regarded them as distinct. In his view, early man's response to his natural environment gave rise not only to myth but also to the worship of stones, trees, other inanimate things (as early as 1764, following the publication, in 1760, of

On the Worship of Fetish Gods by the Président de Brosses in Geneva, Heyne was calling this kind of worship *fetishism*), and ultimately of the stars. At the same time, his response to the achievements of great individuals gave rise not only to myth but also to the worship of heroes and gods. The development of myth was therefore parallel to, but distinct from, that of ritual. Myth and ritual had a common starting point in the concept of the divine, *theos*; otherwise they developed independently. Heyne emphasized that ritual, and not myth, was essential to religion. According to him, the mythical explanation of rites— etiology in its earliest form—did not arise until later.

If myth reflected man's natural environment, if his inhospitable environment exerted a formative influence on the mythopoeic mind, then myths must have varied according to the environment in which they were produced. Heyne stressed the "national" character of the various groups of myths. Similarly, the historical experiences of different peoples, being themselves diverse, are reflected in their myths in diverse ways. Greek myth, moreover, has not come down to us in its primitive form, but as a complex historical conglomerate of old, invented, and imported elements. Over the centuries, as Greek culture developed, this conglomerate underwent many changes. The poets, especially the tragedians, were responsible for some of these changes. The mythologist who bases his interpretation on the oldest form of a myth has to work his way back through numerous distortions and conflations: his is a laborious task that can only be accomplished with the aid of philological and historical criticism.

Heyne shared his realization that myth was tied to region and "nation" with Johann Gottfried Herder (1744–1803).[5] The two men were close friends and exchanged views freely. Although it is not always easy to determine whether a particular view was first expressed by Heyne or by the far less systematic Herder, the outlines of Heyne's concept of myth were fixed by 1763, before Herder began to publish. Herder was fond of the idea that myths are bound to particular peoples. In a journal he kept during a trip in 1769, which was not published until after his death,[6] he went so far as to assert that one has to be aboard a ship to appreciate fully Homer's *Odyssey*. Herder found analogues to the mythopoeic mind of early times in the "savages" of his day and in the "primitives" who sailed with him on his voyage; the latter were sailors, coarse and still untouched by civilization. One thing that sets him apart from the philologist Heyne is what one might call the "sympathetic" quality of his approach to interpretation—a quality that emerges from his journal entry on the *Odyssey*; another is his view of the relationship between myth and language. Whereas Heyne supposed that poetry arose after myth (for he thought that poetry was derived from the verbal forms of, and conveyed the contents of, myth), Herder collapsed myth, language, poetry, and religion into a unity. What impelled early man to utter his first words, Herder believed, was his need to express a religious feeling. The form of this original speech was poetic, while its content was mythical. Myth was not, as Heyne thought, the result of an effort on the part of early man to explain an environment that inspired fear or wonder but an autonomous response of the human mind to the stimuli of its environment: it was not allegory but symbol.

Herder, like Heyne, owed much to the English theologian Robert Lowth (1710–87), who, in his Oxford lectures, which were published at Göttingen in 1753, had analyzed the Old Testament as a work of literature, employing the same literary-historical criteria that one might use to analyze a poem from pagan antiquity.[7] Whereas Heyne, as a philologist, regarded the Old Testament as having developed from old myths, Herder, as a theologian, regarded it as coeval with mankind, as having been revealed to man from the start. Moreover, the discovery of the Norse *Edda* (1753) and the publication of the poems of the Gaelic bard Ossian (1760–63; these were in fact written by James Macpherson, who falsely claimed to have translated them from old manuscripts) made a deep impression on Herder, as it did on many of his contemporaries. In these poems, it was thought, were powerful and primeval myths expressed in a poetic form—myths, furthermore, that arose somewhere else than in the ancient Mediterranean region: they offered evidence not only of the original unity of myth and poetry but also of the local and national character of myth.

The Eighteenth-Century Forerunners of Heyne and Herder

Modern reflection on myth did not begin with Heyne and Herder. Until the end of the seventeenth century, the prevailing approach to myth had been to interpret it allegorically: myths, it was thought, contained veiled truths about the moral and natural worlds. In the eighteenth century, myth was dismissed as irrational, and that ruled out the possibility of allegorical interpretation.

The dismissal of myth was an incidental consequence of the exploratory voyages of the preceding century. Among the "savages" of America and Africa, the explorers encountered customs and tales resembling those of antiquity, and the travel writers and missionaries of the sixteenth and seventeenth centuries habitually turned to the ancient authors for analogues to these recently discovered oddities. In time, scholars were bound to recognize the value of doing just the opposite—of using data gained from the observation of present-day "savages" to explain ancient data. Consequently, the ancient authors were discredited.

The process was accelerated by the celebrated "quarrel of the ancients and moderns." For the moderns, who wanted to impugn ancient authority, the comparisons of ancient tales to those of "savages" came at a most opportune moment. Moreover, the intellectual climate of the Enlightenment was averse to allegorical interpretation, indeed, to any interpretation that bore so much as a hint of allegoresis. Finally, the notion that Greek myth was a collection of bizarre fabrications could also be used by the rationalists as a weapon in their general attack on religion. The recognition that myth was shared with primitive cultures highlighted the absurdity of religion. Pierre Bayle (1647–1706) was one such detractor of myth; in his *Historical and Critical Dictionary* (1697), a fundamental text of the Enlightenment, he amused himself and his readers by portraying myths as absurdities.[8]

With the allegorical interpretation of myth discredited and the myths of antiquity dismissed as aberrations from reason, the scholarly study of myth had reached an impasse. A new and, as it turned out, fruitful orientation was offered in a treatise that can be called, without exaggeration, the cornerstone of modern mythology: *On the Origin of Fables* by Bernard de Fontenelle (1657–1757), Corneille's nephew. Published in 1724, it was written much earlier, perhaps as early as 1690.[9] Fontenelle affirmed the rationalist view of myth as absurdity; indeed, what gave impetus to his reflections was the apparently absurd nature of Greek myths, or, as he called them, *fables*—a word that corresponds to the Greek *mythos* and the Latin *fabula*: they were "nothing but a collection of chimeras, dreams, and absurdities." However, unlike Pierre Bayle and others among his contemporaries, who dismissed these myths as absurd, and unlike the philosophers of antiquity, who interpreted them allegorically, claiming to discover truths hidden beneath what they regarded as a morally offensive literality (see Chapter 8), Fontenelle explained myth historically, by recovering its origins in prehistoric times. Myth, he proposed, was the invention of the first human beings, and it reflected their peculiar mental constitution. Andrew Lang and Lucien Lévi-Bruhl would hold the same view some two hundred years later.[10] Like them, Fontenelle reconstructed a "primitive mentality" on the basis of a study of contemporary "savages." Incredibly "ignorant and primitive," like the "Kaffirs, Laplanders, and Iroquois," early man faced an unfamiliar natural world and tried to explain it in the only way he could: empirically. Since his experience was limited, so was his explanation. At the source of a river early man imagined some- one drawing water incessantly and in superhuman quantities— in this way, according to Fontenelle, the river god was invented. An innate passion for storytelling and a tendency to exagger- ate—qualities that can be observed among "savages"—were determinants in the generation of the fantastic tale.

Fontenelle's interpretive model is still being employed today. To explain myth, Fontenelle supposed, one must recover its ori- gin, and to recover the origin of myth one must reconstruct the mentality of prehistoric man. Fontenelle's reconstruction was remarkably sophisticated—much more so than many similar at- tempts in later times. He conceded that the "savages" of his day did not represent early man precisely, that even they had a past, and that they were far less "primitive" than early man. Despite these concessions, Fontenelle believed that the mentality of early man was not fundamentally or qualitatively different from that of modern man. Early man explained the world empirically, much as we do. What sets us apart is that we have at our disposal a considerably larger store of experience from which to draw in analogical argumentation. Had the "savage" been able to avail himself of such a head start, he would have come just as far as we have.

The year in which Fontenelle's treatise finally appeared, 1724, saw the publication of another work that was to be significant for the history of mythology. François Joseph Lafitau (1670–1740), a Jesuit missionary active among the Indians of North America, gave his book the expressive title *The Customs of the American Savages Compared to the Customs of the Earliest Times.*[11] He based his model for this "early era" on the Canadian Iroquois. The erudite father compared Iroquois institutions and myths with an unprecedented number of institutions, customs, and myths from the ancient Mediterranean region. He discerned many similarities, which he traced back to a common point of origin: Indians and Europeans were the descendants of the sons of Noah. Neither this conclusion nor the comparative method were original with Lafitau—scholars had been tracing one people or another back to the sons of Noah ever since they first sought to explain parallels between the Old and New Worlds. Rather, what was significant about Lafitau's book was the sheer mass of data collected in it. Its abundance of information made it what Frazer's *The Golden Bough* was to the twentieth century—to the layman, an accessible and spectacular presentation of a new method and its results, and to the specialist, a rich source of information.

Neither Lafitau nor Fontenelle dealt explicitly with the interpretation of individual myths. That was the domain of a large number of scholars who agreed on only one thing: that myth was to be reduced to an extrinsic thing. Allegoresis rapidly gave way to euhemerism: myths were traced back to historical events. The term *euhemerism* refers to the theory of Euhemerus of Messene, who, at the beginning of the Hellenistic age, argued that the gods of Greek myth were deified human beings, rulers from early Greek history.[12]

While most scholars were following the euhemerist trend, others were striking out in new directions, developing the arguments that would eventually be employed by Heyne and Herder. Perhaps the most important innovators were Fréret in France, Vico in Italy, and Hume in England. Of these, the significance of Nicolas Fréret (1688–1749) is the most difficult to assess. As a member of the Académie des Inscriptions et Belles-Lettres from 1714, and its permanent secretary from 1742, Fréret became influential through lectures given at the Académie and personal contacts: he should occupy a more prominent place in the history of mythology than can be proved from the available evidence. Fréret stood on the shoulders of Fontenelle, but he concerned himself primarily with the interpretation of individual myths. He was able to reduce only a small portion of the myths that he studied to reflections of history; the rest, which he called a "confused collection of marvels and absurdities," included not only ethical and physical explanations of the world but also sheer figments of the imagination. Fréret attributed the bizarre form of these myths to the *génie national des Grecs* (this recalls Herder's notion of the "national" character of myth; Herder was in Paris in 1769, after Fréret's death), and this bizarre form often made it impossible to interpret individual myths with certainty. The imagination was, for Fréret, one of the sources of myth; later scholars would turn it into a formative principle. Even when he was dealing with myths that originated in history, Fréret parted company with the euhemerists of his day. He did not think that such myths reflected specific events but processes in the history of culture and of religion: Hesiod's three divine generations—the first under Uranus and Gaea, the second under Cronus and Rhea, the third under Zeus—reflected three theological systems among the early Greeks, and the tale, which is at least as old as Homer, of the Thracian king Lycurgus's persecution of the young Dionysus and his maenads reflected the resistance of the inhabitants of northern Greece to the introduction of the cult of Dionysus. Nothing shows more clearly how far ahead of his time, and yet forgotten, Fréret was than the fact that, well over a century after his death, his views were virtually restated by Erwin Rohde, and are still found in present-day handbooks—under the name of Rohde, not Fréret.[13]

The influence of Hume and Vico was more widely felt than Fréret's. In 1725 the Neapolitan Giambattista Vico (1668–1744) published the first edition of his *New Science*, in which he set forth the principles of a general science of human society; two revisions followed in 1730 and 1744.[14] In Vico's view, myth was early man's first utterance after his rebellion against revealed religion. It arose not as a protoscientific explanation of nature but as a result of man's awakening in fear of the divine. The divine, according to Vico, was man's projection of his own primal and intense passions onto the real substances that surrounded him: myth therefore arose "from man's fear of himself." In the beginning, myth took the form of a mute (i.e., prelinguistic) pointing to the "divine substances" (Vico supposed that the Greek *mythos* was cognate with the Latin *mutus* and, in the manner of later nature mythologists, that the gods stood for the real things of man's physical environment). When myth was expressed in language, it at once took the form of poetry, for early man was by nature sensual and imaginative. Vico based his theory on his observation of contemporary "savages," whom he found not in distant lands but in his own country, as Herder was to do later: for Vico, the peasants of Cilento represented primitive man.

For David Hume (1711–76), as for Vico, myth was only one among many interests in a broad philosophical program. In *The Natural History of Religion* (1757) Hume argued that myth was the beginning of religion, and that it bore traces of the psychic forces that made that mythical beginning, for all its absurdity, possible. Like religion, myth arose as man's fearful reaction to his surroundings; frightened by some unfamiliar object, he transformed it into a powerful being, a deity. From the worship of natural objects it was but a short step to the deification of prominent men. Hume's view of myth is significant chiefly because it was endorsed by Heyne and because Hume studied myth not for its own sake but as a way of learning about the human mind.

Fontenelle, Fréret, Vico, and Hume were among those who prepared the way for Heyne and Herder. Many of the ideas of Heyne and Herder were anticipated by their predecessors—not just the view that myth originated in prehistoric times, when man was still like a "savage" or, as is now often said, thought like a child. What made the contributions of Heyne and Herder new was, above all, the seriousness and the sympathy that characterized their attitudes toward myth. No longer was myth a bizarre and absurd product of the savage mind. Heyne viewed myth with detached interest, whereas Herder approached it sympathetically, attempting to feel his way into it. Succeeding generations of scholars, well into the twentieth century, took no attitude fundamentally different from Heyne's observational or Herder's tactile one.

The Romantics

Herder, perhaps inspired by Vico, understood the first linguistic expression of myth as primitive poetry. This notion was further developed by Karl Philipp Moritz (1756–93) in *A Treatise on the Gods or The Mythical Poetry of the Ancients* (1791).[15] Deeply influenced by Goethe, Moritz held that myth is "of the nature of poetry and art"; it was not a culturally irrelevant aesthetic creation but the human imagination's compelling answer to "the power that produces the world." In Moritz's work there is no mention of fear and astonishment, which gave rise to myth in Heyne's theory. Moritz also progressed beyond Herder, who had taught that early man possessed a sense of the divine in addition to his sense of fear; fear, Herder had argued, was merely the impulse that prompted the psyche of early man to explain his surroundings. Moritz's supposition that myth arose as an explanation not of natural phenomena but of the forces that produce them ruled out allegoresis. For allegorical interpretation in effect destroys the aesthetic images that are the essence of myth and "in so doing injures the delicate tissue of the imagination, so that the interpreter is left with nothing but contradictions and inconsistencies." The interpreter of myth, not myth itself, is to blame for these aberrations. This approach survived in *A Treatise on the Greek Gods* by Friedrich Gottlieb Welcker (1784–1868), a friend of Wilhelm von Humboldt (Welcker's book was not published until 1857–63). Welcker, who, as Otto Gruppe wrote, "breathed new life into the religious thought of the Greeks, for which he had a keen sense," was later echoed approvingly by none other than Ulrich von Wilamowitz-Moellendorff, the greatest of all classical philologists.[16]

Lévi-Strauss has pointed out that only two modes of explanation are available to the scientist: reductionism and structuralism. With Moritz, however, the study of myth produced a third approach (though hardly a mode of explanation in the strict sense). Moritz dispensed with analysis altogether in favor of a purely aesthetic view of myth. Thus, myth was emancipated from religion in its historical dimension and was seen in relation to a diffuse, general religious *feeling*: Moritz was only a short step from the romantics. Herder, disagreeing with Lessing, had also insisted that ancient myth be included in the poetry of his day—not as subject matter but as a hermeneutic instrument with which the mythical vision of the world could be learned by the poet. The romantics at Heidelberg, the circle of the Schlegel brothers, shared Herder's view. What the new poets wanted was not just to teach myth but, above all, to create a new kind of myth, a synthesis of myth, religion, and art—notwithstanding Herder's assertion that myth is always a collective creation. Besides the myths of Greece, those of India served increasingly as sources of inspiration for this new kind of myth.[17]

Among non-Mediterranean myths, the myths of India were second in their influence on European thought only to those of northern Europe, which were known from the *Edda* and the Ossianic poems. Translations of Iranian and Indian texts had been available to westerners for some time: the *Zend-Avesta* appeared in 1771, the *Bhagavadgita* in 1785, the *Hitopadesa* in 1788, the *Sakuntala* in 1789, the *Upanishads* in 1801. The romantics mastered these texts, which seemed to be of great antiquity and replete with wisdom. In them they believed to have found a body of myths that far surpassed that of the Greeks: even the Greeks were affected by the romantic break with tradition. Although the romantics were not concerned with chronology and history, they were concerned with language. As early as 1802 Friedrich Schlegel was studying Sanskrit.

On the heels of the romantics came the theoreticians, first J. J. Goerres (1776–1848), posthumously infamous as the father of German nationalism, and then his friend and sometime colleague in Heidelberg, Friedrich Creuzer (1771–1858), who, owing to his four-volume work, *The Symbolism and Mythology of Ancient Peoples, Especially of the Greeks* (1810–12), occupies an equally ignominious place in the *chronique scandaleuse* of German scholarship than Goerres, from whom he drew his inspiration.[18] When it first appeared, Creuzer's work was warmly received by some, bitterly and maliciously attacked by others. It was soon shown to be untenable in its construction of history and unscientific in its method of interpretation. Creuzer proceeded from the assumption that Indian myth and religion were historically prior to Greek myth and religion. He believed that the primitive ancestors of the Greeks were taught by Indian priests ("missionaries came to the Greenlanders," as Karl Otfried Müller later put it). Being otherwise unable to communicate with these proto-Greeks, the priests used symbols; misunderstood symbols turned into myths. To interpret these myths, Creuzer supposed, one had to be naturally gifted: Creuzer had no clear and scrutable interpretive method.

Creuzer was out of step with the times in which he lived. But he did recognize a difficulty in contemporary scholarship: while scholars were moving away from the interpretation of myth as mere allegory, they still assumed that the ultimate cause of myth lay in some natural phenomenon or historical event; mythologists, in other words, were still perilously close to allegoresis and euhemerism. Creuzer proposed a radical solution to this problem: he replaced nature with the artificial symbols of Indian missionaries. (Later mythologists would look for such symbols in the depths of the human psyche.) Moreover, Creuzer's symbolism involved the rejection of an important new approach. Heyne and Herder had argued that myth and language were closely connected; they attributed the specific form of myth to the limitations of primitive language. Creuzer, like Friedrich Schlegel and others, understood myth as a language in its own right, a form of symbolic expression. Accordingly, he set himself the task of elaborating a "grammar" of myth analogous to the grammar of a language. As it turned out, he was frustrated in his attempt to elaborate the etymology of myth, for he did so without first elaborating its phonology. Thus, his grammar was doomed from the start.

In 1819, when the second edition of his book appeared, Creuzer's symbolist theory had already gone out of fashion. The reaction against "Indiamania" had begun. Disabused of the notion that the study of Sanskrit would help him to create a "new myth," Friedrich Schlegel now undertook to put the study of Indian myth on a more sound philological and historical basis. His book, *On the Language and Wisdom of the Indians*, which appeared in 1808, marked his personal departure from romanticism. In it he laid the foundations for a new field—Indo-European studies—from which would issue such divergent interpretations of myth as those of Max Müller in the nineteenth century and Georges Dumézil in the twentieth.[19]

The Science of Myth in the Nineteenth Century

Perhaps the greatest mythologist of the nineteenth century was the classicist Karl Otfried Müller (1797–1840). Müller's influence, which is comparable with that of Heyne, whose chair at Göttingen he occupied from 1819, may be attributed especially to his *Prolegomena to a Scientific Mythology* (1825). While the title of his work suggested a comprehensive treatment, Müller dealt almost exclusively with Greek myth, which, largely as a result of his book, came to be regarded as myth par excellence and would continue to be so regarded for the rest of the century.[20]

Müller cultivated the fertile ground tilled by eighteenth-century scholars. Like his predecessors, he believed that myth was an inevitable form of expression belonging to an earlier, childlike phase of human development. But he did not disparage this childlike phase; he believed, like Herder, that every age had its own value, its own dignity and, like Heyne, that myth and poetry arose not at once but at different times. As a philologist he saw that Homer, the first poet whose work we possess, worked within a long tradition of mythmaking. Myths can be interpreted (hence he speaks of a "science" of myth), and interpretation still meant discovering what gave rise to myth, its cause. This cause lay, Müller thought, partly in the "ideal," in the human imagination, partly in the "real," in man's physical and historical environment, which remains visible through the veil of the mythopoeic imagination. Thus, Müller arrived at a fresh and sophisticated view of the relationship between myth and history.

Like the euhemerists, Müller held that the cause of myth was sometimes to be sought in history, and he stressed that every historical period gave rise to its own brand of myth. The myths of Homer's quasi-feudal society were manifestly different from those of the simple farmers of prehistory, whose chief concerns were the fertility of their crops and the cycle of the seasons. For example, Müller believed that the myths of Demeter, the "Earth Mother," and her daughter Kore, the goddess of nature in both its flowering and its withering, were produced by the latter, prehistoric group, and that those myths which deal with the Olympian gods under Zeus were produced by Homeric society. In drawing attention to historical factors in the production of myth, Müller was preparing the ground for later historicist theories. At the same time, he began to investigate geographical and political factors. German particularism and the German desire for unification may have heightened Müller's awareness of these conditions. Herder had already sought connections between myths and the local history of particular peoples, while Heyne had called for the study of Greek myths that referred to particular places. Müller added that not just peoples but also places had their own bodies of myths, and that the process whereby Greek myths were dispersed and ultimately systematized was an incidental result of the process whereby Greece was unified politically, first in the clan, then in the tribe, and finally in the nation. Just as the myths of prehistoric farmers were preserved, though perhaps becoming, as Müller wrote, "quite distorted and obscure" in the process of transmission, so were those of prehistoric territorial groups. Thus, the interpretation of myth afforded insight into the early history of mankind, as Müller himself demonstrated repeatedly in his *History of Hellenic Tribes and Cities.*[21] The method employed by Fritz Schachermeyr in *Die griechische Rückerinnerung,* which appeared in 1983, is fundamentally no different from that of Müller.

Müller elaborated the legacy of the Enlightenment and of romanticism into a synthesis that would give nineteenth-century scholarship its historical and scientific orientation. But this achievement was not without its shortcomings, the gravest of which was a neglect of the relationship between myth and language. Müller regarded these as distinct. He wrote that "religion," with which myth is linked, "is second only to the creation of language among man's intellectual achievements."[22] The notion that the form of myth is determined by the form of language is absent in his thought. He was willing to concede only that misunderstandings of language could give rise to myths, as in the case of the myth of Pelops, which he explained as a fabrication resulting from a misunderstanding of the laudatory epithet "ivory-shouldered" applied to the historical Pelops (see Chapter 7).[23]

Among those who transmitted Herder's ideas to Karl Otfried Müller, perhaps the most important was Jacob Grimm (1785–1863), the founder, along with his brother Wilhelm, of Germanic philology and ethnology and, late in his life, Müller's housemate in Göttingen. The Grimm brothers examined Germanic myths in an effort to corroborate Herder's thesis, according to which myth bore the marks of the locality in which it was produced and of the people that produced it. They found support for this thesis less in Nordic myths than in German folktales and folk songs, which they regarded as reflections of an ancient mythology. Thus, the stories of Germany acquired a value not inferior to that of Greek myths. Common features of folk compositions (or, at least, the origins of such features) were not explained as resulting from the influence of one tale or song on another; instead, they were traced back to a protomythology, which they related to known bodies of myth much as they related the Indo-European protolanguage to known languages.

The next generation of scholars continued in this direction. The most compelling arguments for an Indo-European protomythology existing before the Indo-Europeans split into separate tribes and language groups were put forth by Adalbert Kuhn (1812–81) in Berlin and Friedrich Max Müller (1823–1900) in Oxford. Kuhn's *The Origin of Fire* and Müller's *Comparative Mythology* appeared at about the same time (in 1859 and 1856, respectively). These men found the key to Indo-European mythology in the *Rigveda*, the publication of which had begun in 1838: there, they believed, myths were captured virtually in the making. They regarded some myths as patent allegories of nature; and relying on the findings of comparative philology, in particular the derivation of the name of the supreme deity—Dyaus, Zeus, Jupiter—from a root meaning "celestial light," they sought the explanation of all myths in a phenomenon of nature: for Kuhn, that phenomenon was the thunderstorm, whereas for the more sensitive Müller it was the dawn (Müller was the son of the author of *Die schöne Müllerin* and himself the author of a tender love story).[24]

With Kuhn and F. M. Müller, mythological research reverted to natural allegoresis (as we have seen, it was just this quest for hidden meaning from which Heyne and Herder had struggled to liberate the study of myth). To explain how so many different myths could result from the impression of dawn on the early Indo-Europeans, Müller fell back on the notion that the mind of early man was of a peculiar nature and on the notion that the early Indo-Europeans were incapable of abstraction and thus developed a language that was sensuous and concrete; for instance, they described the rising of the sun as its birth, its setting as its death. Myth, in his view, was the result of a "disease of language." Nouns were originally predicates or attributes of natural phenomena (the expression *maiden dawn,* for example, denoted the early dawn). But since many nouns were used to describe the same phenomenon, and since each noun bore many meanings (the noun *maiden* denoted a young female person, the dawn, and many other things), misunderstandings were inevitable. These misunderstandings gave rise to myths. Etymologies showed that the individual myths of a people originated in the era of Indo-European mythopoesis and revealed the paths of their transmission.

These etymologies soon proved far too contrived. Nature mythology made myths into "spirited chatter about the weather," as Lewis Richard Farnell derisively remarked. Meanwhile, German folklorists and British comparative anthropologists were approaching myth from new perspectives.

The German scholar Johann Wilhelm Emanuel Mannhardt (1831–80), a student of Jacob Grimm, was, in the early years of his career, an adherent of the comparative mythology of Adalbert Kuhn and Max Müller. But when most of the comparatists' etymologies proved dubious and consequently the distribution of myths was seen as a problem, Mannhardt turned to the popular tradition, in which he saw the soil, as it were, in which each of the various national mythologies had taken root. Like Herder and Vico, Mannhardt saw the source of mythology, the mythopoeic mentality, not in "savages" but in ordinary people. The collection of folkloristic data soon induced him to devote just as much attention to customs and rites as to legends and folktales. Mannhardt was the first to explain Greek rituals on the basis of the rural customs of northern Europe (*Ancient Forest and Field Cults,* 1877). His book led scholars to recognize the explanatory value of agriculture in the area of Greek religion; and in it he linked the study of myths with that of rites. To be sure, neither of these ideas was fundamentally new—K. O. Müller had placed agriculture at the beginning of humanity and thus attached primary importance to it; Heyne had emphasized the significance of rituals for religion. But only now were these ideas beginning to have consequences.

One of Mannhardt's contemporaries, Hermann Usener (1834–1905), the founder of the scientific study of religion in Germany, independently recognized the importance of folklore and peasant customs. Usener thought that myths and rituals reflected the cycle of the seasons, the guide that the farmer followed in carrying out his various agricultural tasks. His emphasis on light and sun, to which Usener reduced many myths, shows the enduring influence of the nature mythologists.[25]

In England, meanwhile, the ethnological approach to myth had been revitalized. The Englishman, after all, stood at the center of a colonial empire, and English officials, officers, and missionaries were sending home detailed reports of what they had seen in distant lands. Like the explorers of the seventeeth and eighteenth centuries, English scholars realized that there were similarities between the myths of primitive peoples and those of "advanced" civilizations, and, again like their predecessors, they fell back on the notion that these similarities were survivals from an earlier phase of cultural development. But the ethnologists had a new heuristic instrument at their disposal. The theory of evolution, which had proved so fruitful in the areas of geology, archaeology, and biology, was now applied in the area of mythology. The mythical "survival" assumed a role analogous to that of the fossil in geology and biology. Edward Burnett Tylor (1832–1917) gave the theory its most lasting form in *Primitive Culture* (1871). But its most prominent and influential exponent was James George Frazer (1854–1941), a classical philologist at Cambridge.[26]

While others were content to detect, in an ill-defined evolutionism, traces of what they considered to be thought at its most primitive level—Andrew Lang (1844–1912), for example, whose work was widely read in his day, found evidence of this primitive thought in totemism—Frazer constructed a general evolutionary model, according to which man's understanding of his natural surroundings has developed in three stages. For Frazer, myth was significant primarily because it afforded a glimpse into an early stage of human thought, as Hume had argued, and as Ernst

Cassirer was still arguing in this century (*The Philosophy of Symbolic Forms*, 1923–29).[27] In the first stage, man attributed natural phenomena to the power of magic; in the second, he attributed them to the will of gods; in the third, he began to view nature as an object of study. In other words, man has ascended from an age of magic to one of religion and, finally, to one of science. Frazer was interested mainly in the age of magic, when, he suggested, man's explanation of nature depended on a misunderstanding of causality. In the age of magic, man believed that he could ensure his survival and prosperity by using magic to control the personified forces of nature (in the age of religion, he submitted without resistance to the transcendent gods). As a farmer, early man was concerned mainly with the fecundity of his crops and animals, and therefore his rites and myths also dealt with fecundity. As "survivals" these rites and myths persisted into the age of religion and persist even today, in the age of science. Frazer acknowledged his dependence on Mannhardt. In the preface to the first edition of *The Golden Bough*, his main work, he wrote: "without [the works of Mannhardt] . . . my book could scarcely have been written."

Frazer never presented his theories in a systematic way. His aim was to persuade his readers not by a concise presentation of his theories but by the sheer mass of data gleaned from virtually every culture known to him (*The Golden Bough* grew from two volumes in the first edition [1890] to twelve in the third and final edition [1912–15]). And persuade them he did: Frazer was generally accepted as an authority by his anglophone readership. His influence was wide; in fact, *The Golden Bough* was read nearly as much by students of literature and art as it was by ethnologists.

Students of social anthropology eventually found fault with much of what the master said; among classical scholars, however, Frazer's influence endured, in part because of the impact of his work on the students of Usener in Germany and their followers, who believed that his views were convergent with their own. To

Albrecht Dieterich (1866–1908), Usener's son-in-law and follower, and especially Martin Peer Nilsson (1874–1967), it was obvious that the myths and rituals of the Greeks were anchored in the thought of farmers. Nilsson's magisterial *A History of Greek Religion* (1940; third edition, 1965) disseminated and canonized this theory. Andrew Lang found the fertility theory ridiculous; he referred to its exponents collectively as the "Covent Garden School of Mythology" (after London's largest vegetable market). Today the most widely known formulation of the theory remains that of Nilsson.

In retrospect, the lines dividing social anthropology and nature mythology do not appear to have been nearly as sharp as Mannhardt and Frazer supposed. Both groups assumed that myth was a product of the human mind, and both reduced myth to a statement about nature. But whereas the nature mythologists sought to reduce myth to a particular natural phenomenon, Frazer's school saw nature in its relation to man *qua* farmer, whose main concern was the fertility of his crops. Not surprisingly, the European city dweller, who had begun, in the wake of the urbanization that followed the industrial revolution, to idealize his rural beginnings, found Frazer's view, with its emphasis on the simple life of the farmer, very attractive. But from a scholarly standpoint Frazer's theory carries no conviction, if only because farming is a relatively recent innovation in the chronology of human evolution, coming about, as it did, in the eighth and seventh millennia B.C. in the Near East and much later in Central America. In fact, *Homo sapiens* and his predecessors had been roaming the earth, hunting and gathering to sustain themselves, long before the advent of agriculture. Recently, Karl Meuli and Walter Burkert have suggested that vestiges of preagricultural life can be found in myth and ritual; indeed, they place the decisive formative phase of both myth and ritual in the age of prehistoric hunters.

Thus, the two prevailing theories of myth in the nineteenth century were the fertility theory of Mannhardt and Frazer and the theory, less expressly ascribed to Karl Otfried Müller, according to which the basis of myth is to be found in history. These theories persist in the twentieth century and to this day are not without their exponents. Each is a species of reductionism: each explains myth by referring to an extrinsic thing, something to which the mythical narrative can be reduced once it has been stripped of its fantastic trappings. The tale as such is not taken seriously. The reduction of myth to history was especially popular among classicists. In embracing historical reductionism they were reacting against the highly speculative theories of the nature mythologists, the Cambridge school as represented by Frazer and especially Jane Harrison, and the comparative method employed by that school: historical reductionism did not require them to look beyond their own clearly demarcated area of study. With historical reductionism, moreover, they could be certain of having ancient opinion on their side, at least from the time of Hecataeus of Miletus, who interpreted myth in a rationalistic manner (see Chapter 6). The discoveries of Heinrich Schliemann, who, taking the *Iliad* as his guide, unearthed Troy, Mycenae, and Tiryns, lent credence to the historicist argument that mythical narrative can report historical fact (see Chapter 3).

Yet there is little to recommend this kind of reductionism. The historical reductionist usually explains away essential features of the myth—the elements of its plot and the details of its narrative—as if these features were a mere nuisance; moreover, the procedure whereby myth is traced back to historical reality is highly arbitrary, as a recent interpretation of the tale of the Trojan horse shows. The myth of the wooden horse, the stratagem that ultimately enabled the Greeks to conquer Troy, is regarded as the result of a transformation of a historical event, the capture of Troy by the Greeks after the walls of the city were toppled by an earthquake: the horse, the argument runs, was sacred to Poseidon, the god of earthquakes. It is true that horses and earthquakes fell within the province of Poseidon, but they did not do so exclusively. The horse was also sacred to Athena, and Poseidon was responsible for more than just earthquakes. Moreover, the interpreter never asks why the tale was told in such fantastic terms. Apparently he still believes, with Fontenelle, that myth was the product of a primitive imagination predisposed to exaggeration.[28] Even myths that reflect historically real events, such as the tale of the return of the Heraclids, which purports to explain the ethnic and political transformation of the Peloponnesus from the Mycenaean to the archaic periods (see Chapter 6), can be compared only generally, if at all, with historical reality as reconstructed on the basis of archaeological and linguistic evidence.

The New Romantics

The nineteenth century produced a third approach to myth, which, by contrast with the fertility and historicizing theories, was not a kind of reductionism, and was never in the mainstream of scholarly opinion. This approach was rooted in the romantic movement. In 1856, just before the field of mythology began to be inundated with interpretations of myths as reflections of natural phenomena, there appeared in Berlin the *Introduction to the Philosophy of Mythology* of Friedrich W. J. Schelling (1775–1854), a book that was somewhat lost in the intellectual landscape of the day.[29] Schelling spent much of his life dealing with myth; his earliest works, written while he was at Tübingen (1792–93), show the influence of Heyne and Herder; later, he joined the circle of romantics at Heidelberg. With those poets Schelling shared the belief that myth is both the earliest form of man's artistic expression and his ultimate artistic aim, in which the sensible and the ideal, the mundane and the divine, after undergoing a painful separation while the ideal "finds its way to itself," are reunited. His confrontation with Hegel, whose chair in Berlin he assumed in 1841, eventually led him to change his view of myth, and it is this view that is expressed in the *Philosophy of Mythology*. According to that work, myth is still an inevitable and involuntary form of expression, but no longer can it reconcile the sensible and the ideal; rather, it is situated at the point at which mankind and divinity are farthest apart from one another; at the same time, it begins the contrary movement leading to their reconciliation. Myth becomes a historical datum, embedded in a specific era of human history, and yet not reducible to an extrinsic thing; it is the symbolic expression of the anticipation of the ideal in man. Schelling offered a radical solution to the problem that had so engrossed Creuzer before him: he divorced myth from all external events.

For Schelling, then, myth is the inevitable form in which man conceives the divine (or in which the ideal is revealed to the thinking man of that time when mankind was at the maximum point of separation from divinity). Schelling was not heard amid the clamor of the early nature mythologists. His approach had no followers, at least in the area of Greek mythology, until the twentieth century. The scholar who remained closest to Schelling was Walter Friedrich Otto (1874–1958). Otto held that myth is "one of the forms in which . . . the divine is revealed," equal in value to ritual, which is forever reenacting the divine epiphany, and to the erection of temples and of cult statues, which are "immediate revelations of the divine." Otto could see myth only from an aesthetic and religious point of view. Karl Kerényi (1897–1973) took a position not far from that of Otto; he was Otto's close friend, though not his student in the strict sense. Kerényi regarded myth as an independent "form of thought and of expression," as "reality resolved into forms that express the divine," like music or poetry—except that myth, for him, remained bound to an early phase of human development. Ultimately, Kerényi's thought extended beyond this notion.[30]

Mythology from Fontenelle to Frazer

Many theories of myth were proposed during the two centuries that separated Fontenelle and Frazer. Looking back at this period, one is struck less by differences than by the persistence of certain underlying assumptions. The mythologists of the eighteenth and nineteenth centuries clung to the notion that to explain myth one had to discover its origin, which, they believed, lay in the childhood of mankind. Accordingly, the interpretation of myth always seemed to involve reconstructing the life of early man. Requiring a basis for this reconstruction, the theorists of this period turned to the so-called primitive peoples of their own day, to children, and to the simplest peasants of Europe, all of whom, it was thought, resembled early man in some respects.

There were few fundamentally different answers to the question of the origin of myth. Some held that myth was man's response to his natural and social environment, or to historical events, or to both. This manner of explanation was reductionist: myth was said to have originated in, in effect was reduced to, a natural phenomenon, the social environment, or a historical event. Others believed that myth was man's response to the divine: myth, in their view, is irreducible. Similarly, Vico's suggestion that myth is man's response to himself cannot be reduced. These answers were also variously combined. Moritz, for example, argued that man projects the divine onto the things of nature. Here a reduction is possible only in a limited sense and tells us nothing about the peculiar nature of myth.

Many mythologists stopped there. To explain why early man reacted in this distinctive way, expressing himself through myths that often seemed bizarre and absurd, they pointed to his distinctive mentality, arguing that such oddities were all that the mind of early man could produce, either because his intelligence was limited (Creuzer offered an extreme version of this explanation), or because his linguistic faculty did not enable him to express himself otherwise, or for both these reasons. Whatever explanation they offered, these scholars invariably saw myth as sensuous, concrete, and vivid by comparison with modern modes of thought, which tend toward the abstract and conceptual—a view that tended toward a critical or even negative evaluation of their own contemporary culture.[31]

Finally, scholars had to explain why myths are found among different peoples in similar forms. Logic permits two explanations: dispersal from a common central point or spontaneous and parallel development under similar circumstances. If the first explanation was accepted, one had to establish the point from which myth originally sprang, and the paths of its dispersal. The notion, support for which was found in the Bible, that all myths issued from Israel was superseded by the Indo-European hypothesis, according to which most European languages were descended from a single mother tongue. The Indo-European hypothesis did not, however, explain how myth first came into being. The second explanation—that homologous myths developed spontaneously—rested on the assumption that the human mind is unchanging and that comparisons may be drawn between natural and social environments.

CHAPTER II

NEW APPROACHES TO THE INTERPRETATION OF MYTH IN THE TWENTIETH CENTURY

The questions and answers of the eighteenth and nineteenth centuries continued to give direction to scholarly inquiry into myth well into the twentieth century. We have already seen how the fertility and historicizing theories of myth—the two most important kinds of reductionism—were revitalized, especially by classicists, and how Schelling's notion of myth was developed by Otto and Kerényi. Even the "new" approaches have their roots in earlier lines of inquiry. Thus, neither the advocates of the psychoanalytic interpretation of myth nor those of the Cambridge myth-and-ritual theory are interested in the surface structure of the mythical narrative, which they regard as fantastic; instead, they seek to understand myth by ascertaining its origins. What, then, makes these approaches new? To begin with, their scope is no longer limited to Greek myth. Myth is no longer the preserve of classicists; consequently, Greek myth no longer occupies the key position it once did. The myths of "primitive" cultures and the sciences that deal with them, namely ethnology and social anthropology, have given impetus to, even supplied the foundations for, new theories. Unlike the classicist, the conventional ethnologist pays little attention to the historical dimension of mythical narration, and consequently ahistorical, or synchronic, modes of analysis have become prevalent—first functionalism, then the various kinds of structuralism. Only gradually have scholars begun to look more carefully at the narrative as such. Currently, they are exploring the structure and typology of mythical narratives, the rules that govern the narration of myths, and the ways in which those rules may be formalized; few ethnologists have shown interest in the history of mythical narratives.

Myth and Psychoanalysis

Even those who know little else about Sigmund Freud (1856–1939), the founder of psychoanalysis, associate his name with the "Oedipus complex." In *The Interpretation of Dreams* (1900), the Viennese neurologist asserted that this complex stems from the repression, in early childhood, of libidinal feelings for the parent of the opposite sex and that these feelings are accompanied by the desire to suppress the parent of the same sex. Freud regarded the myth of the Theban king Oedipus, who unknowingly kills his father and marries his mother, as evidence of the workings of the psyche: in the myth, and in its dramatization in Sophocles' play, are recorded the events of every individual's mental life, which otherwise manifest themselves only in dreams.[1] In general, *The Interpretation of Dreams* postulates that folktales, myths, sagas, jokes, and popular tales are related to dreams in form and content. Later, Freud understood myths more precisely as "distorted wish dreams of entire nations, the dreams of early mankind" (*Totem and Taboo*, 1912–13). The myth of Oedipus is not just a dream inspired by a wish; it also preserves the memory of real, "Oedipal" events in the primeval horde, in which the sons of an oppressive father rose up against their oppressor, expelled or killed him, and wished to take possession of his women. Unlike Oedipus, however, they eventually felt guilty and would have nothing to do with the women; to this extent, the myth retains the character of a wish dream. Despite his frequent use of myths, Freud never developed a coher-

ent theory of myth per se: that was left to his student and colleague Karl Abraham (1877–1925), who argued that, if dreams
preserve and fulfill the memory of repressed desires, myths are
"fragments of a people's childlike inner life," because they contain "the wishes of the childhood of mankind." Adducing a
single myth, that of Prometheus (see Chapter 4), Abraham demonstrated that myths and dreams make use of the same formal
mechanisms.[2]

Abraham's theory offered a satisfactory answer to the question of the relationship between myths and dreams—a problem
with which nineteenth-century scholars had occasionally grap-
pled—and might have contributed to the understanding of myth
in formal terms, had it not been beset with difficulties. It was
based on two long-standing assumptions, both of which can be
traced back to the Enlightenment: namely, that myth belongs to
the childhood of mankind, and that the mentality of this "childhood" may be likened to that of children. The latter assumption
has been refuted by Jean Piaget; modern anthropologists are up
in arms against the former. Moreover, the theory transfers the
problems and processes of the individual's mental life to entire
societies, which, in Abraham's view, dream collectively; but a
collective is greater than the sum of the individuals who constitute it, as research in social anthropology and group psychother-
apy has shown. Finally, the theory involves the claim that the
mythical image can be explained intuitively by the interpreter,
without consideration of the peculiarities of its cultural context.

Freud's second, historicizing view of the Oedipus myth can be
seen as an attempt to resolve these difficulties. In amending his
earlier view, however, he deprived it of much of its psychoanalytic character, creating, in the end, a new myth—the myth
of what happened, once upon a time, in the primeval horde.
Later, Géza Roheim (1891–1953), the Freudian anthropologist,
offered an explanation of myth that was more in keeping with
the principles of psychoanalysis. He proposed that a large number of myths arose from the dreams of individuals, which they

recounted to others.[3] Roheim's hypothesis is impossible to prove empirically, and it is fatally reminiscent of Creuzer's symbolist missionaries. Moreover, Roheim did not ask why dreams were appropriated by the collective in the first place, or whether they were altered fundamentally in the course of their transmission. Yet his answers to these questions would have been crucial to his project.

A quite different approach was taken by another, dissident student of Freud, Carl Gustav Jung (1875–1961).[4] Though heavily indebted to Freud in his early works, Jung eventually parted company with his master and developed a theory of his own, which seemed to make headway. Essentially similar images and symbols, Jung held, recur in myths, folktales, and dreams, because inherent in the human mind is the tendency to represent certain inherited, "archaic" patterns, which he called "archetypes," though he noted that these representations "often vary greatly in detail, without forfeiting their basic form."[5]

Thus, Jung progressed beyond the notion of a mythopoeic childhood of mankind. The ability to create myths, he asserted, lies in each one of us. From Jung's mythopoeic mind it is but a short step to Lévi-Strauss's *esprit humain*, with its fundamental ability to express itself in symbols, of which myths are copies. Myths are created from the immanent store of archetypes; it is in this way that they become expressions of the human spirit. It is not difficult to understand why Karl Kerényi gave up his early views of myth, which he had borrowed from Schelling and Otto, in order to apply Jung's theory of archetypes to Greek myth.[6]

But there is a crux here. Whereas, for Schelling, Otto, and the early Kerényi, the mythical images that well up from the human spirit are manifestations of the divine and the constancy of the mythical images is guaranteed by that of the divine, Jung dispensed with the notion of transcendence altogether. In so doing, he had to offer his own account of the origin of the archetypes. He saw them as "an instinctual tendency." If the archetypes are instinctual, then they must be transmitted just as biological programs are, that is, as pieces of genetic information. That takes us into the realm of the unverified.

Moreover, Jung hardly got past the hypothetical stage; he only began to furnish the massive body of empirical evidence required to prove the existence of the archetypes. His quite impressive comparative studies seldom range far beyond European culture. Much work remains to be done in this area. Still, these archetypes, even if it could be proved that they exist, can account for static symbols, at best; they cannot explain the narrative sequences that constitute myth. To put it in figurative terms, Jungian theory could establish that the same main characters recur in all the plays ever written and still tell us nothing about the plot of any single one of them. Finally, even if we believe in a collective unconscious, the archetypes must be seen in relation to the individual psyche, its problems, and its experiences. Why myth plays such a prominent part in the social life of the cultures in which it resides is a question that remains to be answered.

Myth and Society: From Myth-and-Ritual Theory to Functionalism

That some myths account for societal institutions was obvious even to ancient mythologists. They called such myths *aitia*, "explanations." Etiological myths offer explanations not only of religious phenomena but also of just about everything else. The myth of Apollo and Daphne is an *aition*. The god Apollo was attracted to Daphne, a beautiful nymph, and pursued her. Just as she was about to be captured, she prayed to Earth, her mother, who transformed her into a laurel tree (the Greek word for which is *daphnē*). This myth explains how the laurel tree came into being, and why it is sacred to Apollo. By telling something about the past, myths explain something about the present (this is a point to which we will return). When the modern interpreter traces a myth back to a social institution—when, for example, he argues that the myth of Oedipus is derived from the sacral kingship, as Gilbert Murray did[7]—he is going a decisive step further. For he is explaining not the function of the myth but its origin—an origin, moreover, in an institution that did not exist (the interpreter says: no longer existed) in ancient Greek society.

According to the myth-and-ritual theory in its extreme formulation, myths arose to explain rituals: in creating myths, the ancients sought to explain religious rites that they did not understand. This theory was developed by the so-called Cambridge school, which drew its inspiration from Sir James George Frazer. Frazer, in turn, had been inspired by his friend, William Robertson Smith (1846–94), a theologian and Arabist at Cambridge, who in his fundamental book *Lectures on the Religion of the Semites* (1889) had stressed the significance of ritual in the history of religion (this Heyne had already done) and even asserted that ritual was, at least to some extent, genetically prior to myth. Frazer was in the habit of drawing comparisons between myth and ritual, and he often saw the origins of myths in ritual practices. He believed, for example, that the myth of the "dying and rising god," which is found in many cultures, is a reflection of the ritual of the sacral kingship (ultimately, of course, the myth was thought to be derived from the vegetative cycle). Jane Ellen Harrison (1850–1928), perhaps the most brilliant representative of the Cambridge school, was the first to elaborate this idea fully.[8]

Every known myth, Harrison thought, originated in a ritual. Myth was, according to the first version of her theory, misunderstood talk about rites. She believed, with Frazer, that rites were largely coextensive with fertility magic (*Prolegomena to the Study of Religion*, 1903). Eventually, Harrison grew dissatisfied with the notion, then current, that myth was merely the result of a misunderstanding (shades of Max Müller, the mythologist at Oxford), and altered her theory. In this she was inspired by the work of Émile Durkheim (1858–1917), the father of French sociology.[9] Durkheim developed a general theory of religion, which he outlined as early as 1907 in a lecture held at the Sorbonne and presented more fully in *The Elementary Forms of the Religious Life* (1915). He saw myth as a part of religion. His theory may be summarized as follows. By living and acting within a group, the individual experiences a power that transcends him, the power of the collective, which he tries to imagine as objectified religious forms; thus, social facts and institutions are dramatized as rites, explained and amplified by myths; conversely, the narration of myths and the performance of rituals confirms the individual in his belief in the gods and at the same time binds him more closely to the group. Borrowing from Durkheim's theory, Jane Harrison explained myth as the representation of collective ritual. She was the first to recognize the significance of initiation rites in Greek mythology and religion. She set forth her arguments in *Themis* (1912), with its telling subtitle *A Study in the Social Origins of Greek Religion.*

In consequence of the First World War, which left many European intellectuals (not least among them Jane Harrison) disenchanted with the past, the approach to myth as the representation of initiation ritual long went underappreciated by most classicists. Not until the 1960s, which saw a reawakening of interest in social phenomena, did the myth-and-ritual theory show to its best advantage. The theory then entered a second phase. British scholars, to be sure, had been applying the theory in the study of the Near East and in ethnology long before then, and they were the first to see the problems that it entailed.

It was not difficult to find flaws in the extreme form of the myth-and-ritual theory, according to which every known myth originated in a ritual. There are myths without rites and rites without myths—the two seem able to exist independently. Witness the major Greek myths: the Oedipus myth in its totality cannot be reduced to a ritual. Moreover, there is no lack of cases in which a myth was evidently not originally linked to a ritual, or in which several myths accompanied the same ritual.

It follows that unknown myths cannot be reconstructed on

the basis of known rites, and that unknown rites cannot be reconstructed on the basis of known myths. Such derivations, despite their quasi-mathematical appearance, have never been possible because no one has ever been able to pinpoint the relation
of myth and ritual. Rather, the two seem to develop along
roughly parallel lines; the *aition* takes up a single point, but it
apparently develops autonomously according to the laws of narration (see Chapter 5).

It therefore seemed advisable to abandon the strict version of
the theory, according to which every myth grew out of some
ritual. Once this version had been rejected, the theory as a whole
lost its appeal. Mythologists decided to dispense with the question of the origins of myth entirely and to concentrate on the
relation of myth and ritual in historical times. If necessary, they
were prepared to inquire into the laws governing mythical narration and into ritual procedures. This called for a fresh theoretical orientation. Mythologists gave up the historical and genetic
approach in favor of a functionalist or structuralist one.

In the field of anthropology or, more specifically, Anglo-
Saxon social anthropology, this reorientation is associated with
the name Bronislaw Malinowski (1884–1942), Frazer's most distinguished pupil. Reacting against Frazer's evolutionism and his
"armchair anthropology" (so called because Frazer had spun his
theories in his study at Cambridge and had had no direct contact
with the cultures about which he wrote), Malinowski set himself
two aims: to study ethnological cultures directly and to focus his
inquiry on the meaning of institutions in their societal context.
Both the hands-on approach and the line of inquiry were new,
and the one presupposed the other. Myths, he thought, were
charters ("charter myths"), culturally relevant explanations,
reasons for all that was important in the social life of a community. Myths define group membership as well as matrimonial
rules, land distribution as well as ritual procedure.[10]

Yet this approach was limited. The functionalist made no attempt to explain the peculiar form of the mythical narrative; his

view of myth was perhaps too unidimensional and rational (this may be seen as a reaction against Frazer); so far as Greek myths were concerned, functionalism could scarcely be applied monolithically. Although many myths have a clearly delineated charter function, the major, culturally central myths of the Greeks do not all evince an etiological function in this narrow sense.

Georges Dumézil (1898–1986), the founder of the "new comparative mythology," took a different tack. Strongly influenced in his youth by Durkheim and Harrison, he, like them, was convinced that myths and rites were somehow closely interrelated. He did not, however, postulate the historical priority of one to the other, for he believed such questions to be unanswerable because of the length and obscurity of human prehistory. Nonetheless, he thought it possible for us to make observations about the historical development of myths and rituals. He reconstructed lost Indo-European institutions on the basis of known myths and rituals of the Greeks, Iranians, and eastern Indians as well as those of the Celts and the peoples of ancient Italy. Dumézil thus resurrected the old project of Max Müller and Adalbert Kuhn. The Greeks occupied a prominent place in his early works; later, he developed a theory according to which all the fundamental institutions of the early Indo-Europeans can be arranged in three basic classes, that of the kings and priests, that of the warriors, and that of the farmers and craftsmen. While there is some evidence for this *trifonctionnalité* among the Italo-Celts and the Indo-Iranians, there are few traces of it among the Greeks. The list compiled by Dumézil is short, and the only myth included in it is that of the judgment of Paris—and even this example does not carry conviction. Dumézil's students have made little headway.[11]

The Structures of Myth and of Mythical Narrative

The investigation of the structure of a myth—the isolation of its constituent elements and the analysis of their interrelationships—is conceivable in various forms. After all, even Usener's suggestion that myths reflect the cycle of the seasons involves the comparison of structures; so does the myth-and-ritual theory. But what is today known specifically as "the structural analysis of myth," or "structuralism" as applied to myth, goes back to the French anthropologist Claude Lévi-Strauss (1908–).

Nowhere, with the exception of one programmatic article, "The Structural Study of Myth," published in 1955 and often reprinted, has Lévi-Strauss presented his theory in a succinct manner. He has been concerned with a practical approach, the most impressive example of which is his four-volume work *Mythologiques* (1964–71), rather than with the exposition of a theory. Consequently, much of his theory must be inferred from his practice. Here it is apparent that his thinking has developed further since 1955—and not without inconsistencies.

Myth, for Lévi-Strauss, is a mode of communication, a communicative system, like language, for example, or the exchange of commodities. Culture, generally, is a series of interwoven communicative systems. In "The Structural Study of Myth," Lévi-Strauss proceeds on the assumption that language and myth are analogous, and employs the instruments of the structural analysis of language to understand myth.[12] These instruments he borrows from the work of the Genevan linguist Ferdinand de Saussure, who, in lectures given between 1906 and 1911, drew a distinction between *parole* and *langue*: the former refers to current usage, the latter to the rules governing current usage. Applying this distinction to myth, Lévi-Strauss argues that all known myths constitute a mythical *parole*, except that this *parole* has transhistorical validity. Mythical *parole* is valid not just for the present but also for the past and for the future (mythical *parole* owes its stability to its eternal validity). The mythologist's task is to uncover mythical *langue*, the system of fixed structures underlying *parole*. *Langue* accounts for the universality of certain mythical patterns, that is, it explains why some patterns, prima facie capricious figments of an individual mythmaker's imagination, are astonishingly similar in so many different cultures. Just as language is composed of isolable, inherently meaningless phonetic signs, or phonemes, which take on definite form only when opposed to other phonemes and take on significance only in combination with other phonemes, so myth is composed of isolable, inherently insignificant signs, which Lévi-Strauss calls *mythemes*. The mytheme "Oedipus marries his mother" is insignificant in itself; it takes on significance only in combination with the other mythemes of the Oedipus myth. In effect, the myth is resolved into its constituent mythemes. These mythemes are then rearranged so as to reveal a "deep structure"; the "surface structure" of the myth, the order in which the mythemes occur in the narrative, is ignored. In his much-cited (and much-berated) essay of 1955 Lévi-Strauss chose the myth of Oedipus to illustrate his method. He himself felt somewhat uneasy about his reading of the Oedipus myth, likening himself to a "peddler demonstrating his gadgets." In a later article, *The Story of Asdiwal* (1958), he gave a more precise description of his method: the structure of the myth is evident on various levels, or in various "codes," which convey the same message; only by investigating closely the real experiences of ethnological cultures can one decipher the codes.[13] In the myth of Asdiwal Lévi-Strauss distinguished four such codes: the geographical, the technoeconomic, the cosmological, and the sociological. The significance of the myth, he argued, lies in its structure, not in the environment to which it refers (when we seek the significance of the myth in reality, we inevitably grant too much importance to one of the codes). If there is a significance outside the myth, it is to be found in the human mind and nowhere else, for the structures of myth reflect the structures of thought: that is the ultimate reason for the universality of certain mythical patterns. The structures, in formal terms, are logical relations—oppositions, inversions, parallelisms. In particular, Lévi-Strauss attaches great importance to binary oppositions, which, he believes, are operative as much in myth as in computer language or in the "language" of genetic information.

Indeed, it was just this desire to understand the workings of the human mind that first led Lévi-Strauss to investigate myth. As an expert in the area of kinship studies, he saw that ethnological cultures are governed by systems of rules so complex that they can only have been produced by a mind highly adept at classification. Myth, prima facie a product of the "savage mind" at its most arbitrary and irrational, posed a special challenge for him: he sought to demonstrate that in the making of myths the "savage mind" differs from the modern not in quality but only in the materials it employs, much as a stone ax is distinguished from a steel one not in degree of technological complexity but in the materials used to make it.[14]

Lévi-Strauss's theory of myth, it has been noted, precludes the discovery of any significance in myth other than its own structure. His practice, however, is inconsistent with his theory. He classifies the mythemes according to criteria not of form but of content, and must therefore give them intrinsic significance (whereby he abandons the notion that mythemes are analogous to phonemes); at the same time, he also relates all myths to an extrinsic reality. His assertion that the myth of Oedipus mediates between two opposing notions, the affirmation and denial of autochthony (between the notion that Oedipus is born of the earth and the notion that he is, in fact, born of two human parents), involves reference to an extramythical reality, as does his assertion that the myth of Asdiwal enacts various matrimonial paradigms. These assertions grant special importance to one of the codes—the sociological code. Thus, Lévi-Strauss has done just what he warned against doing in *The Story of Asdiwal*.

Lévi-Strauss modifies his practical approach in *Mythologiques*. In this work he analyzes myths not in isolation but in bundles (complexes). Comparing the structures of the myths in these bundles, he finds that they are marked by parallelism, opposition, or inversion. The structures are, as it were, hypermythemes in a transcultural system spanning South and North America; in this system one basic myth manifests itself in 813 variations. The mytheme proved too difficult to isolate; henceforth, the minimal unit of myth is to be the mythical symbol. Lévi-Strauss detects these mythical symbols with the aid of ethnography. His careful detective work is one of the most attractive things about these four volumes. But his greatest achievement is the discovery of universals, abstract relations among the mythical symbols that have importance virtually the world over, such as the "culinary triangle" raw/cooked/spoiled and its analogue roasted/smoked/boiled, or the oppositions nature/culture and tobacco/honey.

The major objections to Lévi-Strauss's analyses may be reduced to two. First, the theory renders all paths from structure to significance impassable: every assignation of significance must seem arbitrary. The discovery of structures is an act of analysis that must be performed independently of the search for meaning. Second, even in *Mythologiques* the analyst forgoes the surface structure of the narrative, which is a linear sequence, in favor of a deep structure, as though the narrative were of little importance. Is it the purpose of storytelling, then, to give listeners the means by which they might deal with the problems posed by subconscious structures? This is nothing short of absurd. As one critic put it, "Lévi-Strauss has perhaps found the melody, but he has certainly lost the harmony." This is one of the consequences of the erroneous notion that language and myth are analogous, of the fact that phonemes and mythemes are nearly equated. But myth is not a mode of communication analogous to language. Nor is it a metalanguage, as Marcel Detienne once thought. Instead, language is simply one medium, the privileged medium, in which myth finds expression.[15]

Lévi-Strauss's enduring contribution is the notion of structure. He has shown that myths can be richly structured; that mythical structures find expression at various levels (in various codes); and that these levels refer to structures in physical and social reality. While he has demonstrated that one can detect the mythical structures only by elucidating, with painstaking attention to detail, the value that individual symbols have within a given culture, he has also discovered transcultural relations among the mythical symbols. This is not to say that, with Lévi-Strauss, we have finally arrived at the essence of myth. Structural analysis is one of the many methods of elaborating the meaning of myth and therefore can be, and has been, applied to Greek myth. For example, in a minimal application of the structuralist method, G. S. Kirk has shown that the opposition nature/culture, so important to Lévi-Strauss, is operative in the Cyclopes episode in the *Odyssey*, and that the Cyclopes serve to valuate both poles.[16]

In the area of Greek mythology, Lévi-Strauss's structuralism has been most fruitful in the work of Jean Pierre Vernant (1914–) and those in his Parisian circle.[17] There structuralism was adopted in various ways: cautiously by Vernant (who was influenced primarily by Louis Gernet and secondarily by Lévi-Strauss), wholeheartedly by Marcel Detienne. Like Lévi-Strauss, Vernant has been engaged in the pursuit of structures—not those of myth or of *esprit humain*, comprehensible in terms of highly abstract and pseudomathematical formulas, but the "implicit categories" of the Greek conception of external reality and of the self, the network of those symbols with which the Greeks made their world intelligible. Although Vernant regards myth as an especially important area of study, he does not limit himself to this one area: all social institutions may be investigated by the structuralist. The emphasis that Vernant places on society is the legacy of Durkheim, to which he is heir as the student of Louis Gernet. Vernant does not accept Lévi-Strauss's resolution of mythical tales into transcendent structures; unlike Lévi-Strauss, he begins with literary texts—Hesiod's rendition of the Prometheus myth, for example. To be sure, he, too, requires that the significance of the mythical symbols be sought in the context of Greek society. The result is an ethnology of the Greeks, exemplified by his inquiries, with Marcel Detienne, into the significance of the coot (*aithuia*) in connection with the myths of Athena (*Cunning Intelligence in Greek Culture and Society,*

1974) or Detienne's work on aromas, fragrances, and perfumes (*The Gardens of Adonis*, 1972). In the meantime, Detienne has begun to move away from his initial position of close adherence to the views of Lévi-Strauss.

Long before Lévi-Strauss, the Russian folklorist Vladimir J. Propp (1895–1970) had arrived at a structuralist view of traditional tales. Propp, however, was concerned not with the deep structure divorced from the surface structure but with the surface structure itself. He saw his project not as an end in itself but as a "preparation for a historical study of the folktale." In *Morphology of the Folktale*, which appeared in 1928, Propp examined an entire corpus of folktales of a particular kind: Russian fairy tales. Typically, a hero is sent out, or goes out voluntarily, in search of someone or something; he succeeds in finding that someone or something, often with the aid of magical objects; he is pursued by someone; he manages to escape, along with the person or thing that is the object of his quest, from his pursuer, again with the aid of magical objects. Propp elaborated a plot scheme common to all these tales, a sequence of thirty-one functions (called morphemes or motifemes by some), the building blocks of the plot. These functions are determined neither by the identity of the characters that perform them nor by individual motifs. The sequence of these functions is fixed, though not all of them need occur in every tale.[18]

The impact of Propp's book began to be felt just as the structuralist movement was beginning to gain momentum. The English translation appeared in 1958, and French, Italian, and German translations followed. The influence of Propp's book was twofold: it gave rise, on the one hand, to general analyses of traditional tales according to their plot structures and, on the other, to attempts to isolate corpora of structurally similar tales from other cultures.

As for the general analyses, no one has yet succeeded in establishing a satisfactory "grammar" of traditional tales, or even the rough outlines of one. All too often, such attempts seem to get lost in a jumble of pseudomathematical formalization. The second continuation of the Proppian approach seems more promising. In particular, Walter Burkert (1931–) has sketched a number of narrative patterns in Greek myth. One such pattern, which he calls the "girl's tragedy," consists of a sequence of five morphemes: a girl, making the passage from childhood to adulthood, leaves her home (I), lives in idyllic seclusion (II), is surprised and impregnated by a god (III), suffers humiliation and is punished (IV), gives birth to a son and thus is relieved from her suffering (V). The myth of Io, the Argive maiden, is paradigmatic: she is a priestess in the sanctuary of Hera in Argos (I/II), is impregnated by Zeus (III), transformed into a cow by Hera, who is jealous of her, and, goaded by a horsefly, is made by the goddess to wander far and wide (IV), until Zeus causes her to change back into a woman, and she gives birth to a son, Epaphus (V). Yet another type can be reduced to the sequence "contravention of an interdiction/punishment": the hunter Actaeon sees Artemis bathing (I), is punished by the goddess, being transformed into a stag and torn apart by dogs (II).[19]

Significantly, none of these narrative patterns belongs exclusively to the traditional tale. Propp's quest pattern turns up in other kinds of narrative, and even the sequence "contravention of an interdiction/punishment" is not confined to myths. The essence of myth, therefore, is not to be sought at the level of narrative structure (that the general method has been unsuccessful might lead us to the same conclusion); our preliminary definition of myth also dispensed with this approach.

The Myth-and-Ritual Theory Revised

The monolithic derivation of myth from ritual, as we have seen, was beset with insuperable difficulties.[20] Since Harrison's day there has been no shortage of attempts to show that individual myths or groups of myths are connected with certain rituals or ritual types. Indeed, such attempts are still being made. In the wake of Jane Harrison's *Themis*, scholars have focused their attention on initiation rites and myths. A single example, the myth of Theseus and the Minotaur, may serve to illustrate the general hypothesis, and the problems associated with it.

Having grown to manhood in Troezen, Theseus, the son of the Athenian king Aegeus, returns home to his father just as the Athenians are about to send off their annual tribute of seven boys and seven girls to the Cretan king Minos. The children are to be cast into the Labyrinth and devoured by its sole occupant, the Minotaur, a monster that is half man, half bull. Theseus sails with them, and, once on the island, wins the love of Ariadne, Minos's daughter. When she learns that Theseus intends to slay the Minotaur, she gives him a ball of red thread, instructing him to unravel it on his way into the Labyrinth. Theseus does just that, slays the monster, thus saving the children, and finds his way out of the maze with the aid of the thread. On the return journey he deserts Ariadne on the island of Naxos. In his sorrow, Theseus forgets to replace his ship's black sails, which signify failure, with white ones, which signify success. As the ship appears in the distance, Aegeus, thinking that his son has died, plunges to his death. Theseus then succeeds his father as king of Athens.

The basic structure of this narrative accords with that of male initiation rituals. The hero's journey to a distant land, his brush with death, his slaying of a monster, his erotic encounter, and his succession of his father correspond to the elements of the typical initiation ritual: the removal of the initiates from their villages, their apparent death, their encounter with demons from another realm and with the erotic, and finally their return as adults. There are also similarities of detail: the young age of the participants, the black sails. The latter recall the colors with which the typical initiate is marked and the black capes worn by Athenian ephebes, who were, after all, initiates. Finally, the Attic myth is surrounded by *aitia* that also refer to initiation, as H. Jeanmaire first demonstrated.[21]

These similarities raise several questions. Given the structural correspondences between this myth and initiation ritual, are we to assume that they are genetically related? Did the myth arise from the ritual? If not, are they related in some other way? To take a different approach: can we, following Propp, reduce the individual mythical narrative to a basic structure that can be formalized (i.e., a sequence of functions)? Can the gap between myth and ritual be bridged in this way?

In a later book, *The Historical Roots of the Fairy Tale* (1946), Propp himself concluded that the sequence of functions that he had elaborated in his study of the folktale matched that of the typical initiation ritual. This is so, Propp thought, because folktales are derived from initiation rituals. Propp's method was not unlike Jeanmaire's: he compared individual motifs with the stages of ritual, and he leaped arbitrarily from narrative structure to ritual. Since the appearance of Propp's book, not much headway has been made in this direction. And there is yet another pressing question: if myth is derived from ritual, how is it that myth retains its structure even after it has emancipated itself from ritual, whose structure it supports? Lévi-Strauss would have answered that the structure of the human mind guarantees the constancy of the structure of the narrative. For those who cannot accept this answer, Walter Burkert, following Propp, has proposed a bold alternative.

Burkert regards the narrative types as "programs of action" corresponding to elemental biological or cultural realities, such as Propp's structure in the program of the animal hunt, or that of the "girl's tragedy" in the series of events that occur naturally in a girl's life (namely "puberty, defloration, pregnancy, and delivery"), or that of the pattern of crime and punishment in the most elemental cultural institutions. These programs of action guarantee the constancy of the plot, ensure that we can appropriate it without difficulty, and thus are responsible for the nearly universal distribution of many narrative types. At the same time, such elemental programs also structure ritual. Male initiation rites can be brought into accord with the pattern of the Proppian formula, whereas female initiation rites follow the pattern of the "girl's tragedy": for this reason some myths and rituals are connected without difficulty, whereas others exist separately.

Thus, while Burkert's explanation solves a number of vexing problems, it also calls into doubt those studies in which it is assumed that some myths were originally connected with rituals but eventually broke away from them. Angelo Brelich (1913–77), for example, attempted to show that this was the case with initiatory themes in Greece in his *Paides e parthenoi* (1969).[22] Alternatively, one could attempt to show that the vestiges of such a connection can be detected in myth—that, for example, Theseus was the patron of the ephebes in Athens, that the Athenian ephebate was a transformation of an old initiation ritual, and that, at the same time, the structure of the myths about Theseus, and their motifs, regularly refer to initiation. For the time being, though, Burkert's explanation must remain tentative. Only after all occurring narrative patterns have been isolated and attributed to corresponding programs of action will it be possible to assess his hypothesis. For, like Jung's theory of archetypes, his theory tolerates no exceptions.

The Semiotic Approach

Other approaches to myth developed alongside structuralism but have not been widely received in classical studies; they may be grouped under the somewhat loose heading of semiotics. So far as cultural studies are concerned, the most influential approach has been that taken by Roland Barthes (1915–80) in his *Mythologies* (1957).[23] For Barthes, who draws inspiration from Saussurian semiology, myth is a system of signs, like language (in this respect Lévi-Strauss and Barthes are in agreement—especially the later Lévi-Strauss; it is no accident that the title of his four-volume *Mythologiques* echoes that of Barthes' slender but seminal book). Myth, in Barthes's view, is not a language but a metalanguage, a secondary sign system built upon the primary sign system that is language: the linguistic sign, which consists of a signifier and a signified, becomes the signifier of myth, constituting, in combination with a new signified, the mythical sign. The proper name Theseus, for example, is a linguistic sign made up of a sound pattern and a signified; in the myth of Theseus, this sign in turn becomes a signifier that, in combination with a new signified (e.g., the exemplary Athenian ephebe, the embodiment of all Athenian ephebes), produces the mythical sign "Theseus." At the same time, Barthes demonstrates that this semiotic system does not grant too much importance to language, for the same formalization may explain a propagandistic photograph of a black soldier saluting the French flag. Thus, Barthes parts company with those who see mythology as addressing itself primarily or solely to linguistic, narrative manifestations of myth.

In a modern and enlightened society, which is devoid of myths in the traditional sense, this approach holds promise, and one of the reasons for the influence that Barthes's *Mythologies* has exerted lies in his polemical contention that even modern societies have their myths. On the other hand, ancient and traditional societies, in which myth is characterized primarily by its narrativity and in which the linguistic expression of myth has a privileged status, proved rather difficult to reach by way of this approach. Moreover, whereas observers of modern society such as Barthes have little difficulty in recognizing the signified of a mythical sign, the student of an archaic and ultimately alien society often lacks the knowledge necessary for such recognition and must rely on the methods of ethnology, especially those demonstrated in Lévi-Strauss's *Mythologiques*, where the signified of a mythical sign is derived from an analysis of the oppositions into which the sign is inscribed.

Thus, during the last two decades of classical scholarship, fruitful results have been achieved through the application not of extreme semiotic models but of moderate structuralist and semiotic ones. Models derived from Lévi-Strauss and especially Jean-Pierre Vernant have been applied to Greek myths by several scholars, in the United States by a group associated with the periodical *Arethusa*,[24] in Europe by, above all, Claude Calame. Calame has devoted his efforts almost exclusively to the narratological analysis of myth. He sees myth as linked with, and often indistinguishable from, other narrative forms; for the theoretical underpinnings of his work he relies heavily on A. J. Greimas.[25] As for classical semioticians in America, Charles Segal's conception is typical: "From a semiotic point of view . . . myth is a narrative structure whose sign- and symbol-systems are closely correlated with the central values of a culture, especially those values which express a supernatural validation, extension, or explanation of cultural norms."[26] Segal emphasizes that narration, that is, language, is the privileged medium of mythical expression, and that myth has close and vital ties to the value system of a culture or, as I would prefer to say, a society. Moreover, he implies that any analysis of myth must begin with an analysis of mythical signs read against their specific cultural background. Narrative analysis, in this approach, depends on a more fundamental cultural, even ethnological analysis.

A radical departure from these positions is now on the horizon. The view of myths as bound to specific cultures raises the question whether myths really are as universal as mythologists, from the early eighteenth century onward, have supposed. Investigations of the terms used in mythology have raised the same question. Detienne's *The Creation of Mythology*, the original French edition of which appeared in 1981, began to raise doubts; later, Calame's study of the semantics of the word *mythos* in ancient Greece and my own study of Heyne's invention of the term *mythus* pointed to the ethnocentricity of our terminology. These studies have shown that myth is a construct that arose in Europe during the age of Enlightenment. Whereas they do not refute the universality of myth, such a refutation, though disturbing, is not inconceivable.[27] It is entirely possible that in speaking of "myths" in non-European societies we are projecting our own conceptions, which go back to fifth-century Athens, onto those societies.

CHAPTER III

MYTH AND EPIC POETRY

Myth and Homer

Our first witness to Greek myth is Homer. In the *Iliad* and the *Odyssey* we encounter, for the first time in the history of Greek literature, the gods and heroes that constituted myth as the Greeks themselves knew it, and as we know it now. Since Homer's day, Achilles and Hector, Paris and Helen, Zeus, Hera, Poseidon, and Athena, the Cyclopes and the Giants, the Centaurs and the Sirens have engaged the minds of westerners, and they continue to do so today.

And yet the *Iliad* and the *Odyssey* are not naïve mythical narratives: that notion, still current, depends on the false assumption that what is archaic is also naïve. On the contrary, they are carefully considered and elaborately composed works of art. The Greeks attributed them to a great poet, Homer, the blind singer from Chios, who was so real to them that they did not hesitate to sculpt his portrait. The main action of the *Iliad* covers only a few days in the last year of the Trojan War; the poem has the well-knit structure of a play.[1]

Yet it encapsulates the entire ten–year conflict. By showing us the destructive anger of Achilles, the *Iliad* affords insight into the problematic nature of heroic existence, which is the focal point of epic poetry. Even more ambitious than the *Iliad* in its structure, though not in its view of the world, is the *Odyssey*, which deals with the homecoming of Odysseus, plunderer of Troy. In the *Odyssey*, two narrative strands run side by side: one is the fate of Odysseus, the other that of his son Telemachus, who leaves home to seek news of his father. Not until the poem has passed its midpoint are these two strands brought together, when the narrator tells of Odysseus's return to Ithaca, where for years suitors have been wooing his wife Penelope. The narrative as a whole is not linear: the action begins in the last year of Odysseus's wanderings, and his travels of the preceding years are described in a flashback at the court of the Phaeacians.

The Homeric poems, then, are highly reflective works of literature. And like all works of literature, they require explanation. To begin with, Homer is not the "author" of the *Iliad* and the *Odyssey* in the sense in which, say, Leo Tolstoy is the author of *War and Peace*: the origin of the ancient poems is uncertain. Still, their uniformity supports the assumption that each of them was composed by a single, though not necessarily the same, person (an assumption that does not rule out later interpolations), presumably toward the end of the eighth century B.C., at the earliest. Apart from the question of authorship, it is clear that the *Odyssey* is the later of the two poems: both its form and its content indicate that its author was familiar with the *Iliad*. As works of verbal art, they come under the heading of "literature," but we have no way of knowing whether their creator (or creators) was (or were) literate. In any case, scholars no longer dispute that the formal characteristics of the artificial language of epic poetry can only be understood within the context of a tradition of oral poetry. The oral poet improvised. That is not to say that he created an entirely new poem with each performance, for the tradition placed at his disposal a wide range of formulas, set phrases recurring frequently in certain positions in the line, which vary from the combination of noun and epithet (e.g., "rosy–fingered Dawn") to an entire line of verse (e.g., "and they put their hands to the good things that lay ready before them"). Also supplied by the tradition were typical scenes, replete with corresponding phraseology: the harnessing of a hero's horses before his departure, for example, or the arrival of a stranger. Finally, the tradition gave the bard entire plots, such as the structures underlying the tales of Achilles, Meleager, and Odysseus: the hero retires from the fighting and consequently his companions suffer, but eventually he reenters battle and is victorious. Such plot structures may be compared with the patterns, analyzed by Propp and others after him, that underlie traditional narratives in general.

Myths in the Homeric poems may be arranged in three groups: large–scale myths about the Trojan War, myths about individual gods and heroes, and myths that do not deal directly with the Trojan War. To begin with the first group: the *Iliad* and the *Odyssey* were among several poems that took their subject matter from a myth, or group of myths, about the Trojan War. These poems, which formed a part of the so–called Epic Cycle, covered the entire war, including its prehistory and aftermath, with some overlaps. Unfortunately, all the others have been lost, and are known only from fragments or epitomies.[2]

The *Cypria* recounts the events that led up to the Trojan War. Gaea (Earth) complained to Zeus that the weight of mankind was too great for her to bear, and he promised relief. The wedding of Peleus, a mortal man, and Thetis, a sea goddess, afforded him an opportunity to fulfill his promise. Previously, Zeus and Poseidon had wooed Thetis, but they had been dissuaded from pursuing her by an oracle warning that she would bear a son destined to be greater than his father. At the wedding, Eris (Strife) threw a golden apple into the midst of the guests. The apple bore the inscription "For the fairest"; a quarrel arose among Hera, Athena, and Aphrodite, with each goddess claiming the apple for herself. Eventually, they agreed to make Paris, a

Trojan prince, arbiter of their dispute. All three goddesses offered Paris bribes; Aphrodite promised him the most beautiful woman on earth as his wife—this was Helen, wife of Menelaus, ruler of Sparta. Paris awarded the apple to Aphrodite and proceeded to abduct Helen. Menelaus determined to retrieve his wife and requested the assistance of his brother Agamemnon, ruler of Mycenae. Previously, before Helen's marriage to Menelaus, Helen's suitors had agreed to lend assistance to whomever she chose to be her husband, in the event that he should ever require it. With the aid of the suitors, Agamemnon raised a powerful army, and with it he sailed to Troy and laid siege to the city for ten years. It is at this point in the myth that the *Iliad* begins. The *Aethiopis*, in turn, picks up where the *Iliad* leaves off: after Hector's death, Memnon, an Ethiopian king, fought on behalf of the Trojans. Achilles killed him, and was himself killed by Apollo and Paris. The story of the capture of Troy through the ruse of the wooden horse is told in the *Iliupersis* ("Sack of Ilium"), which is followed by the *Nostoi* ("Homecomings") and the *Odyssey*, which deal with the trials of the Greeks on their return from Troy: not all of them arrived home unscathed.

In the form in which we have them, the epic poems that make up the cycle are post–Homeric. Yet it seems that "Homer" was familiar with the history of the entire war, for in both poems he frequently alludes to its prehistory and aftermath, from the marriage of Peleus and Thetis (*Iliad* 18.432–34; 24.534–37) to the judgment of Paris (*Iliad* 24.28–30; cf. 3.399–412), the wooden horse (*Odyssey* 8.502–15), and the murder of Agamemnon on his homecoming (*Odyssey* 1.35–43). The poet of the *Iliad*, in particular, deploys his knowledge of the whole span of the war quite deliberately. In the first half of that poem he refers to the prehistory and beginning of the war, in the second to its end and aftermath. Thus, he creates the illusion, extolled even in antiquity, of temporal depth: the entire war is condensed into the few days of the main action of the poem. From antiquity, too, comes the observation that the only way to understand a myth that is not recounted per se but to which several allusions are made is to piece together those allusions. The poet had in his mind a coherent picture of the mythical past.[3]

If a myth is defined as a traditional narrative, the contents of the epic poems about the Trojan War may rightly be called myths: they are tales that are reshaped constantly and passed on within a (poetic) tradition. The myth transcends the form that it takes in any one text. This is true of the *Iliad*, the *Odyssey*, and the other poems in the Epic Cycle: they are individual renditions of transcendent myths. They are also individual in the sense that all of them (with the exception of the *Cypria*) have come down to us under the name of a particular author. Thus, even Homer can be regarded as an individual poet, whatever his name may have meant to the Greeks. Presumably, even those versions of the Trojan myth that preceded the Homeric poems were individual and distinctive in this sense: like all oral compositions, they bore the imprint of the singer's personality and reflected the conditions of his performance and the expectations of his audience. The relationship between oral epic poetry and myth was therefore no different in principle from that between any literary work and the myth or myths that it relates.

The difference between the bardic and the later, nonbardic narration of myth lay in the degree to which the myths were tied to the audience, and therefore also in the degree to which the myths were culturally relevant. The myths of the epic singer (*aoidos*), as he is represented in the Homeric poems, were tied to the audience in a relatively loose way: the audience was composed of a small number of aristocrats; the poetry was enjoyed virtually as a dessert; every performance was unique. Thus, the myths of oral epic poetry had a low degree of cultural relevance. By contrast, in the case of later, nonaoedic mythical narration (such as that of tragedy), myths were narrated on special occasions before a large group: told in this setting, the myths were bound to, and their narration controlled by, the entire group. The values and norms represented in the myths were relevant to, and shared by, that group. At the end of the archaic period, the Greeks regarded Homer as their teacher par excellence. His poems were not just contingently valid expressions of the Greek conception of the gods and of the past; they were sources of information in many fields of knowledge. At this time, epic poetry had the cultural relevance that was characteristic of mythical tales generally in Greece, and the recitation of epic poetry was an integral part of festive occasions such as the Panathenaea in Athens. This was not yet the case with the *aoidos*, the oral poet as he is portrayed in the Homeric poems. It is true that the Homeric *aoidos* tells traditional tales of gods and heroes (*Odyssey* 1.338), and that he even lays claim to a degree of relevance or validity when he invokes goddesses "who know all things" as the sources of his inspiration (e.g., *Iliad* 2.485; *Odyssey* 8.479–81). Still, his performance is "that which enchants mortals" (*brotōn thelktēria*: *Odyssey* 1.337); it is a form of entertainment performed after a banquet attended by noble men (*Odyssey* 1.150–55; 8.485–543) or at the conclusion of athletic games in the land of the Phaeacians (*Odyssey* 8.254–369). Achilles even sings an epic song (*klea andrōn*) to himself (*Iliad* 9.186). It is reasonable to suppose, although it cannot be proved, that what gave the bard such freedom in his treatment of the traditional material—the freedom that made the *Iliad* such an outstanding achievement—was the fact, indicated by the foregoing examples, that the ties between poetry and social life were still relatively loose. To be sure, the difference between the cultural relevance of oral epic poetry and that of later mythical narrative was merely one of degree, not a fundamental one.

The individual heroes and gods of the Homeric poems have their own stories, which are not confined to Troy. The singer usually alludes to these stories instead of recounting them in detail.[4] The myths of Zeus, for example, are presented indirectly:

the poet of the *Iliad* alludes to his birth (13.354–55), his struggle against Cronus and the Titans (14.203–204), Cronus's captivity in Tartarus (8.478–81; 15.224–25), and the division of the world among Zeus, Poseidon, and Hades (15.187–93). Myths of this kind were systematized by Hesiod (see Chapter 4).

There are more tales about the youth of Nestor than about that of any other hero in the Homeric poems. When he was still quite young he slew Ereuthalion, the huge "club fighter" (*Iliad* 7.132–56), without assistance. As a youth he also took part in the Pylian assault on Elis, carrying away much livestock as booty. To prevent his son from taking part in the subsequent war with the Eleians, Nestor's father hid his horses. But Nestor could not be thwarted so easily; he went to Elis on foot, captured the horses of the Eleian king, nearly defeated the Actorione-Molione (Siamese twins who rode in a chariot), and finally returned to Pylos amid cheers *(Iliad 11.669–761)*.

Here, too, we may assume the existence of an epic tradition, on which "Homer" was dependent. The portrayal of Nestor as a warrior who wishes to prove himself in battle, and does so, is entirely consistent with the epic conception of the world. The Pylians presumably had their own epic poetry in the form of short songs organized around a single hero, Nestor, such as is documented in other, non-Greek epic traditions.[5] The earliest visual representation of the Actorione-Molione dates from the middle of the eighth century, and their myths were told before and after the *Iliad*. Finally, Nestor's standing epithet *hippota* ("who fights on a chariot") points to this kind of epic poetry: only in a limited sense is the epithet applicable to Nestor as he appears in the Homeric poems. The myths of Nestor show just how complex was the tradition that preceded Homer: embedded in the tale of his theft of the Eleians' livestock is the statement that Nestor's eleven brothers were all slain by Heracles when he waged war on Pylos (*Iliad* 11.689–92). Thus, Nestor's mythical biography is closely connected with that of Heracles, the story of whose life is also adumbrated in the *Iliad*. It emerges, in the course of the narrative, that he was the child of Zeus and the Theban Alcmena (*Iliad* 14.323–24), that he fetched Cerberus from the underworld (*Iliad* 8.362–69), and that he sacked Laomedon's Troy (*Iliad* 5.638–42, 648–51).

This takes us to the third group of myths found in the Homeric poems: myths that are not linked directly to Troy. These are, for the most part, little more than allusions (rarely longer narratives) told as exempla, mythical paradigms, by a single person.[6] It is not clear how these shorter myths were related to the non–Homeric tradition, the evidence for which is later than Homer, but they deviate from the Homeric tradition in ways that are almost always significant. The myth of Meleager is a case in point. It is told in some detail by Phoenix, the old tutor of Achilles, in the ninth book of the *Iliad* (9.524–99). Phoenix's purpose is to persuade his pupil to give up his anger and return to the fighting.

> Two peoples of northwest Greece, the Aetolians and Curetes, were fighting over Calydon, the principal city of the Aetolians. The cause of the fighting was the anger of Artemis: when the ruler of Calydon forgot to offer her the firstfruits of the harvest, the goddess felt slighted, and sent an immense boar, which ravaged the land. A large hunting party set out. Meleager killed the boar, but a quarrel broke out between the Aetolians and Curetes over the prizes, the head and skin of the boar. So long as Meleager fought in defense of Calydon, the Curetes could achieve nothing. But then he slew one of his mother's brothers, who was evidently a Curete. In a grandiose scene, his mother cursed him, and in anger he withdrew from the fighting. The Curetes launched a violent assault on Calydon. The appeals and gifts of prominent men, and even of his family and friends, did not induce Meleager to relent. Only when his city was in flames did he intervene to save it. By waiting so long, however, he forfeited the gifts.[7]

Meleager's situation in the paradigm is remarkably close to that of Achilles in the *Iliad*. Like Meleager, Achilles is angered at an offense against his dignity and retires from the fighting; consequently, the enemy begins to gain ground. To him also comes a delegation of prominent men, army leaders and close friends, promising gifts. Again like Meleager, he sends the delegates away and does not relent until the camp is in flames. Phoenix's paradigm is, however, inconsistent with the tale of Meleager as it is known from other sources, where it is said that the quarrel over the spoils arose between Meleager and his mother's brothers. According to these sources, Meleager wanted to give the spoils to Atalanta, the only woman in the hunting party. There was a dispute, and in anger Meleager slew his uncles. His mother was enraged, just as she was in Phoenix's version, but, instead of merely cursing her son, she avenged the murder of her brothers, in the following manner: at the birth of Meleager, the Moerae, the goddesses of fate, had predicted that the child would be handsome and brave, but that he would live only so long as a certain log burned in the hearth; at that time, his mother had extinguished the brand and hidden it; under the present circumstances, she brought it out and placed it in the fire. As the log crumbled to ashes, her son perished.

There can be little doubt as to which of the two versions of the Meleager myth is older typologically. In many other tales, mostly from the eastern region of the Mediterranean, but also from Lithuania and Iceland, a fateful piece of wood, or occasionally a candle, has a similar function. The ritual associations of the myth point in the same direction: the burning of a log was a part of a huge fire ritual performed annually in Calydon. Homer changed the story, and his motive is obvious: had his mother burned the log, the hero could never have made his angry withdrawal, which is in fact all that matters in the Homeric context. Homer selected the tale of Meleager because it was similar, in its main lines, to that of Achilles in the *Iliad*: the wrath of the goddesses (Artemis in the tale of Meleager; Hera and Athena, whom Paris offended, in the tale of the Trojan War) was the ultimate cause of the quarrel, the insult to the hero's sense of honor its proximate cause. But he had to change it radically in order to be able to use it.

Thus, Homer's use of myths that were not about the Trojan War was idiosyncratic. The tale of Meleager is not an isolated case: elsewhere, too, myths were altered to fit the context. As mythographical sources the Homeric poems should therefore be used with caution. It is not always possible to check the Homeric version of a myth against a parallel tradition, or to recognize distortions resulting from his adaptation of a myth to suit the purposes of his narrative.

Moreover, we cannot know whether such tales of non–Homeric content were told in epic verse; if they took some other form, we can only guess what it was. Cross-references in the Homeric poems to epic cycles other than the Trojan one—the Theban cycle (e.g., *Iliad* 6.223) or the story of the Argonauts (*Odyssey* 12.69–72)—are rare. Unfortunately, in most cases evidence for an autonomous tradition of oral epic poetry is entirely lacking (in the case of the stories about Nestor we can at least infer such a tradition). In those relatively few cases in which such evidence does exist, it comes from a much later source.

The tales of Heracles are a case in point. Homer, as we have seen, was aware of substantial parts of the Heracles myth, and from later sources we learn that Heracles was the subject of several epic poems. Perhaps the most famous of these was the one composed by Panyassis of Halicarnassus, the uncle of the historian Herodotus, early in the fifth century.

Recently discovered papyrus fragments have revealed another form in which such epic traditions could survive. There are allusions in the *Iliad* to Hera's persecution of Heracles after his expedition to Troy—that the goddess made him drift to Cos in a storm (*Iliad* 14.250–56) and that he suffered on that island (*Iliad* 15.26–28, 30). The papyrus fragments tell more about these trials. Heracles was compelled to fight against the Meropes, the aboriginal inhabitants of Cos, an island off the southwestern coast of Asia Minor. The hero would have been overcome by them had Athena not come to his aid. The epic poem in which these events were narrated was the *Meropis* ("Tale of the Meropes"). It is an anonymous work, and it probably belongs to the classical period, at the earliest.[8]

The *Meropis* is the earliest example of a kind of poetry that has long been known to have existed: "local epic poetry," poetry that described the mythical past of a particular city or region. Unfortunately, only scanty fragments of such poetry have survived. It is certain that many of these local epic poems belonged to the archaic period; we know nothing, however, about the circumstances of their composition. The subject matter of the *Meropis* was evidently known to the composer of the *Iliad*, and the hypothesis that this local poem and the *Iliad* were being narrated and transmitted at roughly the same time is an attractive one. Local myths are traditional tales that preserve the history (in the archaic sense) of a place and in this way shape the self–image of its inhabitants in the present. The set form of hexameter verse may have lent greater permanence to the mythical contents than a loose prose narrative would have.[9] Admittedly, specifically epic themes such as one finds in the stories of Nestor are lacking in the *Meropis*.

The myth of Meleager illustrates just how difficult it is to ascertain whether a particular mythical narrative was told in verse or in prose when the tradition to which that narrative belonged has been lost. Even after all conceivable Homeric alterations have been removed from the myth, traces of heroic epic poetry remain. Hunting and warfare are eminently heroic undertakings, quintessentially epic themes. Although Meleager bears no epithet that would place him in an epic tradition, his city is twice called "lovely Calydon" (*Kalydōn erannē*) (*Iliad* 9.531, 577). The epithet "lovely" is both inconsistent with the description of the city elsewhere in Greek epic poetry and inappropriate to the city's location, which is in fact mountainous. It is possible that, in assigning this epithet to Calydon, the epic tradition preserved the memory of a time when the territory of the city still included the fertile coastal plain. Phoenix introduces the story of Meleager's rescue of Calydon as one of the "exploits of the heroes of the past" about which "we used to hear" (*Iliad* 9.524–25). That, too, points to a tradition of epic poetry. References of this kind are absent in the tales of the log; whether they, too, were handed down in the form of epic verse or in some other poetic form we cannot know. Another version of the Meleager myth may go back to a tradition of heroic epic poetry: Hesiod relates that Meleager was killed by Apollo (fr. 25 MW). That recalls the death of Achilles or Hector, and rules out the motif of the burning log. It is uncertain whether Hesiod invented this version or borrowed it from an epic account.

The Origins of Greek Myth

Once we accept that myths were among the subjects of the pre-Homeric epic tradition, we cannot avoid the question of the provenance of those myths. This is not to say that we should indulge in perilous speculation about their distant origins. But we may consider suggestions about possible stages in the prehistory of Homeric poetry, and these suggestions will be limited to heroic myths, for in discussing myths about the gods we suddenly find ourselves, wherever oriental models are not forthcoming (see Chapter 4), in a jungle of hypotheses about the origin of Greek religion.

The most influential hypothesis concerning the origins of heroic myths is still that of M. P. Nilsson. Nilsson argued that these myths were traceable to the Mycenaean period (his programmatic title, *The Mycenaean Origin of Greek Mythology* [1932], is misleading so far as it suggests that all Greek myths date from this period). He noted a correlation between the significance of a city in the heroic myths and its significance in the Mycenaean period. In his view, heroic myths originated in the history of Mycenaean Greece. In some cases, however, he could not reduce the myth to history, and often he had to assume the existence of folktale motifs, that is, of traditional narration.

Nilsson's hypothesis has gained wide acceptance, especially among German and British mythologists. The decipherment of Linear B by Michael Ventris (1952) seemed to corroborate it. Many proper names occurring in myth and epic poetry were already present in Mycenaean Greek—with the difference that in the Mycenaean texts they were borne by ordinary people: smiths, shepherds, or slaves. Just this fact, however, can be taken to prove that the myths are post-Mycenaean. For it is hardly conceivable that so many mythical figures shared their names with ordinary people. In the historical period, the names used in the myths were no longer borne by ordinary people—precisely because they were being used in the myths. Even Nilsson's main argument has been weakened. We know of mythically significant sites that do not have a great Mycenaean past (the cities of Argos or Sparta, or Ithaca, where Schliemann searched in vain for Odysseus's palace); we also know of Mycenaean settlements or palaces that have no discernible myths (Gla in Boeotia, Asine in the Argolid, or Miletus). Myth tells us no more about the Mycenaean colonization of Ionia than it does about the Mycenaean conquest of Minoan Crete.

If Nilsson's thesis concerning the correlation between mythical and Mycenaean cities cannot be endorsed without qualifications, neither can his thesis concerning the relationship between myth and history. Myth and epic poetry do not draw a reliable picture of the Mycenaean world, even if certain details in the Homeric poems seem to belong to that world. The title *wanax*, which Agamemnon bears in the *Iliad*, is indeed the word for king in Mycenaean Greek and in later times was used nowhere but in epic poetry; Homer does indeed describe a boar's tusk helmet not unlike the one often worn, so far as we can tell, by Mycenaean warriors; finally, Pylos, the realm of Nestor according to the Homeric poems, is indeed known from the remains of its palace and its tablets. But the picture of Mycenaean Greece implied in these facts is far from accurate. Every petty Mycenaean king was called *wanax*: the title was not reserved for the lord of Mycenae (as yet there is no archaeological evidence to support the claim that he bore this title). Homer regards the boar's tusk helmet as a costly antique rather than as an item of standard equipment, and it may be that somewhere such a helmet did in fact survive the "dark age," to be admired and described by a bard. The Homeric poems do not accurately describe the geography of Mycenaean Pylos as we know it. These inconsistencies are not surprising—so long as we place the beginning of the tradition of heroic myths and of heroic epic poetry after the end of the Mycenaean period. The notion that myth faithfully preserved the memory of historical events from the Mycenaean period thus proves groundless.

A glance at perhaps the most important question for the student of Homeric myths—that of the historicity of the Trojan War—makes this notion even more doubtful.[10] Before Heinrich Schliemann, taking the *Iliad* as his guide, excavated Troy and Mycenae, it was generally agreed that the war never happened. In 1906 Wilamowitz could still dismiss attempts to historicize the poem with the remark: "scholars do not get excited about the matter, nor do they take it seriously."[11] In view of the tangible results of Heinrich Schliemann's excavations, scholars were quick to change their minds. Since Schliemann's day, several generations of historians have tried to show that the story of the war was rooted in the history of Mycenae or Asia Minor. Only quite recently have doubts about the historicity of the war re-emerged, and they are grave indeed.

The most compelling argument in favor of the historicity of the Trojan War is an archaeological one. According to this argument, the stratum known as Troy VIIA, one of many strata representing successive settlements on the site, was destroyed not long after 1200 B.C., approximately the date assigned to the war by the majority of ancient scholars. But the ancient date is worthless, for it is the result of pure speculation on the basis of half–mythical genealogies and kings' lists (no reliable Greek tradition reaches back farther than 800 B.C.); besides, there were other ancient opinions on the date of the war, and they diverged widely. Furthermore, while we know that Troy VIIA was destroyed by force, we do not know what that force was. It is entirely possible that the city was hit by an earthquake, followed by a conflagration. But it is impossible to prove that it fell under an attack, much less that its attackers were Greeks.

Another argument for the historicity of the Trojan War rests on the assumption that, in general, epic poetry tends to be linked to historical events. For example, the *Song of Roland* is said to be based on Charlemagne's Spanish campaign, the *Nibelungenlied* on the power of Burgundy and the expansion of the Huns. There is, however, no lack of counterexamples. That the *Epic of Gilgamesh* has a basis in history, for example, is disputed; that the Finnish *Kalevala* has such a basis is unthinkable. More important, we know from independent historical sources that epic poetry, when it does represent a historical event, tends to distort it, and often does so violently. From such sources we learn that Charlemagne's Spanish campaign was a small-scale affair, and that his rear guard was attacked by Basques, not by Saracens; that the Burgundians never fought against Attila; that the king of the Huns and the Goth Theoderich (Dietrich von Bern) were not contemporaries. "No one in his right mind would go to the *Song of Roland* to study the battle of Roncevaux or to the *Nibelungenlied* to learn about fifth–century Burgundians and Huns. I do not see that the situation is any different with respect to the battle at Troy" (M. I. Finley).[12]

If the myth of Troy does not offer a single piece of evidence for the historicity of the Trojan War, it also does not offer any conclusive evidence to the contrary. Given Nilsson's observation that the significance of a locality in the heroic myths is related to its significance in Mycenaean times, which, with some qualifications, holds true, and given the presence of Mycenaean proper names in the myths, one may reasonably suppose that those myths, in one form or another—as stories either told by the Mycenaeans themselves or, somewhat later, about them—were connected with the Mycenaeans. If we assume that those tales which dealt with the Mycenaean period only began to be told after the collapse of Mycenaean civilization, then it was the impressive ruins of Mycenae, Tiryns, or Troy that gave rise to the connection between the myths and the Mycenaean cities, and we should expect to find in the myths no survival, apart from the place names, from the Mycenaean period. That would explain why Miletus, which was also a Mycenaean city, was of little interest to the epic bard: it lay beyond the reach of the Greeks of the "dark age," and not long after the collapse a fresh group of colonists built their settlement over the old one. In the particular case of the Trojan War, we do not possess enough information to make a decision. It is possible that the Trojan War was a Greek campaign against the citadel of Hissarlik on the Dardanelles. No historian, however, has ever adduced a convincing motive for such an expedition, and Mycenaean logistics would hardly have been adequate for a siege, even one lasting no more than a few weeks. A second possibility is that the "war" was a local conflict on a small scale, perhaps in central Greece, as the names Ilion and Troy suggest; that this conflict was memorialized in poetry that eventually took on epic proportions; and that the connection between the war and the ruins of Hissarlik was made by Aeolian immigrants. A third possibility is that there was never any conflict at all: many of the elements of epic narration can be brought into accord with a ritual pattern.[13]

Furthermore, even though the epic poet assures us that he is reporting the tradition "accurately" (*atrekes*) and that this "accuracy" (*atrekeia*) is guaranteed by the Muse, the tradition preceding him, being purely oral and therefore not controlled through comparison with a standard fixed in writing, was prone to mutation. Ethnological studies have shown how quickly myths can respond to changes in the environment to which they refer—in some cases extensive mutation occurs within as little as a generation. So long as its content remains vital and of vital significance, a society's oral tradition adjusts itself to the requirements of the day, unbeknownst to its upholders. Examples to the contrary may be found, but it would be rash to count the tradition surrounding Troy in the "dark age" among them.

Of course, the peculiar nature of myth or poetry does not lie in historical connections, be they real or not. What leaves a lasting impression on the reader of the *Iliad* is, among other things, the magnificent image of Apollo, who sends a plague on the Greeks, or Zeus's love nest on Mount Ida, and what makes the Trojan War memorable is Zeus's great plan, the quarrel among the goddesses and the judgment of Paris, the capture of the city through the ruse of the wooden horse: these events cannot be reduced to history (see Chapter 1). Similarly, the principal heroes of the *Iliad* are not historical figures: although Agamemnon and Menelaus have genuinely Greek names, the lives that they lead in myth are far removed from everyday affairs, from historical reality. Attempts to reduce these heroes to historical personages have been no more successful than attempts to make the description of Homer's Ilium fit the ground plan of Troy VIIA. Helen was never a mortal woman but a goddess who received cult in several places. Odysseus also had a cult, perhaps as early as the Bronze Age, and was worshiped without interruption into the historical period. Finally, there is Achilles: the issue of a mortal man, Peleus, and a sea goddess, Thetis, he was vulnerable in only one place, his heel, by which Thetis had held him over the fire that renders a person immortal; he was raised by the centaur Chiron, possessed divine horses capable of speech, and bore armor forged for him by the divine smith Hephaestus. The name Achilles, though attested in the Mycenaean period, is attached in the myth to a figure that is essentially not historical but mythical—just as mythical, indeed, as the whole group of tales that deal with Troy.[14]

The word *mythical* is vague, and requires definition. By *myth-*

ical we do not mean simply "nonhistorical," "fictional." It was demonstrated long ago that the figure of Achilles recalls the ephebe, the young Greek warrior at the stage of life between adolescence and adulthood. According to this argument, parts of the myth of Achilles—that he was raised by a half-bestial, half-divine centaur and that he hid for some time among the daughters of Lycomedes on Scyrus, disguised as a girl—reflect the practices and myths of primitive initiation. Moreover, there are similarities between the Homeric description of Achilles and that of the young Irish warrior Cû Chulainn, which correspond to the martial ecstasy, the *wuot*, which has been shown to be characteristic of the Indo-European warrior.[15] The exploits of Nestor's youth—his battle with the monstrous club fighter, his theft of the livestock, and his capture of a chariot of his own,[16] all of which lead to his acclamation in Pylos—bear comparison with those of Cû Chulainn's youth. Cû Chulainn slays a monstrous spirit with a hockey stick, proves himself by stealing cattle, and finally tricks his uncle Conchobor into giving him his armor. After he has accomplished these things, the hero emerges as a full warrior. Once again, it appears that these details reflect the institution of Indo-European warrior initiation, perhaps even of Indo-European mythical narration, for the episode in which the young hero fights a monster can only be understood as a mythical narrative.[17] Finally, scholars have called attention to the fact that tales in which a hero, his honor injured by the ruler of a city, lays siege to that city and ultimately takes it through a ruse (often disguised as an animal) are not uncommon in the corpus of myths from the Caucasus, and the suggestion has been made that these myths are Eurasian analogues of the Trojan myths. The ritualized capture of a city is an element of some European festivals involving young men, and this fact is another indication that the roots of the tale lie in Indo-European customs.[18]

Even as some scholars were detecting Indo-European rituals and an Indo-European narrative tradition in the epic poetry of the Greeks, comparative linguists were pursuing the elements of an Indo-European poetic language. They have discovered that Greeks, Indians, and Iranians employed the same metaphors for poetic creation and have taken this fact as proof of the existence of an Indo-European poetic tradition. The linguists also found Indo-Iranian expressions that correspond closely to the Homeric expressions *klea andrōn* ("famous deeds of men") and *kleos aphthiton* ("imperishable fame"). Thus, there was evidence not just for Indo-European poetry but also for Indo-European heroic poetry, in which the theme of "the glory of men" was no less prominent than it is in Homer.[19]

Scholars pursuing two independent lines of inquiry, then, have made a compelling case for the existence of an Indo-European epic poetry, the formulas of which found their way into the artificial language of Homer, and for certain Indo-European institutions, perhaps even for myths based on those institutions. Thus, the narration of myth in the epic poetry of the Greeks can be seen in a historical context extending as far back as the third millenium B.C., to a time long before the height of Mycenaean civilization.[20]

The traces of Mycenaean civilization in the Greek myths now take on a new aspect. They are no longer to be understood as indications of "the Mycenaean origin of Greek mythology." Instead, we have to imagine that, in the post-Mycenaean period, the Greeks preserved the memory of a Mycenaean civilization— so magnificent and yet so suddenly toppled—in the following manner: old myths that once belonged to the oral tradition of epic poetry were localized, that is, they became associated with Mycenaean power centers, and old heroes received the names of great Mycenaeans. Links were established between myths and localities on the one hand, myths and persons on the other. In this respect the Greek poets were not unlike the Irish bards, who linked their tradition to Ulster and Cû Chulainn.

The Mycenaeans themselves may have narrated myths, perhaps in the form of epic poetry.[21] At the moment there is no evidence to support this claim. Mycenaean texts have revealed a number of divinities, recipients of offerings, most of whom belong to the later Greek pantheon. It is reasonable to suppose that myths were told about these gods, too, but the texts, which are without exception administrative in nature, furnish no proof to this effect. No names of heroes are to be found in the lists of offerings, apart from Trisheros (a general title) and Ipimedeja. It is tempting to equate the latter with Iphimedeia (the binomial personal name was already being used in Mycenaean times): the linguistic analysis is far from certain, but the names Iphimedeia and Iphimede are at least as old as Hesiod's *Catalogue* (frr. 19, 23 MW).[22] There is little evidence to suggest that myths were being represented pictorially in the Mycenaean period. In the visual representations that we do possess it is difficult to distinguish heroes from ordinary men (Attic vase painters, by contrast, sometimes identified the figures that they depicted with inscriptions). Well-known Mycenaean vases from Cyprus and northern Syria show men riding in chariots, a fight with a giant bird, and departing warriors. There is no way of knowing whether these vases illustrate particular Greek myths. They may be scenes from everyday life, or representations of Near Eastern myths.[23]

The conviction of modern scholars, and nearly all ancient ones, that myths in epic poetry preserve the memory of historical events has made us aware of one peculiarity of this kind of poetry. It poses as a kind of history: it is governed by a fictive, reasonably coherent chronology. The fathers of those who fought at Troy belonged to the generation of Heracles, who attacked Troy under Priam's father Laomedon (that it is Priam's sons, not Priam himself, who fight against the Greeks does not strain the chronology beyond credibility); to that generation also belonged those who fought at Thebes and the Argonauts. Myths not about the Trojan War tend to be introduced as memories. As such they gain a certain authenticity: in telling the myth of Meleager, Phoenix is reporting past events; the tale of Bellerophon, who rode the winged horse Pegasus, is integrated into the genealogy of the Lycian lord Glaucon, who fought at Troy (*Iliad* 6.145–211).

This kind of historicization is characteristic of those mythical tales, such as the epic poem, which combine diverse, and originally independent, mythical subjects into a single tale that encompasses them all. If such an imposing mass of data is to be organized, it must be imbued with rationalism; what emerges from the rationalization of the data is a chronology of the myths. Rationalism is also characteristic of the narrative style of the Homeric poems, in which the excessively fantastic, fabulous, and magical is studiously avoided. Even if we accept that heroic poetry generally poses as history, or even originates, as the *Nibelungenlied* or the *Song of Roland* did, in historical events, the realism of the Homeric poems is unusual. Admittedly, this realism is more apparent in the *Iliad* than in the *Odyssey*. The scene in which the horse Xanthos speaks to Achilles, foretelling the death of the hero—"when it had uttered these words, the Erinyes checked its voice" (*Iliad* 19.418)—is typical: the unnatural is a momentary aberration and is at once "corrected." So, too, in the myth of Meleager, the magical log of the myth as it is known elsewhere is replaced in Homer by Althaea's curse—here the logic of the narrative converges with realism. As for the *Odyssey*, we should not let ourselves be misled by the monsters and the magic: most of the episodes in which we encounter the supernatural belong to Odysseus's account of his wanderings, which take place outside the known universe, a place to which Odysseus was transported by a storm that raged for nine days (*Odyssey* 9.82). What is perhaps the most impressive monster in the poem, the giant, one-eyed Cyclops, occupies the richly detailed and realistic world of the dairy farmer. The Cyclops is the inverse of the average person of Homer's day: the monster knows no laws, does not eat grain, and lives apart from others. Indeed, he and his ilk know neither the cultivation of grain nor "assemblies in which counsel is taken . . . [and] traditional rules," neither navigation nor trade (*Odyssey* 9.106–15).

The epic tradition ends with the generation of the sons of those who fought at Troy. There followed an age of uncertain events, a "dark age" for the poets, too, until the onset of historical memory not long before 800 B.C. Nonetheless, the epic poet declares that he can span these centuries by "remembering" with the aid of the Muses. Such declarations are found in the epic poetry of many peoples. It is also possible that the poet is claiming to reproduce the beginning of the tradition, the heroic age, with historical accuracy. Such a claim presupposes a desire for such historical knowledge. The moment at which that desire was first felt by the Greeks came in the eighth century—the first century of flourishing since the collapse of Mycenaean civilization and the intervening period of relative poverty and isolation.[24] The earliest temples known to archaeologists were built at this time; contacts within Greece multiplied and were increasingly regarded as normal; Greeks began to colonize territories to the east and west, far from the Greek mainland; Ionian traders advanced into the Black Sea. As they came into contact with other cultures and achieved greater inland mobility, they grew aware of themselves as an independent group, as Hellenes. The foundation of the Panhellenic Olympic Games, traditionally assigned to the year 776 B.C., is a sign of this growing awareness. In the second half of the century the heroes of epic poetry began to be worshiped in the fallen Mycenaean cities and at Mycenaean tombs. Survivals from the past began to raise questions, the answers to which took the form of the tales of epic poetry (not necessarily that of Homer, that is, of the *Iliad* and *Odyssey* as they are known to us). In the epic tradition was found a history that was common to all Greeks. It is not surprising that epic poetry about the Trojan War met with such a strong response. The myth of Troy found expression in a supreme artistic achievement, the *Iliad*, but it was also appealing for other reasons. It told of a Panhellenic expedition against non-Hellenic peoples, and it offered an explanation for the passing of the heroic age: in accordance with Zeus's plan, the heroes killed one another off at Troy, as a fragment from the opening of the *Cypria* shows (F 1 *EGF.*).

CHAPTER IV

THE ORIGIN OF THE WORLD AND THE GODS

Hesiod's *Theogony*

Nearly contemporary with the Homeric poems, and no less important for the study of Greek myth, was another epic poem, the *Theogony* ("The Origin [and Descent] of the Gods"), by Hesiod of Ascra in Boeotia. Unlike Homer, Hesiod was unquestionably a historical figure. A later work, the *Works and Days*, gives biographical details, and the *Theogony* opens with a prologue in which the poet tells of his personal encounter with the Muses. They explained to him, he says, that they could tell many lies, but also the truth, and they gave him the ability to sing about the past and the future. Hesiod claims to have heard the truth in person.

The *Theogony* is therefore just as reflective and carefully planned as the *Iliad* or the *Odyssey*. To be sure, creation myths—accounts of the origin of the world and the gods—are firmly established in the mythical traditions of many cultures. In this respect Hesiod's poem was no different: it was not produced ex nihilo but was based on a tradition. As a bard, too, Hesiod stood in a poetic tradition. To a large extent, his language and formulas are consistent with those of the Homeric tradition, and there are points of contact between his myths and those of Homer. To what extent he was dependent on a Boeotian tradition of epic poetry is a point of contention.[1] Hesiod's peculiar talent was not so much for innovation as for the selection, disposition, and combination of traditional material. On the other hand, the *Theogony* soon became a part of the rhapsodes' repertory, and insertions and accretions have been ascribed to the rhapsodes, but it is uncertain how extensive they were (in the past, their number may often have been overestimated). In the oral rhapsodic tradition, a plot was unlikely to be transmitted without alteration. This may have been especially true of the *Theogony*, whose plot is not so densely and purposefully woven as that of the *Iliad* or the *Odyssey*.

> Hesiod's account of the origin of the gods begins with Chaos (Chasm). Then "broad-chested Gaea" (Earth) came into existence, and Eros, the principle of sexual reproduction. From then on, every new creature (with some exceptions) would have a father and a mother. For the time being, however, there was a shortage of sexual partners. From Chaos were formed Erebus (Nether Darkness) and black Nyx (Night). The children of Nyx were bright Aether (Upper Air) and Hemera (Day). Gaea gave birth to Uranus (Sky), the Mountains, and finally Pontus (Sea). Gaea and Uranus united to become the first couple. Their children were the Titans, the one-eyed Cyclopes, and the enormous Hecatoncheires (Hundred-Handers): Gaea and Uranus, half-formed forces of nature, had a tendency to produce hulking offspring. Terrified at the hideousness of his children, Uranus prevented their emergence from Gaea by copulating with her continuously. In answer to his mother's pleas, and with her aid, Cronus, a child of Uranus and Gaea, severed his father's genitals with a "toothed sickle" (175). Uranus parted from Gaea, the children were freed, and Cronus made himself ruler over the second generation of the gods. Such is Hesiod's version of a widespread myth ac-

cording to which sky and earth were separated at the beginning of creation.[2] From the blood that dripped upon Gaea
from Uranus's wound were formed the Giants, the Erinyes
(goddesses of retribution), and the Dryads (tree nymphs).
From the foamy semen that gushed from his severed organ,
which Cronus had flung into the sea, grew the goddess
Aphrodite (*aphros* means "foam"; cf. 195–98).

The rather lengthy account of the first generation of the
gods is followed by more genealogies: the progeny of Night
(mostly dark powers such as Sleep, Death, and Strife), the
water or sea deities descended from Gaea and Pontus, the
children of the Titans, and finally the offspring of Cronus
and Rhea, his sister. As a father, Cronus was no better than
Uranus. He had learned of an oracle foretelling that one
of his sons would overthrow him, and to prevent this he
swallowed them as they were born. But the future predicted
by oracles is fixed. Rhea tricked Cronus by giving him a
stone wrapped in rags to swallow in place of their youngest
son, Zeus, whom she hid on the island of Crete. Zeus grew
up quickly and overthrew his father "by wiles and force"
(496), causing him to disgorge the stone along with his
brothers and sisters (in Hesiod's day this stone marked the
navel of the world at Delphi). He then freed the Cyclopes,
whom Cronus had imprisoned beneath the earth, and he
received from them the thunderbolt as an expression of
their gratitude.

Still more genealogies follow. Hesiod tells how each of
the rebellious sons of the Titan Iapetus was punished by
Zeus, ending with Prometheus. Zeus chained him to a col-
umn; an eagle fed on his liver by day, but the liver regener-
ated itself by night; much later, he was released from his
torment by Zeus's son Heracles. To explain this bizarre punishment, the poet tells at length how Prometheus attempted
to deceive Zeus. The date that Hesiod assigns to this attempt is an odd one: "when gods and mortals reached a

settlement at Mecone" (535–36). On that occasion, Prometheus divided up a slaughtered ox, placing to one side the meat and entrails, which he wrapped in skin and paunch, to the other the bones, which he concealed in savory fat. Zeus protested that the division was uneven, and Prometheus invited him to choose between the two portions, whereupon Zeus at once claimed the outwardly more appetizing one. From that time on, mortals have been immolating the bones and the fat as offerings to the gods, and eating the meat and entrails themselves. Zeus, Hesiod emphasizes, deliberately made the wrong choice, for he was brooding evil designs against mortals (the revision shows that Hesiod was working with an older source). In retaliation Zeus concealed fire from mortals, but Prometheus stole it and gave it back to them. Zeus countered by sending them woman, a "beautiful evil" (*kalon kakon*, 585): Pandora, as she is called elsewhere. Since that time, whoever marries embarks on a potentially ruinous adventure, whereas whoever does not will have no children to nourish and care for him in his old age, and his possessions will be divided among strangers after his death.

Zeus's struggle with Cronus and the Titans dragged on for ten years, and there was a deadlock until Zeus, again on the advice of Gaea, freed the three Hecatoncheires and enlisted them as his allies. In the subsequent clash, heaven and earth rumbled, Olympus and Tartarus quaked. Zeus deployed the thunderbolt (perhaps for the first time), and the Hecatoncheires drove the Titans into Tartarus and fettered them there.

A description of Tartarus and its inhabitants (a passage that some scholars consider spurious) is followed by an account of Zeus's last battle. After the expulsion of the Titans, Gaea bore the monster Typhoeus, who rose against Zeus. It is unclear what Gaea's motives were in producing this rebel, for up to this time she had been the loyal counselor of the younger gods. Typhoeus would have become ruler of mortals and immortals, Hesiod says, had not Zeus thundered and scorched him with lightning. Defeated, the monster was cast into Tartarus. From him originated the harmful winds; the beneficial ones, Notus, Boreas, and Zephyrus, had been produced by Eos (Dawn) long before then. Zeus, his regime finally secured, assigned to the gods their various privileges or functions (*timai*).

There follows a long catalogue of Zeus's marriages. His first wife was Metis. On the advice of Gaea and Uranus, Zeus swallowed her to forestall the birth of a son who would depose him. Afterward he became pregnant with Athena, who was born from his head. His subsequent unions are listed—first those with other goddesses, then those with mortal women. The marriages of the other male Olympians are also mentioned. An epilogue-like distich (963–64) is followed by a second invocation (965–68) introducing a catalogue of goddesses who bore children to mortal men: this ending (from 963 to the end of the poem) is obviously an appendage that served to link the *Theogony* with the *Catalogue of Women* (see Chapter 6).

The foregoing synopsis shows that the *Theogony* gives prominence to Zeus and his regime: the poem is an interpretation of the present universal order, over which Zeus presides. There have been three generations of divine rulers since the creation of the world. The first is that of Uranus and Gaea, the second that of Cronus and Rhea, the third that of Zeus. The gods of the first generation, under Gaea and Uranus, constitute the physical framework (Earth, Sky, Sea, and Mountains). Also to this era belong the enigmatic and inimical monsters of the distant past, who were subdued by the children of Cronus and the heroes Perseus, Bellerophon, and Heracles. Carefully distinguished from the children of Uranus are the descendants of Night, the daughter of Chaos. They are Bright Air and Day, but also the destructive and eerie powers that lurk in the depths of all being. With the appearance of the gods of the second generation under Cronus and Rhea, the cosmos becomes mobile. Sun, Moon, and Stars, Rivers and Winds are formed, as are the intellectual principles, which form the foundation of the present era: Themis (Divine Justice), Mnemosyne (Memory—she who preserves tradition, without which human society ceases to exist), Metis (Resourcefulness), and the ambivalent forces Glory, Victory, Strength, and Violence. Not until Zeus overcomes Cronus and his monstrous henchmen, however, does the world become the one that the Greeks of Hesiod's day would have recognized as their own. Zeus, the son of Cronus, and the grandson of Uranus, is the third in a line of rulers, each of whom must use force to depose his predecessor. In each case, a son's act of violence is justified as a requital for an atrocity on his father's part. By swallowing Metis, Zeus becomes the first ruler to make his regime secure. In addition, by single-handedly defeating Gaea's son Typhoeus, he frees himself from Gaea's control.

Zeus's prominence in the *Theogony* corresponds to his prominence in the pantheon of a Greek polis. The privileges or functions (*timai*) that he apportions are expressed, in the world of mortals, in sacrifices and prayers to individual gods. The cultic role characterizes even those gods of the distant past who were actually worshiped by the polis, above all Cronus and Gaea. So far as the polis cult was concerned, Cronus was excluded from Zeus's world, just as he is in the *Theogony*. It is true that Cronus received sacrifices—at the Athenian Cronia, for example. But these sacrifices were made only when Zeus's order was temporarily suspended—when, during the interval between the end of one year and the beginning of the next, there was a carnivalesque interregnum. This accounts for Cronus's ambivalent status in myth, where he is not only Zeus's adversary but also the ruler of the golden age. This temporary release from everyday obligations aroused feelings of extraordinary happiness.[3] Similarly, Gaea, the only deity of the first generation regularly to receive cult, was not worshiped as the beneficent "Earth Mother" (as she was once seen by romanticizing historians of religion) but as an ambivalent deity, a somewhat eerie power on the margin of the polis religion, to whom curiously taboo-laden sacrifices were made.[4]

What is missing in this account of the origin of the world and of the gods—the bipartition is alien to the thought of Hesiod, for whom the world *is* the gods—is the origin of mankind. Human beings suddenly appear at the division of the sacrificial animal at Mecone, where they are curiously obscure behind their champion Prometheus. The first human beings—to borrow a piece of information from the *Works and Days*—lived during the reign of Cronus; they had been created by the gods of that era, the Titans. If the appearance of mankind reaches back to that distant time, then Zeus had to deal with it from the start. This may explain why the Titan Prometheus defended them. (Later, from the fourth century on, Prometheus was represented as the creator of mankind, indeed of all living beings, and it was on this later account that Goethe, among others, based his Prometheus poem.) What took place between Prometheus and Zeus was of great importance for the men of Hesiod's time. However men understood their earliest status, the sacrifice at Mecone was seen as integrating them into Zeus's world. The events at Mecone also explained the tripartite division of their existence into the religious (sacrifice), the technological (fire and the arts derived from it), and the cultural (Pandora and the family). The division of the sacrificial victim does not just explain the normative Greek sacrifice, with its uneven and offensive distribution of the offerings; it also defines the attitude of mortals toward the gods. Men approach the gods offering sacrifice, and not without fear, for they remember that the sacrifice is the result of an act of deception. The fire that Prometheus brought to men was a part of the sacrifice (the offerings were, after all, roasted on the altar). The possession of fire was also a cause for anxiety, and it had been jeopardized since Zeus was no longer as munificent, nor as careless in his munificence, as he once was. Again, the *Works and Days* offers an explanation. By concealing fire from mortals, Zeus deprived them of their *bios* (42), their "livelihood," and since then they have had to toil arduously and unremittingly. In addition to sacrifice and labor, there was woman, that is, the necessity, for a man, of marrying and begetting children, if he was to avoid suffering in his old age and vanishing without a trace after his death, without his name remaining bound to family property. The Greeks generally regarded sacrifice, fire, and marriage as characteristic of the human condition. (These were the elements of civilization, philosophers would later say, that were absent in early times, when men lived like wild animals, and that were absent among the "savages" who could still be found at the fringes of the known world.) What Hesiod is offering here, in an apparent excursus at the center of the *Theogony*, is a definition of mankind under Zeus, one that is essential to the poem. Compared with this definition, physical creation is of secondary importance: religious and cultural integration is what defines humanity.[5]

The Eastern Background

If Hesiod was an organizer and interpreter of traditional tales, then the question arises: can these traditional tales be recovered, at least in part? One clue comes from the *Theogony* itself, where Hesiod says that Zeus was not deceived by Prometheus at Mecone (550–53). The passage is manifestly a revision, that is, a reinterpretation of an already existing tale. Although there is no way of knowing what his sources were or to what extent he diverged from them, similar tales explaining the distribution of the slaughtered animal are known from ethnology. The myth of the theft of fire and that of the separation of heaven and earth were probably also traditional, for these subjects are found in many cultures—again, the specifics are lacking. What Homer tells us about the gods is no less informative than what Hesiod says. The exploits of the gods (*erga theōn*) formed a part of the oral tradition of the epic bard no less than those of men (*Odyssey* 1.338). As one might expect, stories about heroes are more abundant in epic poetry than are stories about gods; in particular, references to the history of the Olympians are rare. Homer says repeatedly, however, that Zeus's sovereignty was threatened by Cronus, whom Zeus banished along with the Titans into lowermost Tartarus (*Iliad* 8.478–81; 14.200–204, 273–74; 15.225), and by Typhoeus, whom he struck down with his lightning bolt in the land of the Arimi (*Iliad* 2.781–83). Zeus is the eldest and wisest of the sons of Cronus; he shared his dominion with them (*Iliad* 15.187–93); for this reason even Poseidon has to obey him (*Iliad* 15.165–66; this datum—that Zeus was the eldest child of Cronus and Rhea—is consistent with the Hesiodic account, so long as, in determining the ages of the children, one reckons from their second birth or, more properly, disgorgement from Cronus's stomach). In the *Iliad* it is stated explicitly that Cronus is their father (Zeus bears the epithet Kronion or Kronides, the "son of Cronus") and that Rhea is their mother (*Iliad* 15.187–88), whereas the Titans are sons of Uranus, *Ouraniōnes* (*Iliad* 5.898). The succession Uranus—Cronus—Zeus is therefore as old as Homer. By contrast, the Homeric poems do not mention the ancestry of the pair Oceanus and Tethys, to whose protection Rhea entrusted her daughter Hera during Zeus's struggle with Cronus. Homer does say, however, that Oceanus and Tethys are the origin (*genesis*) of the gods (*Iliad* 14.201, 302). This is our earliest piece of evidence for a non-Hesiodic theogonic tradition. In the *Theogony,* Oceanus and Tethys are called Titans, parents of the rivers and Oceanids, curiously parallel to Pontus and his descendants. Such aberrations tend to occur in myths about the first generation of gods. This may be explained by their remoteness from the current regime. In general, the more remote the myth is from Zeus's universal order, the looser are its ties to cult, and it is just these ties that restrict mythical speculation.

While there are no complete theogonic myths in the Homeric poems, such myths are found not far from the Greek world, in the Near East, in Anatolia, on the Syro-Phoenician coast, and in Mesopotamia, and they are at least as early as the Greek epic poems that have come down to us. The parallels between these mythical tales and Hesiod's *Theogony* attracted the attention of scholars long ago. In particular, the Hittite tales about the god Kumarbi, the "Hittite Cronus," caused quite a sensation. The most important of these is the *Kingship in Heaven* (*ANET* 120–21),[6] which took written form in the thirteenth century B.C. It is a succession myth not unlike that of Hesiod's *Theogony*. The first king in heaven was Alalu; he was overthrown by his vizier Anu (Heaven), who in turn was overthrown by Kumarbi. As Anu fled upward, Kumarbi bit off his phallus. Having thus been made pregnant, Kumarbi gave birth to the storm god Teshub, among other children. The ending is fragmentary; other tales report, however, that Teshub deposed Kumarbi and banished him, along with his retinue, to the underworld. Kumarbi sought vengeance on Teshub. According to the *Song of Ullikummi* (*ANET* 121–22), the sequel to the *Kingship in Heaven*,[7] Kumarbi impregnated a huge rock, and in this way begat Ullikummi, a monster made of diorite, who grew up rapidly and threatened Teshub's palace and regime. Not until Teshub, using the sickle with which heaven and earth had once been separated, severed Ullikummi from Upelluri, who had been carrying him on his shoulder (Upelluri was a giant who supported heaven and earth, like the Greek Atlas), was he able to put the monster out of action (presumably—again, the ending is fragmentary).

The Hittite tales, like Hesiod's *Theogony*, trace a line of divine rulers, each of whom deposes his predecessor by force, down to the reign of the youngest god. One of the kings is "Heaven," Anu. Like Uranus, he is deprived of his phallus and flees upward (to be sure, the myth of the separation of heaven and earth belongs in another context, as the mention of the sickle shows—a sickle is used to sever Uranus's organs, too). Like Cronus, who swallows his children, Kumarbi swallows something—the next generation, as it were, in the form of a phallus—and perhaps a stone as well. Like Zeus, Teshub, the storm god (Zeus is a storm and weather god), must defend himself not only against the preceding generation but also against monsters created by an earlier deity out of revenge (Typhoeus, it was later said, was created by Gaea in retaliation for Zeus's suppression of the Titans).

Yet the differences are inescapable. Unlike Uranus, Anu has a predecessor, Alalu; the "father of the gods" is not Teshub but Kumarbi; Ullikummi is a stone giant, not a multipartite creature like Typhoeus; genealogies, which constitute a way of interpreting the world in Hesiod's poem, are almost entirely absent. More important, Hesiod, on the one hand, seems to preserve a more tightly constructed, typologically older version of the succession myth, for he places the separation of heaven and earth at the beginning. On the other, only Hesiod traces the succession down to the consolidation of the youngest god's regime. By contrast, there is some doubt as to whether the myth of the *Song of Ullikummi* is a continuation of the succession myth of the *Kingship in Heaven*: no direct link can be established between the two.

A different text, the *Hedammu*, tells of another attack by Kumarbi on Teshub's dominion.[8] According to *Hedammu*, Kumarbi begat, in union with the daughter of the sea god, a serpentlike sea monster, Hedammu, who began to devour the earth. Mankind was threatened with extinction, and the gods with starvation, since they were dependent on the labor of mortals for nourishment. Ishtar, the goddess of love, then managed to outwit the monster with her charms (the sequence in which the goddess bathes, puts on perfume, and decks herself out bears striking resemblances to the scene in the fourteenth book of the *Iliad* in which Hera does the same to outwit Zeus (*Iliad* 14.153–223). Hedammu is tempted to the shore and, like Ullikummi, destroyed (presumably—again the ending is not extant).

Thus, Hesiod probably knew closely related Hittite myths, though it cannot be said that he was directly dependent on any of the extant mythical tales, so far as we can make them out from the written record. The same is true of his relationship to the Babylonian creation poem, known after its opening words as *Enuma Elish* (*ANET* 125–26). In the form in which it has come down to us, *Enuma Elish* cannot have been composed before 1100 B.C. Before heaven and earth existed, Apsu and Tiamat were the only gods. Apsu embodied the male, fresh waters, Tiamat the female, salt waters. They had two sets of children: a group of gods whose succession led to the wise Ea, the great-grandson of Apsu, and another group that remained within Tiamat, until Apsu, annoyed at their boisterousness, plotted to destroy them. But the plot was forestalled by Ea, who cast a spell on Apsu, appropriated his power, then killed him and built a temple and a palace over his corpse. To avenge Apsu, Tiamat raised an army of monsters against the younger gods, who were helpless against the threat until Marduk, Ea's son, promised to defend them if in return they promised to make him ruler of the universe. The gods agreed to meet this condition. Marduk routed Tiamat's army and, with the aid of the evil winds, defeated Tiamat in single combat. He split her into halves, from which he fashioned heaven and earth, and went on to create the rest of the cosmos. Eventually he made human beings from the blood of the god Kingu, Tiamat's firstborn and her vizier. Then he gave the gods their places in the cosmos. They in turn built him the city of Babylon, replete with its main temple to his godhead.

For the reader of the *Theogony*, the Babylonian creation poem, like the Hittite texts, is a blend of the familiar and the strange. What is familiar, if more confused in its particulars, is the succession from an elemental force, Apsu, to the supreme god in the contemporary pantheon, Marduk. Also familiar is the way in which the children of the primeval couple were kept inside their mother, until a younger god revolted. Apsu and Tiamat, as water deities, recall the Homeric Oceanus and Tethys; a variant of Tiamat's name in a later Greek text, Tauthe, comes close to Tethys.[9] What is strange is that the cosmos, as mankind knew it, was created only at the end of the succession. Where the Babylonian poem is fundamentally different from the *Theogony* is in the place it assigns to mankind: the gods created man to release them from the need to work. Indeed, at the beginning of the flood story it is said that originally the gods performed agricultural work themselves, until they grew tired of it and fashioned man to do it for them; from then on, man nourished the gods by working and offering them sacrifice—that is, the fruits of his labor.[10] In the Mesopotamian temple economy, doing farm work and serving the gods were one and the same activity. For Hesiod, too, man's place was defined by agriculture and sacrifice. In the economy of the small farmer, however, agriculture and sacrifice were distinct institutions, and there was yet a third institution that defined the condition of man: that of marriage. Man was not created just to help the gods; he had dignity and, in a sense, independence; accordingly, he existed already prior to the accession of Zeus.

Where more material is available, we are able to see that the relationship between Greek and Near Eastern myths could be quite complex. A case in point is the myth, or mythical pattern, in which the supreme god faces a serpentlike adversary.[11] In the Hittite tales, Teshub, the storm god, has to fight not just the monsters Ullikummi and Hedammu—the stone giant and the sea snake—but also the monster Illuyankas, whose name means "snake." In their first encounter, Teshub is vanquished and maimed by Illuyankas, but ultimately he is able to kill the monster with the aid of other gods (*ANET* 60–72). It is possible that Tiamat, the adversary of Marduk in *Enuma Elish*, had the form of a snake; several Akkadian representations show a god slaying a dragon (cf. fig. 4; admittedly, the interpretation of these representations is uncertain). The battle between Marduk and Tiamat in the Babylonian poem may be compared with the battle between Zeus and Typhoeus in the *Theogony*: both accounts ex-

plain the origin of the evil winds, although they do not correspond to one another in all details. Hesiod says that the moist,
unpleasant winds were formed from Typhoeus after he was
overcome by Zeus's thunderbolts (*Theogony* 869; the good winds
had been created by Eos [Dawn] long before then, 378–80). In
Enuma Elish, by contrast, the supreme god, Marduk, creates the
winds to aid him in his struggle against Tiamat (*ANET* 66, tablet
IV, line 45; Marduk had received the four good winds from his
grandfather Anu).

Hesiod's Zeus easily defeated Typhoeus. However, according
to a later account, preserved in the *Library* of Apollodorus
(1.6.3), Zeus was initially defeated and maimed by the monster,
here called Typhon. In northern Syria Zeus was pinned by his
adversary, who cut the tendons from his arms and legs. Not until
Hermes stole and replaced the tendons was Zeus victorious.
After a long chase, Zeus threw Mount Etna on top of him. Oriental influence is apparent elsewhere in this account. In *Enuma
Elish*, Marduk is also called Sirsir, which means "he who heaped
up a mountain over Tiamat" (*ANET* 71, tablet VII, line 70).
Apollodorus's Typhon was debilitated by the "ephemeral fruits."
In one version of the myth (*ANET* 125) of Teshub and Illuyankas, the monster is tricked into eating a huge meal, which renders him vulnerable. In Apollodorus's account, Zeus's initial defeat takes place on Mount Casius in Syria, which is called Sapon
in Ugaritic; scholars have tried to show that the name Typhon is
derived from Sapon. At all events, the setting of the battle in
northern Syria, Typhon's home according to authors as early as
Aeschylus and Pindar, clearly indicates that the myth is of Near
Eastern origin. It is well to remember, however, that no Greek
tale can be derived from the Near East in its entirety, and one
also cannot help but suspect that Apollodorus's version of the
myth was a late importation from that region, since its date is
relatively late. In fact, oriental succession myths continue to be
documented for centuries. The historian Philo of Byblus (*FGrH*
790 F 1–7), for example, writing in the early imperial period,

recounts a myth that is strikingly reminiscent of the Hittite *Kingship in Heaven,* and the Neoplatonist Damascius, following Aristotle's pupil Eudemus (Eudemus, fr. 150 Wehrli), tells of a cosmogony that resembles the Babylonian creation poem. In Damascius's account, Tiamat is called Tauthe, Apsu Apason; Marduk, however, has become Belos, the Babylonian Bel (and the Phoenician Ba'al).

An even more interesting mixture of the familiar and the strange is found in another local Babylonian tale, the fragmentary *Theogony of Dunnu.*[12] It, too, is a tale of succession, beginning with the elemental pair Plow and Earth and unfolding in a long sequence of generations. In later generations the succession is usually effected by a brother and a sister who mate and overthrow the ruling parent or parents. In the first three generations, however, a mother and a son mate, and this is followed by a parricide or a matricide. Thus, Earth seduces her son Amakandu, the Cattle God, who then kills his father Plow; Amakandu's son Ga'um, God of Flocks, marries his mother Sea, who promptly kills her mother, Earth. Whereas in its details as well as in its overall development this tale differs markedly from Hesiod's *Theogony* (and from *Enuma Elish*), several of its motifs are familiar: marriages between siblings, especially between Titans (Cronus and Rhea) and between the children of Cronus (Zeus and Hera) occur frequently in Hesiod's poem; as for the incestuous relationship between mother and son, Gaea mates with her sons Uranus (*Theogony* 132) and Pontus (*Theogony* 238); parricide is absent in Hesiod's poem, but the mutilation of Uranus may be seen as a mitigated form of it. In the last generation mentioned in the fragmentary text of the *Theogony of Dunnu,* a son seizes, imprisons, and succeeds his father, as Zeus does Cronus. The datum that the son "took over his father's dominion . . . at the New Year" suggests a ritual background analogous to that of the Greco-Roman Cronus-Saturnus.[13] Not only does this local theogony remind us of the many local myths that, although they have not come down to us, may have influenced the

Greek tradition; it also shows that often what was transmitted from one culture to another was not so much single stories or motifs as story patterns, narrative strategies, solutions to similar narrative problems. How, after all, was one to initiate a succession tale that began with a single primeval couple? How was one to explain the role of an otherwise unremarkable god in the New Year festival?

This brings us, finally, to the questions when, where, and how the Greeks became acquainted with tales from the Near East. As we have seen, traces of these tales can be found in the poems of Hesiod and, occasionally, Homer; thus, from an early date they were firmly established in the corpus of Greek myths.[14]

Of these three questions, the last—how the tales were transmitted—is the easiest to answer. The many differences of detail between the Greek myths and their Near Eastern sources suggest that the Greeks were introducing orally transmitted material into their own oral tradition. If so, then the extant Near Eastern texts are literary crystallizations of a narrative heritage whose chief vehicle of transmission was the oral performance.[15] We lack information on the Hittite oral tradition, but we do know something about the conditions under which tales were transmitted in Mesopotamia. On the one hand, written traditions are readily discernible in Mesopotamia—much more so than in Greece. Akkadian tales were handed down from scribe to scribe; they show traces of priestly erudition, as in the list of the fifty names of Marduk at the conclusion of *Enuma Elish*. On the other hand, Mesopotamian societies had their singers: we even possess a mythical tale that begins with a fictive dialogue between a bard and his audience, a device by which the former aspires to win over the latter.[16] The numerous variants of well-known myths, in particular the different versions of the myth of the creation of mankind, make it probable that there was a living oral tradition. The phonetically modernized names of the gods (as against those of *Enuma Elish*) in the cosmogony of Damascius also point in this direction. Only in a limited sense can the term *written* can be applied to a culture such as the Babylonian or Assyrian, in which the scribe played an important part as the transmitter of a highly specialized knowledge (since the system of writing was quite complex, and therefore difficult to learn); in such a culture there was much room for the oral transmission of its narrative inheritance.

If Near Eastern myths were transmitted orally to the Greeks, then Greeks must have been in the Near East, most likely in Cilicia. Indeed, we know that Greeks lived and were active commercially in that region in both the Mycenaean and the archaic periods.[17] During these two periods—the period before the collapse of Mycenaean civilization in the early twelfth century and the period of renewed contact with the East after the "dark ages," from the latter half of the ninth century onward—the Greeks were open to oriental influence. There is one consideration that makes the later period more likely. It is surprising that among the tales told by Hesiod we do not find any Canaanite myths such as are known from texts excavated at Ugarit in northern Syria, although the presence of Mycenaeans in Ugarit is well attested. The texts in question were composed in the fourteenth century, while Ugarit itself remained powerful and important until the incursion of the Sea Peoples, who also put an end to Mycenaean power. Had the Greeks taken over the bulk of the oriental tales and motifs at that time, the Hittite and Mesopotamian myths would hardly have been so prominent. Another argument in favor of the second of the two possible periods of influence is that in the ninth and eighth centuries the cities of northern Syria (in the rough triangle between Hama, Ugarit, and Iskenderun), most though not all of which were coastal, stood under the influence of Assyria, while the area to the north of these was occupied by the so-called Neo-Hittites. The latter preserved the Hittite traditions, including, one presumes, the myths, whereas the Assyrians transmitted the Mesopotamian ones. One of the earliest extant objects imported into ninth-century Athens from the East, a bronze cup of Neo-Hittite provenance, is emblematic of the impact of the Near East on Greece.[18] We cannot exclude the possibility, however, that some tales were already being transmitted to Greece during the Mycenaean period.

Theogony and Cosmogony after Hesiod

Hesiod's account of the origin of the world and the gods, including his interpretation of the human condition, never became canonical. What he said about the Olympians, about Cronus and Gaea, had some support in cult, epic poetry, and perhaps also the local myths of individual cult centers. This the Greeks of the following centuries accepted, for the most part, without objection. However, whatever was not rooted in religion, poetry, or myth was open to further speculation. Subsequent cosmogonical and cosmological speculation followed two separate paths. One was that of mythological poetry, the other that of philosophical reflection—in short, Orphism and Presocratic philosophy, about which only a few remarks can be made here.

None of the post-Hesiodic poems about the origin of the world and of the gods has been preserved in its entirety. Allusions to them show how much has been lost, and that the term *Orphic* cannot be applied to them without qualification. The fragments of the works of the choral lyric poet Alcman, who flourished around 600 B.C., include a cosmogony (fr. 5 *PMG*). Most of these poems, however, were attributed to legendary or semilegendary authors, above all the two bards Musaeus and Orpheus.[19] References to poems under their names are attested from the late sixth century onward. Of the two it was Orpheus who, in the course of the following centuries, came to be regarded as authoritative on matters of cosmogony and theogony. Common to all the poems attributed to Orpheus is the lengthening of the line of ruling deities by the addition of one generation or more to both its beginning and its end. Two rulers, Phanes Protogonos ("Phanes the Firstborn") and Nyx ("Night") were placed before Uranus; after Cronus and Zeus was placed Zeus's son Dionysus. Thus, there were six generations in all. With Dionysus was associated an account of the origin of mankind, according to which Hera, out of jealousy, incited the Titans to kill, boil, roast, and devour the child Dionysus, the son of Zeus and Persephone. Zeus, however, struck them dead with a bolt of lightning, and from the soot of the scorched Titans man was formed. The myth, whose first traces are found in Pindar (fr. 133 Snell), explains the nature of humanity: being descended from the insurgent and ungainly Titans, human beings harbor an impulse to rebel against the gods. Thus, the mythical tale was, to a greater degree than Hesiod's *Theogony*, a vehicle for speculative thought, which was expressed in a traditional form. Such a tale was not of general relevance, but was meaningful only for the closed circle of Orphics (*Orphikoi*), if indeed such a circle ever existed.

All this contrasts sharply with philosophical speculation. So far as we can tell, the earliest Greek philosopher was Thales of Miletus, who predicted a solar eclipse, which took place in 585 B.C. Of his cosmology only one statement has been preserved: that the earth floats on water (DK 11 A 12). This statement has been compared with those myths from the Near East in which water was said to have been the origin of all things and in which the earth was occasionally likened to a raft built by the creator on the surface of this primeval ocean. It is entirely possible that Thales, who, as a citizen of one of the leading commercial cities of the day, had many associations with the Near East, took this and other ideas from Mesopotamia; he may have based his prediction of the solar eclipse on data acquired there. The crucial fact about Thales, of course, is that he abandoned the mythical mode of expression. Water, according to him, was not a divine force belonging to the earliest age but a physical element and a cosmic reality. What was being developed here was a model of the world explained on rational rather than mythical grounds.[20]

The shift from the Hesiodic explanation of the world to that of the Presocratic philosophers was a fundamental and momentous one. To say, as some nineteenth-century scholars did, that with Thales man made the leap from the torpor of myth to the clarity of logic is certainly an overstatement. Reacting against this, twentieth-century scholars have emphasized that Presocratic thought had its irrational side, that the theories of the Milesian thinkers bore strong similarities to Near Eastern myths, and that the expressions used by the philosophers in their descriptions of physical principles often came close to those of religion—to Thales, after all, is attributed the (admittedly obscure) statement that "all things are full of gods" (DK 11 A 22). These scholars have also called attention to the many personifications of abstract powers that appear in the *Theogony*.[21] Nonetheless, the shift from Hesiodic or Orphic to philosophical cosmogony— the replacement of gods imagined in human form or personifications with physical elements or abstract principles, and the abandonment of the idea that cosmic events are brought about by gods whose actions resemble those of human beings, in favor of the assumption that underlying these events are purely physical processes—had two consequences whose significance should not be underestimated. With the disappearance of the names of the gods, accounts of the origin of the cosmos were released from their former bonds and associations with religious worship, and thus from the traditions of Greek society. Even when the theogonic poets innovated, they still arranged their statements within the framework of traditional, suprapersonal narration; they employed the traditional names of the gods, and they ascribed their works to great poets of the past. The Milesian philosophers (Thales, Anaximander, and Anaximenes), by contrast, created a new mode of expression. By using appellatives, they set their language apart from that of the tradition and made it wholly their own. Similarly, by writing in prose instead of poetry, they distinguished themselves from their predecessors; at the same time, the new medium enabled them to sort what they were saying into categories that lay within the realm of human experience. These were signs of an incipient trend: less than a century later, the Greeks, relying on their own power of reasoning, would begin to question the cultural relevance of myth (see Chapter 8).

The impulses behind this trend can be traced back as far as the eighth century, long before Thales' day. In the course of that century, with the rise of inland trade, of travel to the East, and of colonization, the Greek world grew increasingly receptive to new influences both internal and external (see Chapter 3 n. 24). Perhaps the strongest single impulse was the emergence of the polis. More and more Greeks took an active part in its formation, despite occasional setbacks, and in so doing they experienced the power of rational argumentation and independent thinking. It is no accident that our earliest piece of evidence for the *boulē*, the democratic council, is an inscription contemporary with Thales, and that it belongs to Chios, a large island to the northeast of Miletus that was famous for the prowess of its seafaring merchants.[22]

Those Presocratic philosophers who came after the Milesians and who employed a mythical mode of expression offer further testimony to this trend. The poem entitled *On Nature* by Parmenides of Elea (before 520 to after 450 B.C.), which offers a rational account of physical reality, opens with a myth in which the author describes how divine horses conveyed him to the palace of the goddess Aletheia (Truth). This journey into the beyond has parallels in Greek religious texts as well as in shamanistic tales, as scholars have emphasized.[23] Thus, the poem poses as mythical revelation. The purpose of the prefatory myth is to give suprapersonal sanction to the doctrine that follows. For the same reason the poem is written in the traditional form of epic poetry. In effect, Parmenides claimed divine inspiration, just as epic poets had done before him. He judged his invention of ontology to be so fundamental to his thought—as it turned out, ontology became a cornerstone of European philosophy—that he could not formulate it as a matter of personal opinion.

Different from Parmenides' poem in this respect was another scientific poem composed in hexameter verse, that of Empedocles of Acragas in Sicily (ca. 483 to 423 B.C.). Unlike Parmenides, Empedocles speaks in the first person throughout, and his doctrine vacillates between the exposition of physics and the narration of myth. Although he does refer to the four elements—his enduring contribution to the history of philosophy—as "fire, water, earth, and the boundless height of air" (DK 31 B 17, 18), he nevertheless introduces them in the guise of gods: "Hear, first, the four roots of all things: shining Zeus, life-giving Hera, Aidoneus, and Nestis, who with her tears supplies mortal springs with water" (DK 31 B 6). By characterizing the elements as gods, Empedocles was attempting to distinguish them (as the eternal elements from which all things are derived) from the four substances—fire, air, earth, water—as they are perceptible to the senses. The "mortal springs" are not identical with the element water but are produced by it; moreover, all four elements are indestructible and eternal—qualities that the religious tradition ascribed to the gods. When Empedocles makes a statement about physical reality in mythical terms—when he allegorizes—he does so with a purpose. It is no accident that he calls the two primal forces Neikos (Strife) and Philotes (Love), which, by mixing and separating the elements, cause the universe to come into being and pass into nothingness (DK 31 B 17, 20–26). They are abstract powers: his purpose in representing them as gods was no different from his purpose in representing the elements as gods.[24]

In the philosophy of Empedocles, mythical figures were mere code words for the things of nature. In Empedocles' day, myth had already been called into question, and the allegorical interpretation of myth was not original with him. The earliest known practitioner of allegoresis was Theagenes of Rhegium, Empedocles' senior by some two generations, who understood traditional mythical narration as a veiled form of physics. (Theagenes, and the trend that he initiated, will be discussed in Chapter 8.)

CHAPTER V

MYTH, SANCTUARY, AND FESTIVAL

Herodotus remarks in a much-cited passage that Homer and Hesiod "composed a theogony [*theogoniē*, i.e., an account of the birth and descent of the gods] for the Greeks, gave the gods their titles, assigned them their privileges and skills, and described their appearances" (2.53). The representation of myth in poetry shaped and influenced the Greek conception of the gods, even those who actually received cult, and this conception cannot be separated from religion. For the Greeks, the gods and heroes were always operative; therefore, they had temples and altars and received sacrifices, prayers, and votive offerings. Exactly how myth and religion were related to one another, however, is not immediately apparent, and has often been a matter of controversy. It is certain that the Greeks never regarded myth as the unalterable manifestation of the divine will, as Christians understand their sacred scripture. Just as certainly, Greek myth did not represent, as Mircea Eliade thought, "the triumph of the literary *work* over religious *belief*."[1] That presupposes an opposition between literature and belief that was alien to early cultures. For myth, of which the privileged medium of expression is language, is governed by the laws of narration; it is itself literature.

Looking beyond the handful of tales that have been counted

as Greek myth since the end of antiquity, we find an abundance
of myths that were tied to sanctuaries, temples, divine images,
and rituals. Here we focus on a single group of myths: those
which had as their setting the sanctuary of Apollo on the small
island of Delos.

Delian Etiologies

The Homeric *Hymn to Apollo* relates in detail the central myth,
that of Apollo's birth on Delos.[2] The text belongs to a collection
of thirty-three hymns written in dactylic hexameter. The
hymns have survived under the name of Homer, but the attribution is fictitious; they are of varying quality, and date from different periods, from late archaic times to late antiquity. The
Hymn to Apollo is a complex work, a blend of two originally
separate hymns, one of which is connected with Delos, the other
with Delphi. Scholars have assigned different dates to these two
sections on stylistic grounds. The Delian part (1–178), it is generally agreed, was written in the seventh century B.C., the second, Delphic part (179–546) somewhat later; the composite work
that has come down to us dates from the late sixth century B.C.,
and was performed on Delos, where the tyrant Polycrates of
Samos celebrated the Delian and Pythian festivals simultane-
ously.

The hymn opens with an account of Apollo's entry into
Olympus. When Apollo first appeared there, bow in hand,
the gods were startled and leapt up from their chairs. Only
Leto, his mother, remained calm by the side of Zeus. She
took her son's bow and quiver, hung them on a golden nail,
and led him to his seat. Zeus, his father, offered him nectar
in a golden cup; thus, Apollo's position as son of Zeus was
made plain to all the Olympians. A short hymn to Leto, the
mother of Apollo and Artemis, effects a transition to an
account of Apollo's birth. The pregnant Leto roamed the

earth in search of a place to bear her child, but nowhere was anyone willing to receive her (all were afraid of the unruly son whom she was carrying) until she reached the small, rocky island of Delos, where, she promised, her son would found his first and most beautiful temple. For nine days the goddess lay in parturition by the Inopus, the island's principal river, and many goddesses came to her aid. The reason for the prolonged labor was that Hera, out of jealousy, had been keeping Eileithyia, the goddess of childbirth, from Leto. At last Eileithyia came, bribed by Iris ("Rainbow"), the messenger of the gods. Then "Leto threw her arms around a palm tree and kneeled on the soft meadow, and the earth smiled beneath her. Apollo sprang forth into the light, and all the goddesses shouted" (117–19). The newborn child was bathed, wrapped in a sheet fastened with a golden band, and he tasted nectar and ambrosia, whereupon, to the astonishment of the goddesses, he broke free from his constraints and spoke: "May the lyre and the curved bow be dear to me forever, and I will prophesy to mortals the unerring will of Zeus" (131–32). Music, archery, and oracular prophecy are Apollo's provinces. One might expect that an account of the founding of the temple would be given at this point; instead, what follows is a description of the great Delian festival, which was attended by all Ionians and at which the Deliades, Apollo's chorus of maidens, sang. As an indication that Leto had kept her promise, an account of the founding of Apollo's temple could hardly have matched this description of the god's magnificent festival.

The myth explains how Apollo's cult was established on the small, barren island. Delos, according to the myth, was the only site that would receive Leto when she was ready to give birth to Apollo. That is why Apollo had a temple on the island. The oldest temple, an inconspicuous stone structure, dates from the geo-

metric period. Leto, too, had a sacred precinct (*temenos*) on Delos, within which stood a sixth-century temple (owing to her
significance in the Delian cult, Leto had the honor, in the opening lines of the hymn, of sitting next to Zeus, where Hera usually sat). Apollo's sister Artemis was also worshiped on Delos;
her temple was erected circa 700 B.C. Even Eileithyia had a *temenos*, and a festival was held in her honor. The palm tree on which
Leto had supported herself during the delivery was regarded by
the Homeric Odysseus as an emblem of the Delian sanctuary
(*Odyssey* 6.162).

In later texts the tale was altered: though closely bound to a
cult center, it was not canonical. What remained stable was the
kernel of the myth—the birth of Apollo beneath the palm tree
by the Inopus. The later addition of an olive tree is to be attributed to the influence of Athens, which wanted to have its own
sacred tree inserted into the myth to strengthen its claim on the
island (from the middle of the sixth century onward, Delos several times came under the sway of Athens). To understand later
variations, one usually has to consider the poet's interests. In the
Homeric hymn, Leto is surrounded by goddesses, this entourage
being appropriate to her rank in the divine realm. Later poets
brought out the pathetic and pitiful sides of the tale. In Callimachus's *Hymn to Delos* (249–63) Leto is ruthlessly persecuted by
Hera's agents Ares and Iris, and when she gives birth on the tiny
island, she does so alone. Similarly in Ovid's *Metamorphoses*
(6.337–42) she is compelled to take flight immediately after the
delivery, carrying her newborn children in her arms (Artemis,
in Ovid's version, is also born on Delos). In Callimachus's poem
the birth is attended by prodigies. Swans, which were sacred to
Apollo, circle the island seven times (seven was Apollo's sacred
number, and his birthday fell on the seventh day of the month,
as did most of his festivals), and then the god is born; in
celebration of his birth, the entire island is bathed in glittering
gold—a baroque exaggeration of the meadows in the Homeric hymn.

However, the myth was bound too closely with the cult site to give a merely superficial explanation of the island's sanctity. The paradox of the myth, that so great a god could be born on so small an island—a paradox that later poets so readily invested with pathos—reflected the paradox of the cult, that so small an island could become the site of so great a sanctuary, where Ionian islanders gathered, far from their own cities, to celebrate their common festival. The notion, found first in Callimachus (*Hymn to Delos* 30–36), that Delos was once a floating island, and thus neither land nor sea, contributed to the paradox. Ovid's explanation of the choice of the site (*Metamorphoses* 6.333–34) depended on this notion. According to him, Hera had forbidden Leto to have her child on land, leaving her no option but the floating island of Delos. Occupying a space between categories, Delos was the ideal location for the celebration of a festival at which many cities were to be united. The island's intermediate position made it virtually impossible for the member cities to engage in disputes and rivalries. Similarly, the Panionion, which served as a political and religious center for those Ionians who lived in the twelve cities on the western coast of Asia Minor, was situated on a slope of Mount Mycale—a remote spot.

Surrounding the major myth of Apollo's birth, which explained why Delos was sacred, were minor myths linked to details of the festival and to other cult objects on the island. Delos's chief attraction was the so-called Horned Altar, which was made of the horns of sacrificed goats. Mentioned along with the palm tree in the *Odyssey* (6.162–63), it was later counted, by some, among the seven wonders of the world (Hesiod, *Theogony* 347).[3] We know from numerous sources that the skulls and horns of sacrificial animals were deposited in sanctuaries, originally by hunters. A trace of this practice was preserved in the myth according to which Apollo himself, when he was only four days old, wove the altar from the horns of wild goats killed by the huntress Artemis, his sister (Callimachus, *Hymn to Apollo*

61–63). It was also said that about the altar young men and women, *kouroi* and *parthenoi*, performed a dance, which the Delians called the *geranos*, or "crane"; that this dance was introduced by Theseus when he put in at Delos on his way home from Crete with the Athenian youths and maidens whom he had rescued from the labyrinth; that the many twists and turns of the dance represented the winding passageways of that mazelike structure; that, during the same visit, Theseus left behind a wooden image of Aphrodite, which had been fashioned by Daedalus, the architect of the labyrinth, and which he had received from Ariadne; that Theseus founded the Delian games, promising to the winner a bough from the sacred palm tree as prize; and that he was the first to crop his hair and offer it to Apollo. A very old wooden statue of Aphrodite, which was thought to have been dedicated by Theseus, was indeed kept in the precinct of Apollo. As for the Delian games, they are described in the Homeric *Hymn to Apollo*: the events were boxing, song, and dance—events that typically belong to festivals of youths and maidens on the verge of adulthood. The hair offering was a feature of Apollo's cult, as many authorities attest.

We should not attempt to coordinate these myths with others. The appearance of the Delian festival during the interval between Theseus's visit and that earlier moment when Leto, according to the Homeric hymn (83–88), vowed that Apollo would have a cult on the island was of little concern to the narrator (or inventor) of the tales of Theseus. On the other hand, we can place the diverse institutions attributed to Theseus in a ritual context, even though these institutions were only included in the myth after Delos came under Athenian rule. We have already noted correspondences between Theseus's voyage to Crete and initiation ritual (Chapter 2); Crete is a transformation of that place in the beyond where young people are molded into adults. Accordingly, Theseus's return from Crete in the myth corresponds to the initiates' return from the beyond, after which they become adults. In ethnological cultures, this passage into adulthood is marked by dancing, contests, and the beginning of normal erotic relations. The hair offering belongs in the same context.[4]

Among the cult monuments in the vicinity of the sanctuary of Apollo were two tombs dating from the Mycenaean period, the so-called *sēma* and *thēkē* (each means "place of burial"). The *sēma* was situated in the precinct of Artemis, the *thēkē* east of the precinct of Apollo.[5] The occupants of these tombs were still being worshiped in historical times. The Greek names go back to Herodotus (4.33–35), who says that the *sēma* contained the remains of two Hyperborean girls, Laodice and Hyperoche. These girls, Herodotus explains, came to Delos under the protection of five young men, bearing offerings in return for ease of childbirth, and died in the sanctuary; since that time, the boys and girls of Delos, before marriage, had been placing locks of hair on the girls' tomb. The *thēkē* was also thought to be the burial place of two Hyperborean girls. These girls, Arge and Opis, had come to Delos even earlier than Laodice and Hyperoche, "along with the gods." The women of Delos went around collecting gifts for them, and sang in their honor a hymn composed by Olen, a Lycian who also was said to have composed the other hymns sung at Delos. In one such hymn Olen had Eileithyia come to Delos from the land of the Hyperboreans, and the pregnant Leto was likewise said to have come from there. Evidently, it was in the company of these goddesses that the first Hyperborean girls came to Delos.

The premarital offering of hair at the temple of Artemis on the promontory of Artemisium accords with premarital rites known from other places at which Artemis or Apollo were worshiped. The votaries brought to Delos by the Hyperborean girls constitute the mythical occasion for an actual offering of first-fruits. This offering did not come from the Hyperboreans, the "people beyond the north wind"; rather, Athens probably had a hand in establishing the practice. As for the collection of gifts by the Delian women, it is a common feature of the worship of goddesses who protect the interests of women, such as marriage and childbirth.[6] In later versions of the myth (Callimachus, *Hymn to Delos* 291–99; Pausanias 1.43.4), complications arise. In them we find not two pairs but either three girls, Upis, Loxo, and Hecaerge (Callimachus) or two, Opis and Hecaerge (Pausanias). The brides cut their hair and dedicate it to the girls, while the grooms offer their first beards to the girls' male escorts, who are apparently thought to be buried in the tomb also. To further complicate the matter, Pausanias (5.7.8) says that Olen wrote a hymn to a Hyperborean girl by the name of Achaea, who came to Delos after Opis and Hecaerge: it is possible that she was connected with a ritual of Delian women, this time in the cult of Demeter, whose title elsewhere was Achaea. The jumble is significant: only the rituals, in this instance the offering of hair by the brides and young men, were fixed, while the myths were variable, even when they were represented in cult hymns.

Another group of myths concerns Anius, the hero in whose cult the political unity of the inhabitants of Delos was expressed.[7] Anius was said to be the son of Apollo and Rhoeo, a granddaughter of Dionysus (while we know that the cult of Dionysus on Delos was important, we lack myths about the god from that source). When Rhoeo's father learned that his daughter was pregnant, he had her exposed in a chest. She was rescued and gave birth to Anius, who, when he had grown to manhood, came to Delos, where he became the founder the island's first settlement and its first king—so far the myth accords with other foundation myths. But it goes on to give an additional etiology. Anius's sons, for their part, became the eponymous founders of various Aegean islands: Andros, Myconos, Thasos. Thasos was torn apart by a dog, and for that reason no dogs were allowed on Delos. Dogs were rare in Greek religion; the sacrifice of dogs was considered barbaric and was associated with Hecate, the mistress of ghosts; a dog bite could be a religious desecration. The sanctity of Delos, which forbade births and burials, also excluded dogs. The myth explains this taboo.[8]

Anius also had three daughters, Spermo, Oeno, and Elais ("Grain Maiden," "Wine Maiden," and "Oil Maiden"), so named because Dionysus had given them the ability to produce grain, wine, and oil, respectively, from the ground or from nothing (all three were called, somewhat one-sidedly, the *Oinotropoi*, "they who turn [anything they please] into wine"): they were the patronesses of the powers that brought forth the staple foods of the Greeks. Their story was continued in the Epic Cycle. The *Cypria* told how Agamemnon's army, on its way from Aulis to Troy, made a stop on Delos, and there received nourishment from Anius's daughters. Much later, Roman poets altered the myth. According to Vergil (*Aeneid* 3.79–83) and Ovid (*Metamorphoses* 13.644–74), among others, the progenitor of the Romans, Aeneas of Troy, was hospitably received by Anius on Delos. Ovid, in particular, made Anius into an enemy of the Greeks. Agamemnon, seeing in Anius's daughters an inexhaustible source of food for his army, tried to kidnap them; in the end, Dionysus was able to save the girls, but only by transforming them into doves.[9] It is possible that this tale of transformation did not have underpinnings in cult.

The Delian myths that we have been considering all had an etiological function: they explained why a particular ritual was performed, why a temple, a special cult statue was venerated, and they usually did so by telling how the ritual, temple, statue, or other cult object first came about. Thus, the temple was promised by Leto; the Horned Altar was built by Apollo; the statue of Aphrodite, the crane dance, and the games were introduced by Theseus. To be sure, the connection between the myth and the institution that it purported to explain was not always so close as it was in these examples. Since the Hyperborean girls were buried in the *sēma*, they received a hair offering: in this case, it was taken for granted that the hair offering was made at the tomb—the sepulchral offering familiar to every Greek. Similarly, since a dog tore apart the young Thasos, dogs were forbidden on Delos. While these myths assigned causes to institutions, they did not fix the moment at which the institutions came into being.

Understanding Mythical Etiology

The relationship between myths and the institutions that they purport to explain requires closer examination. Not every ritual, cult statue, or temple was explained by an *aition*. *Aitia* are found in conjunction with especially important or venerable temples and cult statues, and with fundamental or unusual ritual acts— for example, the ancient temple of Apollo, the ancient statue of Aphrodite, the strange hair offering, or the animal sacrifice, which was explained by the myth of Prometheus (see Chapter 4). If an institution lost that which made it important or unusual, the myth that explained it was often forgotten. The archaic *Hymn to Apollo*, for example, made Leto the founder of her son's temple on Delos. This *aition* was forgotten when, after about 540 B.C., the old temple was rebuilt.

If the etiological myth was not forgotten, it was altered, as the myths surrounding the temples at Delphi show.[10] In the *Hymn to Apollo* we are told that the god himself laid the foundations of the Delphic temple (294–95), which was indeed at least as old as the *Iliad* (9.404–5). The Delphic part of the Homeric hymn had already been composed when, in 548/7 B.C., the temple was destroyed by fire. Thereafter, the myth was changed from an account of the temple's founding into a *Baugeschichte*, a record of temples built on the site—so first in Pindar, who was writing two generations after the fire (*Paean* 8). According to Pindar, the stone temple had three predecessors. It replaced a bronze structure, fashioned by the divine smith Hephaestus. The bronze temple was preceded by one made of feathers and beeswax, the so-called "Feather Temple" (*naos pterinos*), which was preceded, it was later said (the text of Pindar's *Paean* breaks off at this point), by a hut made of laurel thatch (the laurel tree was sacred to Apollo).

It is not difficult to imagine how the new myth originated. Since the stone temple that burned down could no longer be regarded as the one built by the god (for how could the god let the temple that he himself had built be destroyed?), it was said to have been built in a historical period, which followed a quite distant "mythical" one. The bronze temple was built during the age of the epic heroes, who lived in what we would call a Bronze Age—a fact of which Homer was always aware. Earlier still was the curiously dreamlike building made of feathers and wax: it belonged to a golden age, when permanent housing was unnecessary, when honey (which, like wax, is produced by bees) flowed abundantly, and birds and bees were thought to have the gift of prophecy. Finally, the thatched hut has associations with ritual and also carries overtones of a mythical history of culture. Thatched huts belong to rites in which participants enact "life as it was in ancient times" (ho archaios bios), which is prior to culture.[11] The laurel hut and the feather temple therefore correspond to one another semantically, but they must be treated successively in the myth, which purports to be a record of the buildings that occupied the site. It is significant, however, the adjective pterinos in the expression naos pterinos was thought by some to be derived not from pteron, "feather," but from pteris, "fern" (Pausanias 10.5.10): the naos pterinos, in other words, was understood as a kind of thatched hut.

Similarly, ancient cult statues, if they were thought to have special significance, were explained by aitia.[12] The ancient wooden statue of Artemis at Halae Araphenides in Attica was believed to have been the one stolen by Orestes from the land of the Taurians, where it had fallen from the sky. The statue of Artemis Orthia in Sparta, which was just as ancient as the one at Halae Araphenides, was also thought by some to be the one stolen by Orestes. The very ancient, boardlike statue of Hera on Samos was reportedly brought there from Argos by Admete, the daughter of Perseus. The Palladium, the oldest statue of Athena at Athens, supposedly first stood at Troy, where it once fell from

the sky. All these myths were attached to statues that were believed to be of great antiquity (by contrast, no myths, apart from
anecdotes, were connected with the chryselephantine statues
made by Pheidias for the Parthenon at Athens and the temple
of Zeus at Olympia). For the peculiarities of these old statues
special explanations were given. The statue of Hera on Samos
was said to have been taken from her temple during a festival
and wrapped in strips of cloth. Pirates once stole it, but their ship
did not budge until they put the statue back on the beach. The
earliest inhabitants of Samos found it there and, thinking that
it had run away, tied it to a bush. The statue of Dionysus Aisym-
netes in Patrae was kept in a chest. The Patraeans believed that
it was extremely old, the work of Epeius, who built the Trojan
horse, and that anyone who dared to open the chest would go
mad on seeing the statue. Cult statues were often thought to
have special powers. Madness was supposedly also caused by the
Spartan statue of Artemis Orthia from the land of the Taurians.
It was believed that Troy could not be conquered so long as it
possessed the Palladium and for that reason the image was stolen by Diomedes and Odysseus.

Where details are known, the cults surrounding these images
also seem to have been of a peculiar nature. The statue of Artemis Orthia attended the bloody flogging of the Spartan
ephebes, which was regarded as an attenuated form of human
sacrifice. Worn on the arm of the priestess, it was light, but it
grew unbearably heavy whenever those who were doing the
whipping did not use all their strength. Orestes was told not just
to dedicate the statue of the Taurian Artemis at Halae but also
to establish a bloody ritual there; this ritual was a substitution
for his death in the land of the Taurians and was understood as
a transformation of a human sacrifice. At the Samian festival of
the Tonaea, during which the old statue of Hera was set up out
of doors, participants acted out the incursion of nature (instead
of being preserved in the interior of a temple, a thing of culture,
the statue was attached to a tree, a thing of nature), the break-

down of the norms of civilization. The very ancient and eerie cult statue was always a symbol of an exceptional and, often enough, eerie ritual.

Thus, we return to ritual. The myth-and-ritualists, it will be remembered, argued that every known myth originated as an explanation of a ritual (Chapter 2). The foregoing examples suffice to show how one-sided this is, how etiological myths purport to explain all sorts of religious phenomena. Moreover, *aitia* are found outside the sphere of religion, too. Indeed, they account for nearly every conceivable peculiarity of nature and society. However, cult *aitia* occur most frequently among etiological myths, and for that reason alone the connection between myth and ritual deserves special consideration.

In the case of cult *aitia*, as in the case of *aitia* generally, the phenomena that they explain tend to be especially striking. The myth of Prometheus's deception of Zeus at Mecone does not account for the entirety of the normal Greek sacrifice; it explains a single detail, the strange and offensive division of the sacrificial animal. The story of the Hyperborean girls accounts for a hair offering and nothing more: here it should be noted that while the myth deals primarily with a sepulchral hair offering, the ritual that it explains is a premarital one. Such inconsistencies between myths and rituals are not uncommon and are usually significant. At a sacrifice to Demeter in Eleusis the Athenian ephebes used to "raise the ox," that is, they would carry the ponderous, live animal to the altar on their shoulders. The myth traces this ritual back to one of the deeds of Theseus's youth. When the hero, having grown to manhood in Troezen, came to Athens in search of his father Aegeus, he entered the city near the temple of Apollo Delphinius, which at that time was still under construction. Theseus had long hair and was wearing a long chiton, and the men who were roofing the new building teased him, asking what a "girl" like him was doing out of doors, walking alone. Enraged, Theseus unhitched a draft ox from a nearby cart and threw it high over the ridge of the temple roof.[13]

The myth and the ritual share only one feature: a young man lifting up an ox; the specific religious context of the Athenian ritual is lacking in the myth; there the religious context is replaced by one that includes the temple of Apollo Delphinius. This difference is not adventitious: there is an intrinsic connection between the ephebes and the temple of Apollo Delphinius. According to the myth, the sanctuary of the Delphian Apollo is the place where Theseus and Aegeus meet and where Aegeus recognizes Theseus as his son and the successor to his throne. In historical reality, the Delphinium, as the sanctuary was called, was the locus of a judicial court that adjudicated in disputes over citizen's rights, that is, in disputes over the position of the adult male in Athenian society. The myth, then, explains the ephebic rite of "raising the ox": just as Theseus, by performing his feat of strength, demonstrates that he is not a girl but a man, so the ephebe, by performing the rite, makes it known that he has grown to manhood.

Still, the ephebes' act does not correspond to that of Theseus in every respect. Whereas the superhuman hero threw the ox into the air by himself, the human ephebes merely carry it, and they do so not individually but as a group. The myth enlarges upon what is only intimated in the ritual. Such illustration of, one might even say extrapolation from, the ritual act is not uncommon. To take a typical case: in antiquity some rites were understood as attenuated forms of human sacrifice.[14] Taking these myths at face value, evolutionists have filled the prehistory of the Greeks with grim human sacrifices. This view is untenable, as a Spartan ritual shows. In Sparta the ephebes were flogged at the altar of Artemis Orthia. The ritual was reportedly instituted by Lycurgus, the Spartan lawgiver, as a substitute for a human sacrifice, which had a prehistory of its own. Once, it was told, after the Taurian statuette was brought to Sparta, a bloody fight broke out among the participants in a sacrifice at the goddess's altar, and several of them were killed. To punish the Spartans for this sacrilege, Artemis afflicted them with a pestilence. On consulting the Delphic oracle, the Spartans received the response that their atonement would be to spill human blood at the altar annually. The Spartans practiced human sacrifice until Lycurgus devised a way in which the oracle could be satisfied in a less bloody fashion.

Although the myth purports to be an account of the historical background of the cult, it is certainly not historical. There is no evidence to suggest that the flogging ritual, which the myth explains, was of such an early date. First mentioned by Cicero, the ritual was popular in the Roman imperial period, when Sparta's strange customs attracted tourists from all over the empire. In the fourth century B.C. there is no mention of flogging, but there is evidence for a cheese-stealing competition at this time. Two groups of young men would contend with one another at the altar. Some tried to steal a piece of cheese from the altar, others to prevent them from doing so. It was not Lycurgus or any other figure from Sparta's early history who altered the ritual but a Hellenistic reformer. Far from toning it down, he made it sanguinary, turning a relatively bloodless cheese-stealing match into a flogging. Thus, the *aition*, as an explanation of the flogging ritual, collapses. The ritual had no ancient background; instead, what emerges from the sources is that it made a strong impression on visitors: to them, the flogging seemed to be not a festive occasion but a kind of human sacrifice, with eerie and frightening undertones.

The myth does not explain any act in particular. Flogging is not mentioned specifically; if we had to reconstruct the ritual on the basis of the myth, there would be no reason to assume that it took the form of flogging. Rather, the myth gives expression to a general feeling. In this respect, it is not an isolated case. Many other myths, besides those dealing with the sacrifice of human victims, are linked to the rituals that they explain by a general feeling, a mood. The mood that is established in the myth of Apollo's birth on Delos, for example, corresponds to the mood of the festival: just as, in the myth, the birth of the god is a joyful event, one that delights the personified island of Delos, so the festival is a cheerful occasion. Otherwise, however, the myth and the ritual have little in common.

Only occasionally do we have the impression that the purpose of an *aition* is to account for all the details of a ritual. The Homeric *Hymn to Demeter* tells how Demeter came to Eleusis in the guise of an old woman and was brought into the palace of Celeus to serve as a nurse to his little son Demophoon.[15] Wine was offered to her, but she asked for a drink consisting of meal, water, and mint (206–10), the mythical prototype of the *kykeon*, the mixture with which the Eleusinian initiates ended the three-day period of fasting that preceded the actual celebration of the mysteries. Similarly, only after drinking the *kykeon*, whereby the goddess ended her period of fasting (during which she mourned the loss of her daughter Persephone), could she assume her duties as a nurse. The correspondences are close, and yet the ritual act could not be reconstructed from the myth alone: the *aition* is a part of the narrative, which here takes the form of a typical scene, that of the arrival of a stranger (see Chapter 3).

Myth and ritual, then, are autonomous phenomena. Although they may come into contact here and there, each of them is governed by its own structural laws. Myths are narratives, and as such they obey the conventions of the literary genre in which they are told; they are also assembled from narrative patterns, which migrate from one myth to another. Leto must flee from Hera's wrath; so must Io. The birth of Apollo is delayed by Hera; so is that of Heracles. The pregnant Rhoeo is exposed by her irate father; so is Danae, the mother of Perseus. It has already been said that patterns such as these make up the basic structure of a mythical type (Chapter 2). In this light, the philological method of establishing priorities among such motifs and of distinguishing original from later versions seems fraught with problems.

Just as narrative patterns sometimes migrate from one myth to another, so whole myths sometimes migrate from one cult to another. For example, the myth of the conveyance, by Orestes and his sister Iphigeneia, of a very ancient statue of Artemis from the land of the Taurians was told in Halae Araphenides, Sparta, Tyndaris on Sicily, and Aricia in Latium. The myth was adapted to the circumstances of the cults in each of these places. In Tyndaris it was added that Orestes wrapped the statue in tree branches, because a statue wrapped in this manner, that of Artemis Phakelitis, the "goddess in the bundle of withies," was carried in the local ritual. In Aricia the myth was augmented for a different reason. The cult there claimed that the statue was later conveyed to Sparta, because the cult statue of Diana in Aricia in historical times looked markedly different from the one described in the myth.[16]

So far, we have been considering the synchronic dimension, the functions of *aitia* for their contemporary users. But in discussing the Delian myths we have occasionally glimpsed a diachronic dimension: we were able to connect a number of myths with initiation rites. Similar rites are attested in ethnological cultures around the world. In the case of initiation rites in Greece, other institutions replaced them or were superimposed on them. That does not necessarily mean that certain Greek myths were genetically derived from prehistoric, Mycenaean, or even archaic Greek initiation rites. (There are two reasons for making this supposition. First, in the archaic societies of Crete and Sparta, the institutions that regulated the behavior of young people, in particular that of young males, bear strong resemblances to initiation rituals known from ethnological cultures. Second, the myths of Theseus told on Delos, which could not have taken the form in which we know them before the sixth century, retain traces of a ritual context.) But just as Greek institutions can be shown to have analogues in the institutions of ethnological cultures, so Greek myths can be shown to have analogues in the mythical ideology of the rituals found in those cultures. Here myths and rituals exhibit not only correspondences of basic structure but also correspondences of detail that guarantee connections between them.[17]

A notion that underlies many initiation rites in ethnological cultures is that the initiates are transformed by the ritual. The initiates become men: they were boys before undergoing the ritual. This transformation is reflected in a narrative type in which a girl turns into a man. One example of this type in Greece is the *aition* that explains the premarital rites of Leto Phytia in Phaestos on Crete. During her husband's absence, a woman gives birth to a girl. But, because the father wanted a son and threatened to expose a daughter, the child is named Leucippus and is raised as a boy. As the child approaches adolescence, the mother, in despair, calls on the goddess for help—and the girl becomes a man (Antoninus Liberalis, *Metamorphoses* 17). Even more drastic is the type in which the initiates are killed and then reborn. Enacted in various ritual forms, the type is a part of the most widespread ideology of initiation rites. Death and human sacrifice were prominent themes in Greek myth, as our examples have shown. The Greeks placed emphasis on the eerie aspects of ritual, and it was those aspects that their myths purported to explain.

Myth, Sanctuary, and Festival

We began by considering Delos and its myths. The Delian part of the *Hymn to Apollo* shows how the mythical narrative was integrated into the festival. The poet mentions the Deliades, the Delian maidens, who "sing in praise first of Apollo, then of Leto and Artemis" (158–59). That the present hymn has a place in their repertory is shown by the following lines, in which the poet addresses himself directly to the maidens: "Girls, who in your eyes is the sweetest of the singers here, and in whom do you delight the most? You will all answer with one voice," and he goes on to describe himself (169–73). The oldest Delian cult songs, however, were traced back to Olen, as Herodotus reports. In the Hellenistic period Delian inscriptions were still honoring poets, whose works have not come down to us, for their representation of "local myths." The mythical narrative was a set feature of the Greek hymn in its traditional form; its proper place was in the central "epic" section of the hymn, where the poet praised the outstanding abilities of the deity to whom he was making his appeal. Such was its function in the few cult hymns that have been preserved in inscriptions as well as in the cult poetry of the archaic poets, particularly in that of Pindar and Bacchylides, who gave prominence to myths in their hymns and paeans, even myths that were neither local nor closely connected with a sanctuary.

Not only do the maidens of Delos sing of Apollo, Leto, and Artemis; they also praise the "men and women of the past" (160). They praise heroes and heroines; they treat the themes of epic poetry. At the festival, then, myths were told that did not relate to the immediate context of their narration; the myths of cult poetry, by contrast, tended to refer to their cultic context. Delos was no exception. The performance of epic poetry was a part of many festivals; the *Homeric Hymns*, after all, were preludes to rhapsodic performances at festivals of the gods. Myths were also narrated in choral lyric poetry. Stesichorus, the greatest choral lyric poet, was considered the greatest teller of myths between Homer and tragedy.[18] No one doubts that choral lyric poetry was performed at festivals, although in most instances we do not know exactly where or when it was performed. Thus, mythical narration became virtually an aesthetic end in itself, contributing especially to the festivity of the occasion. The poem was a kind of *agalma*, an intangible votive offering to the gods— although Hellenistic poets, after their mythical narratives were performed, occasionally had them chiseled·in stone and set up in the sanctuary.

There were other media of mythical narration in the sanctuary: votive offerings fashioned out of stone and metal, and pictorial representations. These objects were not embellishments of the festival but permanent adornments of the sacred space.[19] The myths told in these media did not necessarily relate to the sanctuary. The east pediment of the temple of Zeus at Olympia shows the myth of Pelops and Oenomaus, the mythical found-ing of the Olympic games, while the west pediment shows the battle of the Lapiths and Centaurs, in which a radiant Apollo intervenes to restore order. At first glance, this seems irrelevant to Olympia. However, by glorifying the victory of the Greeks and their civilization over the chaotic and eerie Centaurs, the west pediment may refer to Olympia as the site of athletic games: the difference between sport and war is merely one of degree, and the athletic games perpetually reenact the same vic-tory. Pausanias gives a detailed description of votive offerings that he saw in the Delphic sanctuary (10.9–31). Many of these are representations of Delphic myths. At least as many, however, represent either the local heroes of the cities that made the dedi-cation or their local myths, and Pausanias names a group of iron statues fashioned by a certain Tisagoras, which showed Heracles fighting the Hydra and which was admired for the peculiarity of its material (10.18.6). All that mattered in this case was that the offering was a costly one.

In this chapter, to be sure, we have hardly discussed the great myths of the classical tradition. It was the lesser *aitia* that had especially close ties with actual Greek religious practice. Many of these are attested only by late authors such as Pausanias, and we cannot be sure how valid they were. Yet the Homeric *Hymn to Apollo* is not the only text that affords evidence of a mythical narrative performed in the context of a festival. Herodotus refers to the hymns of Olen; inscriptions prove that local poets wrote hymns; Euripides tells the *aition* of Halae Araphenides. The nar-ration of etiological myths had been a feature of Greek cult from time immemorial.

FIG. 1. The sack of Troy: (from the left) Aeneas escapes with his father and his son; Cassandra seeks refuge at the statue of Athena; Priam, with the dead Astyanax on his lap, is slain on the altar of Zeus; Hecuba defends herself; Menelaus and Helen. Attic red-figure hydria by the Cleophrades Painter, circa 500–480 B.C.. (*Naples, Museo Nazionale*).

FIG. 2. Heracles and the Actorione-Molione. Boeotian fibula, circa 725–700 B.C. (*Athens, National Museum*).

FIG. 3. Zeus and Typhoeus. Chalcidian hydria, circa 550 B.C. (*Munich, Antikensammlungen*).

FIG. 4. Gods as dragon slayers. Akkadian cylinder seal, circa 2300 B.C. (*Baghdad, Iraq Museum*).

FIG. 5. Artemis, Apollo, Leto, Aphrodite, and another goddess (Delos?). Attic red-figure bell crater in the manner of the Meidias Painter, circa 420–410 B.C. (*Vienna, Kunsthistorisches Museum*).

FIG. 6. Croesus on the pyre. Attic red-figure amphora by Myson, circa 500 B.C. (*Paris, Louvre*).

FIG. 7a. Theseus, under Athena's protection, performs his deeds on the road from Troezen to Athens: (clockwise from Athena) the slaying of Sinis (note the pine branches!); the slaying of Sciron and Procrustes; the slaying of the sow of Crommyon; the slaying of the Minotaur; the taming of the Marathonian bull. Attic red-figure cup by the Cleophrades Painter, circa 500–480 B.C. (*Paris, Bibliothèque Nationale*).

FIG. 7b. Theseus and the wrestler Cercyon. Tondo of the same cup.

FIG. 8. In front of the temple of Artemis in the land of the Taurians, Iphigeneia hands Pylades a letter to Orestes (the goddess is above and to the right of Iphigeneia); on the left, Orestes; above him, a satyr; on the right, a sacrificial attendant. Apulian amphora, circa 350–340 B.C., illustrating Euripides, *Iphigeneia among the Taurians* 728 ff. (*now lost*).

FIG. 9. Orestes is cleansed of blood guilt by Apollo in Delphi; on the left, three Erinyes and the ghost of Clytemnestra; on the right, Artemis. Apulian bell crater, circa 370–350 B.C., inspired by Aeschylus, *Eumenides* 282–83 (*Paris, Louvre*).

FIG. 10. Heracles and Geras ("Old Age"). Attic red-figure pelike by the Geras Painter, circa 480 B.C. (*Paris, Louvre*).

FIG. 11. Jason. Attic red-figure cup by Douris, circa 480–70 B.C. (*Munich, Antikensammlungen*).

CHAPTER VI

MYTH AS HISTORY

Myth and Historiography

Down to the end of antiquity, it was self-evident to most Greeks that heroic myth, if not divine myth as well, related the events of their past, and that this historical reality could be detected in the myths or reconstructed from them. From the late sixth century onward, the Greeks tended increasingly to regard divine myths as veiled representations of physical processes no less real (though not historically real: the divine myths were not regarded as historical until the emergence of euhemerism; see Chapter 8). Plato called the narration of myths "a search for the things of the past" (*Critias* 110a). Ancient historical works usually took the mythical past as their starting point. Herodotus, the "father of historiography" (as Cicero called him), began his history, the main purpose of which was to give an account of the Persian Wars, by considering the ultimate cause of the conflict between Greeks and barbarians. The Phoenicians, in his view, started it all. They abducted the daughter of the king of Argos, Io, and brought her to Egypt; the Greeks retaliated by making off with a Phoenician princess, Europa of Tyre. Then the Greeks put themselves in the wrong by raiding Colchis and seizing, among other things, Medea, the king's daughter. Two generations later, the Asians were avenged when Paris of Troy carried off Helen, the wife of the Spartan king Menelaus (1.2–4). It is true that Herodotus attributed this explanation to "Persian informants" (*logioi*; one wonders how these learned Persians could have known so much about Greek myth); and it is also true that he dismissed it, remarking that, instead of attempting to answer the question whether the enmity between Greeks and barbarians really originated as the Persians claimed, he wished to begin with the man who, he was absolutely certain, was the first to commit an injustice, namely Croesus, the king of Lydia, unquestionably a historical figure. Nonetheless, he did not doubt the historicity of the mythical abductions in principle; he simply preferred beginning with verifiable events to distilling the truth from obscure myths. Later in his work, he accepted without hesitation the notion that the royal dynasties of Lydia and Persia had been established by Heracles (1.7.2). Indeed, he made this derivation the cornerstone of his chronological system by placing Heracles nine hundred years before his own time (2.145.4).

Thucydides, who is generally and rightly regarded as the most rational of the Greek historians, similarly accepted myth as history but doubted some of its details. He was extremely cautious in his treatment of the distant past, because it was something about which nothing could be known for certain ("People," he noted, "accept without scrutiny the stories that they hear from one another about past occurrences, even those occurrences which belong to the history of their own land," 1.20.1). Yet he began his preliminary account of the early history of Athens and Greece with the period that we would call mythical. Here he sometimes exercised his astuteness on the wrong object. For example, his view of Minos, the king of Crete, as a ruthless expansionist led him to suppose that Minos's reason for checking piracy was "to ensure that the king's revenues might reach him more easily" (1.4). In general, the more "modern" Thucydides is far more reliable than the "naïve" Herodotus, so far as the historicity of myth is concerned. Comparing Herodotus's view of Minos with that of Thucydides, however, one might arrive at the opposite conclusion. Herodotus assigned Minos's maritime supremacy to the obscure past, naming Polycrates, the tyrant of Samos (third quarter of the sixth century B.C.) as the first sea ruler "of the so-called human era" (3.122).[1] But this passage is exceptional. For although Herodotus's phrase "the human era" may imply the germ of the notion of myth as something essentially different from history (he was distinguishing "the human era" from an earlier one, which presumably he would have called "heroic"), elsewhere he, like all later historians, distinguished myth from history solely on the basis of the degree to which it could be verified. The remoter the event was, the more difficult it was to substantiate it. Whereas modern historians regard myth and history as distinct or even sharply opposed categories, ancient historians saw them as belonging to a single continuum.[2] Their vocabulary makes this apparent. For Herodotus, *mythoi* were not the tales of Io, Europa, Medea, Helen, and Minos but reports that did not tally with probability and experience, including the notion that the Nile rose when the water of Oceanus is forced into it by winds from the south (2.23). Similarly, when Thucydides spoke of *to mythōdes*, he meant a kind of historical narrative that was fabulous and entertaining. He eschewed this kind of history, endeavoring instead to produce "a possession for all time" (1.22).

Myth was also understood as, or transformed into, history by the contemporaries and predecessors of Herodotus and Thucydides, including the earliest among the latter whose works are not lost to us, Hecataeus of Miletus, who appears to have been active a little before 500 B.C. (*FGrH* 1). In a work later known variously as *Genealogies* (*Genealogiai*), *Researches* (*Historiai*), or *Tales of Heroes* (*Heroologiai*)—the book title had not yet been invented, and the titles represent later attempts to categorize the work— Hecataeus collected, examined, and recounted the tales that constituted the history of the Greeks down to the time of the Trojan War, a period known only from mythical narratives. To be sure, he considered the traditional accounts (*logoi, FGrH* 1 F 1) "ridiculous," but he did not reject them; instead, he distilled from them what he took to be their true meaning, discarding anything that did not measure up to the standards of probability and common sense.

A case in point is the tale according to which Heracles once fetched Cerberus, the three-headed dog that guarded the gate of Hades, from the underworld. Hecataeus did not think that this tale could be taken literally, but he did allow that Heracles could have caught a huge snake named the "Hound of Hades" near Cape Taenarum, the supposed location of an entrance to Hades (*FGrH* 1 F 27). While three-headed dogs dwelling in the underworld seemed highly unlikely, huge poisonous snakes did not. Thus, Hecataeus could reasonably suppose that the myth had been invented by someone who took the snake's name, Hound of Hades, literally. Hecataeus saw the myth as what Max Müller would call a "disease of language." Even more ingenuous is another Hecataean rationalization: Hecataeus challenged the mythical datum that Aegyptus had fifty sons, apparently on the ground that fifty was an unlikely number of children for a man to have had by one wife. Aegyptus, he said, begat "not even twenty, in my opinion" (*FGrH* 1 F 19).

Myth, for Hecataeus, was obviously subject to the storyteller's tendency to exaggerate: as Fontenelle would remark, "we are naturally disposed to exaggerate to an astonishing degree." That is the methodological credo of all those who would read history into myth. Plutarch outlined the rationalist's method at the end of the first century A.D.: "our aim is to purify the fabulous (*to mythōdes*), making it yield to reason and take on the appearance of history" (*Theseus* 1). In 1983, a respected classical historian called this process "the demystification of the historical."[3] Herodotus took a similar approach in the first chapter of his history: it was not, according to him, a huge gadfly sent by Hera that drove Io to Egypt, not Zeus in the guise of a bull that abducted Europa, but traders or pirates. It is a point in favor of

Herodotus's sense of history that he denied responsibility for the veracity of such tales, often by laying them to the account of his Persian or Phoenician informants.

Genealogies

As the title *Genealogies* indicates, Hecataeus's main interest lay in putting the immense mythical tradition of the Greeks into chronological order by means of genealogical data. Other early Greek historians shared this interest (and the title *Genealogies*). Their undertaking was significant, for they assumed that the myths were discernibly interlinked; they saw them not as entities suspended independently in timelessness but as links in a chain. In other words, they saw the myths much as we see historical documents: as pieces of a large puzzle. In ordering the myths, the early historians exhibited two tendencies. On the one hand, they synchronized the genealogies with increasing stringency and precision, so that the sequence of generations in a given family tree would be the same from one myth to the next. On the other, they attempted to bridge the gap that existed between the end of what we regard as the mythical period—the generation of the sons of those who fought at Troy—and the beginning of historical memory and documentation.

The principle of interlinking myths by genealogical means was not original with Hecataeus. Genealogies were at least as old as the Homeric poems. In their most rudimentary form they extend over three generations: every Homeric hero has a father, and sometimes a son as well. Thus, we learn that Nestor's father was Neleus, his son Antilochus; that Odysseus's father was Laertes, his son Telemachus. Longer genealogies were reserved for special situations. The most extensive is that of Aeneas. Before engaging Achilles in single combat, the hero recites his family tree "in order that you may be certain of my lineage," as he says to his opponent (*Iliad* 20.215–41). Aeneas's family history covers six generations. As a collateral relative of Priam and his son Hector, he belongs to the ruling family at Troy, which he traces back to Zeus. This genealogical excursus evokes myths linked with individual forebears, such as Ganymede. There is even a rudimentary history of the city of Troy: Ilium (another name for Troy), situated at the edge of the Scamander Plain and founded by Priam's father Ilus, was preceded by another city, Dardania, situated higher up in the mountains and founded by Dardanus, a son of Zeus.

As Aeneas's genealogy shows, various and even independent myths—the myth of handsome Ganymede, for example, was told for its own sake throughout antiquity—were incorporated into a single family tree. On the other hand, some ancestors, such as Ilus, the founder of Ilium, or Tros, the ruler of the Trojans, appear to have been little more than eponyms; these may have been invented just for the purpose of explaining a proper name. Most important, the interlinking of myths resulted in a chronological sequence within the mythical period, one that extended from Zeus to Aeneas and Hector. The epic bard was obviously more than a teller of tales; he was also a collector and systematizer of myths—this side of his activity is underappreciated. In fact, this systematization, this quasi-historical ordering of mythical data, contributed to the rationality of mythical narration in epic poetry.

Such systematization on the part of the *aoidoi* is much more conspicuous in the *Catalogue of Women*, a hexameter poem preserved, in a very fragmentary state, under the name of Hesiod (frr. 1–245 MW).[4] In the *Theogony*, the genealogical chain forms the basis of Hesiod's vision of the gods and the cosmic forces represented by them; that poem, as it is known to us, ends with a list of the marriages of Zeus and the other gods (886–1022). It is at this point that the *Catalogue of Women* begins. Proceeding from the unions of gods with mortal women, it traces their genealogies through the mythical period down to the generation of those who fought at Troy and occasionally to that of their sons. Each genealogy in the catalogue opens with the fixed introductory phrase *e hoie* ("or like that woman who . . ."), whence the alternative title *Ehoiai*. The individual genealogies are linked by a common ancestry: the heroes and heroines are descended from the original mortal couple, Deucalion and Pyrrha, the children of Prometheus and Epimetheus, respectively, and the sole survivors of the great flood. Their son, Hellen, was the eponymous ancestor of the Greeks, who called themselves Hellenes. The tree branches out, in the next generation, with more eponyms: in union with a sister of Hellen, Zeus begat Macedon and Magnes, who gave their names to the Macedonians and the Thessalian Magnesians; in union with another sister of Hellen, a certain Pandora, Zeus begat Graicus, eponym of the northwest *Graikoi*, from whose name was derived the Latin *Graeci*; Hellen's sons were Aeolus, Dorus, and Xuthus, ancestors of the Aeolians, Dorians, and Ionians, respectively, the three main ethnic and dialectical groups of Greece. This had a definite purpose; it categorized the various groups, related linguistically and culturally, that were on the Greek mainland during the archaic period; it legitimated the boundaries that separated them from one another by assigning their origins to the period immediately after the flood, which marked the beginning of the mortal era; and it provided a map, as it were, with the aid of which one might find one's bearings in the midst of diverse ethnic and political groupings. Similarly, the *Theogony* organized, and indeed made intelligible, not only the gods of cult but also the cosmos in general.

Genealogy may appear to have been just a chain of names and not a form of mythical narration. Yet nearly every name entails a story. Thus, genealogy can be the mainspring of myth, as the *Ehoiai* and the family tree of Aeneas in the *Iliad* show. Genealogy and the narration of myth were even more closely connected in those tales, the earliest of which, so far as we know, were told in late archaic epic poetry, in which a royal house is afflicted with a hereditary curse. Such a curse befell the descendants of Tantalus, the rulers of Mycenae and Argos. The pedigree of Agamemnon's scepter in the *Iliad* (2.101–8) seemed harmless: Hermes gave it to Pelops, who left it to his son, Atreus; Atreus was succeeded by his brother, Thyestes, who in turn left it to Atreus's son Agamemnon. But in later treatments of Tantalus's house—in Attic tragedy, for example—Atreus and Thyestes were represented as enemies:

> A lamb with a golden fleece appeared in Atreus's flock. Instead of sacrificing the lamb to Artemis, Atreus kept it as a warrant of his rule. Thyestes seduced his brother's wife Aerope and with her help stole the fleece. Atreus killed Aerope and banished his brother. Then Thyestes induced Pleisthenes, a son of Atreus, to murder Atreus. But Atreus killed Pleisthenes, not knowing that he was his son. To avenge himself, Atreus pretended a reconciliation and invited Thyestes to a banquet at which he served his brother the flesh of his (Thyestes') children. Finally, Atreus was killed by Thyestes' son Aegisthus. These horrors were attributed to two curses. One was uttered by Pelops when he discovered that Chrysippus, his illegitimate but favorite son, had been murdered by his other sons Atreus and Thyestes. The other was that of the charioteer Myrtilus, and it afflicted the house most dreadfully. Myrtilus helped Pelops to gain the daughter and realm of Oenomaus, ruler of Pisa in Elis, but when he demanded his reward, Pelops killed him. Before he died, Myrtilus called down a curse on Pelops, which carried over to the following generations: Aegisthus seduced Agamemnon's wife Clytemnestra, who slew her husband; Orestes, Agamemnon's son, avenged his father's death by killing his mother, thereby entangling himself in an apparently hopeless quandary (see Chapter 7).

For all its systematization, the *Catalogue of Women* was not thoroughly synchronized (later historians were more exacting). Furthermore, it did not extend beyond the generation of the sons of those who fought at Troy. Only later was the gap between that generation and the beginning of historical memory bridged. This was accomplished gradually, as individual aristocratic families and even entire poleis required ties with the mythical past. To enhance their status in the polis, Greek aristocrats linked their families with the genealogies of the epic heroes, and therefore also with the divine ancestors of those heroes. For example, the Aeneadae, who lived in the Troad, traced themselves back to Aeneas. Many scholars believe that the prominence of Aeneas in the *Iliad* was the result of their influence.[5]

The practice of linking one's family to the heroes and gods of the mythical past was not confined to aristocratic houses. Herodotus (2.143) reports that even Hecataeus claimed descent from a god (in the sixteenth generation); the names of the intervening fourteen ancestors, however, are not recorded. According to Pherecydes of Athens (*FGrH* 3 F 2), the family tree of the elder Miltiades, the grandfather of the Miltiades who led the Athenians to victory at Marathon (490 B.C.), indicates how the gap was bridged. The elder Miltiades traced his lineage back to Philaeus, the eponym of the Philaïdae (an aristocratic family) and the son of the Homeric Ajax, son of Telamon. The twelve generations between Philaeus and Miltiades are hardly more than names to us; at some point, however, historical memory must have begun. Just how far back the memory of the living could reach is indicated by the genealogy of a man from Chios, preserved in a late fifth-century inscription: it spans fourteen generations—over four hundred years—and none of the names can be inserted into any known myth.[6] The memory of this man's family may indeed have gone back to the time when his ancestors immigrated to the island, but we cannot be certain.

The beginnings of the practice of linking historically real genealogies with those of the heroic age described in epic poetry are almost imperceptible. Yet this practice marked a highly significant conceptual development. For once the gap separating the historical and the mythical ages had been bridged, myth ceased, permanently and demonstrably, to be seen as something that took place *in illo tempore* (M. Eliade), in a chronologically vague past, the age of "demigods" (*hēmitheoi, Iliad* 12.23), of Hesiod's heroes. Although these heroes lived in an "earlier age" radically different from the present (*Works and Days* 160), the Greeks had been discovering, identifying, and worshiping their bones and burial places since the eighth century. The age of the epic heroes enters into a datable relation to the present age. Ajax was said to have lived twelve generations before the elder Miltiades, that is, in the mid-tenth century (if we allow three generations to a century). The linking of the heroes of myth with their bones and tombs was perhaps the first step toward the conception of myth as history (Chapter 3): with that step, the heroes of myth were regarded as men of the distant past. With the elaboration of a chronology, the Greeks had a rational way of including the heroic age in their past, which they understood as a quantifiable time continuum.

The oldest genealogical line, that of the Spartan kings, was just as much a form of political history as it was an expression of pride on the part of private aristocrats.[7] The impressive family trees of the Spartan kings Leonidas and Leotychides, who fought as generals in the war against the Persians, are recorded by Herodotus (7.204; 8.131). To a large extent, the personal genealogies of the two kings coincided with the list of the kings of the Spartan dual kingship: Leonidas traced his lineage back to Agis, the progenitor of the Agiad dynasty, Leotychides to Eurypon, the progenitor of the Eurypontids. Ultimately, both kings were said to be descended from Heracles, the son of Zeus. Again, the mythical and historical ages were neatly spliced. The antiquity of these genealogies is uncertain. At all events, the Spartan poet Tyrtaeus, who flourished early in the seventh century B.C., knew of the descent of the Spartan kings from Heracles. It is difficult to imagine that the line had not already been traced back to the mythical period in Tyrtaeus's day; in all likelihood, the whole line dates from the eighth century B.C. For centuries, genealogy remained central in the Spartans' view of their own history.

Plato has the sophist Hippias of Elis boast that, to please his Spartan audience, he had become quite adept at reciting genealogies and other stories about the distant past (*Greater Hippias* 285d). Sparta, old-fashioned and conservative as it was, tended to preserve lore, which, in the archaic period, had been just as highly valued by other poleis.

Mythical Constructions of History

The return of the Heraclids and the Ionian migration are the subjects that show the most extensive use of myths to bridge the gap between the end of the heroic age of epic poetry and the beginning of historical memory and thereby to explain the political and ethnic differences between Greece as it was known from epic poetry and Greece as it was known in historical times. According to the *Iliad* and the *Odyssey*, the Peloponnesus was divided into a number of local principalities—that of Agamemnon in Mycenae, of Menelaus in Sparta, of Nestor in Pylos—while the western coast of Asia Minor was inhabited by Carians, Lelegians, and other non-Greek peoples (*Iliad* 10.428–31). In the first millennium the coast was occupied, from south to north, by Dorians, Ionians, and Aeolians, all of whom had relations on the mainland across the sea. Indeed, the mainland itself was split into various ethnic groups and political units.

Ancients and moderns agree that these changes resulted from population movements. The Dorians, who lived in northwest Greece during the Bronze Age, conquered the Peloponnesus, with the exception of the mountainous district of Arcadia, then migrated by way of Crete to Rhodes, Cos, and the coast of Asia Minor. The Aeolians crossed the northern Aegean, settling on Lesbos and its Asiatic hinterland. The Ionians occupied the area between them. Modern archaeology has shown that in the Bronze Age certain cities in Ionia were occupied by Greeks, but that with the collapse of Mycenaean civilization these cities were destroyed and were not resettled for at least a century. The peculiar nature of the ceramic finds there links the new settlers with Athens.[8] The Dorian migration is more problematic. The prevailing view has the Dorians penetrating into a vacuum created by a wave of invading Sea Peoples, as they are called, who are thought to have passed swiftly through the region around 1200 B.C. The border peoples of northwest Greece, according to this view, took this invasion as an invitation to advance southward. Recently, however, scholars have raised doubts about the migration itself, pointing out that the Dorians left behind no archaeological evidence that would identify them as such, and that traces of the Dorian dialect have been detected in the language of the Mycenaean Linear B tablets; accordingly, these scholars have suggested that the group known as the Dorians was in fact the oppressed population of the Mycenaean period, the vassals, as it were, of the Mycenaean lords. That is going too far. The traces of the Dorian dialect in Linear B are not very conspicuous, and archaeologists have discerned a clear break in the style of decorated pots as well as traces of settlement, at least in Sparta. That indicates an influx of new population elements into Greece. The new elements did not necessarily immigrate en masse; it is more likely that small groups trickled in and merged with the existing inhabitants.[9]

The post-Mycenaean settlement of the Peloponnesus is an entirely different matter. The Greeks referred to this settlement as the "return of the Heraclids," or the descendants of Heracles. Two accounts of this return have been preserved, one in the universal history of Diodorus of Sicily, the other in the *Library* of Apollodorus. Both works are late compilations. In its main lines, however, the tale predates the fifth century B.C.[10]

> The Heraclids, having fled by a circuitous route from their father's arch enemy, Eurystheus, the ruler of Mycenae, went as suppliants to Athens, where Theseus agreed to protect them. Eventually, Eurystheus was slain in single combat by Heracles' son Hyllus. Under Hyllus, the Heraclids

attempted to reclaim the land that was their birthright, but they were unsuccessful—either because an oracle consulted during a drought required that they return only "after the third harvest" or because Hyllus engaged in a duel with a Peloponnesian champion, promising that if he lost the Heraclids would not return for fifty (or one hundred) years, and was slain. The Heraclids spent these years in the realm of Aegimius, a son of Dorus and a friend of Heracles. An attempt to return after only three years was again unsuccessful. The Heraclids realized that Apollo had meant three generations, not three years. When three generations had passed, the Heraclids, joined by Aegimius's Dorians, returned to the Peloponnesus under the leadership of Temenus, Cresphontes, and Aristodemus. But they, too, had to wait, because the Heraclids killed a seer who was sacred to Apollo, whereupon the god issued another enigmatic oracle. They were able to solve it, were successful at last, and cast lots for the three major regions of the Peloponnesus. Temenus received the Argolid; the sons of Aristodemus, who had meanwhile been struck down by a thunderbolt, received Sparta; and Cresphontes, by an act of deception, received rich Messenia.

The myth agrees with what is known about the Dorian invasion from the archaeological and dialectological record only in its main lines—that the historical Dorians, that is, the Argives, Spartans, and Messenians, migrated from central Greece into the Peloponnesus not long before the beginning of the historical period. Even so it agrees only in the case of Aegimius's Dorians, who play a secondary role in the narrative. It is possible that they were imported into it from another, originally independent myth. If that is so, the myths must have been combined at an early date, because all Dorian poleis were divided into three phylai, or tribes, derived from the two sons of Aegimius, Dymas and Pamphylus, and the Heraclid Hyllus.

At all events, the Heraclids finally succeeded in returning to the land to which they were entitled by birth, the land from which they had once been banished by Eurystheus. The myth transformed the historical conquest and settlement of the Peloponnesus into a long and involved struggle for the hereditary realm of the Heraclids. The result was not just an exciting story; it also legitimized the conquest of the Peloponnesus. Similarly, Cresphontes' act of deception legitimized and made morally palatable the later conquest of Messenia by Sparta, which resulted in the abolition of the preexisting social structure. The tale of the settlement of Sparta by the two sons of Aristodemus, who for etiological reasons was removed from history by a thunderbolt, explained the Spartan double kingship, whose two royal houses went back to Agis and Eurypon, the grandsons of Aristodemus. Theseus's intervention on behalf of the Heraclids at once accounted for the cults of Heracles in Attica and gave expression to Athens's claim that it was equal, if not superior, to the Dorians—a claim that was a root of political conflict in the fifth and fourth centuries.

Political etiology was not the only factor in the formation of myths. Myths were also shaped by the requirements of narration and especially of chronology. Hyllus belonged to the generation of those who fought with Agamemnon at Troy. After Agamemnon's death, the rule of Mycenae remained in his family, devolving to his son Orestes and then to his grandson Tisamenus. Only in the third generation after that of Hyllus, that is, fifty to one hundred years after his death, could the Heraclids have won the Peloponnesus. It was therefore necessary to retard their return, and this was effected by the misinterpretation of the first oracle (a narrative *topos*) and by the (characteristically epic) duel between the commanders of the opposing armies. The second retardation is a repetition of the enigmatic oracle (which, unlike the first, was interpreted correctly at the first attempt); it appears to have had a purely narrative motivation.

The myth of the return of the Heraclids explained the dialects and ethnic groups that existed in the Peloponnesus after the Bronze Age, and it legitimated the political groupings associated with them. For just that reason it was regarded as history, as a representation of a real past, but one that had ramifications in the present. Conversely, since no sharp line was drawn between myth and history, one might expect to find historical events expressed in the form of mythical narratives. The tale of the near demise of Croesus, the king of Lydia, as told by Bacchylides (3.29–63, 468 B.C.) and Herodotus (1.86–87), exemplifies the representation of history in myth.[11]

> Croesus, trusting in an ambiguous oracle, made war on the mighty Persians. The unfair match ended in the subjugation of his empire and his capture by Cyrus, the king of Persia, in the summer of 547 B.C. Croesus was to be burned alive. When, as Herodotus reports, he cried "Solon!" three times on the pyre, Cyrus asked him to explain his outburst. From the top of the burning pyre the Lydian said that Solon had once tried, without success, to make him appreciate the maxim that no one should be called happy until he is at the end of his life and that until then he had not grasped Solon's meaning. Cyrus, for his part, reflected on the maxim, had the fire quenched, and made Croesus his adviser.

The choral lyric poet Bacchylides had represented the same historical event some years earlier. According to his version, however, Croesus called on the gods for help, whereupon Zeus at once sent down a rain shower to put out the fire, and Apollo conveyed him and his daughters to the land of the Hyperboreans. Although Bacchylides' version seems more mythical than that of Herodotus—in particular, the miraculous rescue of a man by the gods as a reward for his piety (Croesus had once sent lavish gifts to Apollo's temple at Delphi) is a characteristically mythical feature—it is no less implausible than Herodotus's tale. That the Athenian Solon visited the Lydian Croesus is a chronological impossibility. Herodotus's narrative merely purports to be more rational; it has a different purpose—namely, to illustrate unforeseeable change in human affairs. Around a historical event, the capture of the Lydian king by the Persians in the summer of 547 B.C., have grown up two stories, the exact details of which are beyond our grasp. The stories became traditional: even before Bacchylides wrote his poetic account of the event, an Attic painter had represented the king offering a libation to Zeus. That was the myth as Bacchylides knew it (fig. 6).

If no line was drawn between myth and history, myth remained adaptable to new conditions, so long as it retained its vitality. The myths that dealt with Theseus's visit to Delos were created to legitimate Athenian claims to the island (see Chapter 5). Our authorities for myths about Theseus as an Attic hero are relatively numerous and illustrate how myth was changed to meet the requirements of the day.

Theseus and Athens

In the archaic period Theseus was one hero among others, and some of his adventures were narrated quite often.[12] He is mentioned several times in the Homeric poems. Nestor tells how Theseus fought beside Perithous against the Centaurs (*Iliad* 1.263–70). Odysseus says that he saw Ariadne, Minos's daughter, in the underworld; Theseus, he continues, wanted to bring her from Crete to Athens, but Artemis, at the recommendation of Dionysus, killed the girl on the island of Dia (*Odyssey* 11.321–25). That presupposes the Minotaur adventure. Odysseus would have seen Theseus and Perithous, too, during his visit in Hades, had he stayed there longer (*Odyssey* 11.631). The mention of Theseus and Perithous presupposes the tale according to which the two heroes descended into the lower world to abduct Persephone, the queen of that realm, but were detained there and punished for the attempt. In another Homeric passage Theseus's mother Aethra is listed among the maidservants of Helen (*Iliad* 3.144). That presupposes the tale of Theseus's abduction of Helen, according to which Helen's brothers, the Dioscuri, later came to their sister's rescue and not only freed her but also carried off Theseus's mother, who had been keeping Helen hidden.

The abduction of women and the slaying of monsters: these are the deeds of the Homeric Theseus, and these are also the deeds of Theseus as he is represented again and again in early lyric poetry and in archaic art. The oldest surviving depiction of the slaying of the Minotaur is Corinthian and dates from the seventh century. There is nothing specifically Athenian about Theseus here.

In the last quarter of the sixth century, there was a startling change in the iconography of the hero. Attic vase paintings showing Theseus suddenly begin to appear, and in the metopes on the treasury of the Athenians at Delphi (ca. 500 B.C.) Theseus's exploits are juxtaposed with those of Heracles. Significantly, there are no scandalous abductions of women here, no battles with half-human monsters; instead, Theseus is represented as, above all, a civilizer, who made the road from Troezen to Athens safe for travelers. He is shown clearing the road of all sorts of bandits—among these were Sciron, who hurled wayfarers over a cliff; Sinis, who tore them to pieces by fastening them to young pine trees, which he bent to the ground and then released; Procrustes, who forced them to fit into his bed by stretching them or lopping off their extremities; and Cercyon, a powerful wrestler who crushed his victims (Plutarch, *Theseus* 8–11). Apparently, Theseus's civilizing feats were meant to contrast with Heracles' encounters with wild animals and monsters from foreign lands. Theseus's popularity among the Athenians seems to have reached its peak when, in 476 B.C., the hero's bones were unearthed on the island of Scyros and returned to Athens by Cimon, the son of the Miltiades who led the Athenians to victory at Marathon (Plutarch, *Theseus* 36.1–3; *Cimon* 8.5–7). Theseus was even said to have intervened personally on behalf of the Athenians at Marathon (Plutarch, *Theseus* 35.8).

Theseus's popularity as the slayer of villains on the road from Troezen probably stemmed from an epic poem, the *Theseid*. Composed, at the latest, in the last quarter of the sixth century, the purpose of the poem was to make Theseus into an Athenian hero. There was much to recommend Theseus, whose exploits had been widely known from the time of Homer—at all events, Theseus was a much more attractive nominee for the role than Menestheus, Athens's rather pale representative at Troy (*Iliad* 2.552).

Whether the *Theseid* was written at the suggestion of Peisistratus, the Athenian tyrant, or Cleisthenes, the founder of the Athenian democracy, is a matter of dispute and, in any case, of little importance here. The important point is that, for political reasons, certain episodes in Theseus's mythical career were developed into an epic poem representing the Athenian self-concept.[13]

For the Athenians, Theseus was not, like other heroes, just a doer of prodigious deeds; he was one of their early kings. His adventures vexed the Greeks of later times, in particular the fourth-century Atthidographers. These writers of early Attic history attempted quite recklessly to rationalize the tale, so popular in the archaic period, of Theseus's struggle with the Minotaur. The monster was explained away as a real person, Taurus, an officer of Minos, conquered by Theseus in a sea battle (Demon, *FGrH* 327 F 5) or in single combat (Philochorus, *FGrH* 328 F 17). Cleidemus understood Theseus's Cretan adventure as an invasion, with Athenian support, by Cretan exiles whose purpose was to overthrow the tyrant Minos (*FGrH* 323 F 17). Theseus, thus demythologized and historicized, could no longer be represented as a slayer of monsters.

The *Theseid* may have initiated this rationalizing trend by portraying Theseus as the unifier of Attica and therefore the founder of the Athenian state. The inhabitants of Attica, it was said, once lived in scattered villages, without a common political identity. Under Theseus, they were incorporated into the Athenian polis, with a common political center in the city of Athens. Posterity considered this act of unification, known as synoecism, Theseus's greatest accomplishment. It was celebrated at the Synoecia, a festival that was thought to have been instituted by Theseus.[14] The festival took place on the sixteenth day of Hecatombaeon, the first month in the Attic calendar, immediately after the appearance of the full moon. Various rituals of dissolution and renewal marked Hecatombaeon as the first month of the new year. At the Synoecia, too, a strange sacrificial ritual took place. The participants, instead of roasting the meat communally in accordance with normal practice, brought it home raw: in this way, the Athenians enacted the dissolution of their political unity, which was followed by a fresh start. The myth, according to which the Athenians first lived in scattered villages and then were united under Theseus, traces just this sequence of events, expressed in the code of political action. Here myth and ritual did not necessarily preserve the memory of an actual synoecism from the early history of Attica—even the scholar who asserts that a myth is "a tale that rests on a historical basis" must allow that this synoecism was probably the result not of a single act but of a "long and gradual developmental process."[15] Thus, all that is left of the myth is the basic notion that a great city arose as a result of the unification of several towns; such a synoecism is plausible, whether it is historical or not.

Even more important was the late sixth-century transformation of Theseus from a folktale hero into a quasi-historical politician acting with absolute authority. Extreme democrats of the fourth century (who had a forerunner in Euripides) went so far as to make the king abdicate and introduce the democracy. Theophrastus, a student of Aristotle, even credits Theseus with the invention of ostracism, the vote by potsherd, which was fundamental to the Athenian democracy—undoubtedly with a polemical and antidemocratic purpose, for he goes on to say that the first victim of ostracism was none other than its inventor. Theophrastus's teacher, with greater historical plausibility, says that ostracism was introduced by Cleisthenes, ascribing to Theseus a constitution that "deviated somewhat from monarchy" (*The Constitution of the Athenians* 41.2). By contrast, Thucydides represented him as an absolute monarch who possessed enough power to divest the individual villages of their sovereignty and thus to pave the way for the synoecism (2.15). Plutarch imagined that Theseus went from one aristocratic power center to the next promoting his idea; while the commoners followed him enthusiastically, the nobles did so only with reluctance, in view of his dynastic power (*Theseus* 24.1–2).

To be sure, not every one of these details is the stuff of which traditional tales are made, but the starting point—the notion that Theseus was an Attic king—certainly is, and it is on this notion that the later additions are based. The Theseus myth is presented in a form that every Greek could understand as history. The conception of myth as history goes back at least to the latter part of the sixth century, unless one assigns an even earlier date to the etiology of the Synoecia.

Myth as History

The conception of myth as history—to sum up the results of our survey—was not a late occurrence; nor was it an indication that myth had become an empty shell, as some evolutionists, unable to see the development of Greek thought as anything but the triumph of *logos* over *mythos*, have been far too ready to assume. In fact, myth, especially heroic myth, was regarded as history throughout antiquity. One of the reasons for this attitude was that, in the archaic period, heroic myth took the fixed form of epic poetry, particularly the Homeric poems. Even in the *Iliad* and the *Odyssey* the mythical universe is structured in accordance with chronological—"historical"—criteria. This quasi-historical perspective is consistent with the Homeric tendency toward realism: the realistic Homeric narrator shuns the fantastic and the fabulous (Chapter 3).

Realism, which has been disparaged as the mark of an un-imaginative mind (G. S. Kirk) but also extolled as characteristi-cally indicative of, and rooted in, a pristinely anthropomorphic universe (B. Vickers, rightly and convincingly), is a distinctive feature of Greek mythical narration in general.[16] Monsters, when they appear, are surprisingly tame. Perhaps the most com-plicated one is the chimaera ("in front a lion, in the middle a goat, in back a snake") or Hesiod's Typhon, with its various ani-mal heads. More common are animals such as those against which Heracles fights: a lion with skin that resists iron; a bull and a boar, both unusually large and savage creatures; man-eating horses; a hind with golden antlers. Particularly spectacu-lar are Cerberus with his three heads and the Hydra with its four serpentine necks. Most of the figures of Greek myth, how-ever, are human, and so are their actions, which include not only murder, rape, and cannibalism but also love, friendship, and marriage. Attic vase painting is also of a preeminently anthropo-morphic character: monsters are rare (among Heracles' labors, the struggle with the lion is depicted most often; among those of Theseus the struggle with the Minotaur, another not less than extravagantly fantastic monster). Vases usually show men and women, and we cannot always be sure, in the absence of inscrip-tions, whether a scene is from myth or everyday life. Is the part-ing warrior in every case Hector, the dead man over whose corpse others are fighting always Achilles? The human and in-deed the humane qualities of myth have made epic and tragic poetry the loftiest achievements of both Greek and other litera-tures; these qualities explain the immense impact that Greek myth has had, from antiquity to the present day.

CHAPTER VII

MYTH, CHORAL SONG, AND TRAGEDY

Athenian Tragedy

Fifth-century Attic tragedy, like archaic epic poetry, took its subjects almost exclusively from myth. Tragedies on nonmythical themes were never more than experimental. We hear of two plays on historical themes written early in the century by Phrynichus, whose junior rival was Aeschylus: one dealt with the capture of Miletus by the Persians in 494 B.C. (*Capture of Miletus*, *TrGF* vol. 1, 3 T 2), the other with the repulse of the Persian invasion of 480–79 B.C. (*Persians*, *TrGF* vol. 1, 3 T 1), and we possess a play on the latter theme, Aeschylus's *Persians*, which was produced in 472 B.C.. The title of a play written at the end of the century by Agathon, a young friend of Socrates, also indicates a nonmythical theme (*Anthus* or *Antheus*, *TrGF* vol. 1, 39 F 2a).

Tragedy was also influenced by the treatment of myth in epic poetry. Even ancient authors called Homer the father of tragedy, and Aeschylus reportedly said that he worked with the crumbs from Homer's table (*TrGF* vol. 3, T 112a–b). The tragic poet deliberately situated himself in the epic tradition of mythical narration.

To define tragedy generally as dealing with man's place in the world on the basis of mythical episodes is to state the obvious. Myths had to do with gods and heroes. In the fifth century it was taken for granted, as it had been from time immemorial, that man's place in the world was determined largely by the gods and was incomprehensible without them. The heroes, whom the Greeks regarded as great men from a past that was in some sense real, so exceeded ordinary human dimensions as to become examples, be they commendatory or cautionary. Both heroes and gods received cult, and therefore they were endowed with a cultural relevance that imaginary persons, or even persons of the recent past, rarely had.

More remarkable is that the performance of tragedy was a part of the cult of Dionysus—a fact that even some Greeks found puzzling. Originally, tragedies were staged only on the three days of the Great Dionysia in the month of Elaphebolion (March/April); later, they were added to the Lenaea, which was also a festival in honor of Dionysus, celebrated in the month of Gamelion (January/February). The place of performance was the sanctuary of Dionysus on the southern slope of the Acropolis. The tragic trilogy was followed by a satyr play, whose "heroes" were a chorus of satyrs, Dionysus's half-human worshipers. Finally, in antiquity the origins of tragedy were traced back to elements of the cult of Dionysus. Yet, for all these connections with the cult of Dionysus, only a handful of plays on Dionysiac themes are attested. In general, it was not the myth of Dionysus but heroic myth that furnished the subjects of tragic poetry. More than a quarter of the extant titles refer to myths about the Trojan War, and the Argive and Theban royal houses each account for another tenth. How is this paradox to be explained?

There are two answers to this question. One has to do with the carnivalesque nature of the festival. Dionysus was a god who came from outside and temporarily suspended the activities of everyday life. His festival created a space outside the day-to-day reality of the polis. The actors put aside their own identities, donning masks, high boots (*kothornoi*), and colorful costumes.

Even the walk to the theater of Dionysus, situated as it was on the slope between the homes of the Athenians and the citadel of their gods, removed them, for three days, from their familiar surroundings. This carnivalesque setting, this "carnival time" gave them an opportunity to reflect critically on, and to call into question, all that was familiar to them: the polis, the people, the gods. At the same time, it fostered in them a sense of solidarity, which rendered such reflection and questioning tolerable. From this perspective, the festival of Dionysus seems the ideal occasion for the performance of tragedies.[1]

The other answer has to do with the origin of tragedy. This takes us into a maze of difficulties; indeed, the problem is one of the most controversial in the history of Greek literature.[2] In antiquity two theories were prevalent. The first was that of Aristotle, who traced the origin of tragedy to satyr drama and the dithyramb, a song in honor of Dionysus. According to the second, commonly known as the post-Aristotelian or Hellenistic theory (the name is misleading, for the rudiments of the theory were already being discussed in the fourth century), tragedy grew out of certain rites belonging to the cult of Dionysus in Attica. Modern theories abound. They may be divided roughly into two groups: the literary-historical theories, according to which tragedy grew out of the dithyramb or a presumed subsidiary form, the "satyr dithyramb," and the ritualist theories, according to which tragedy originated in the cult of Dionysus or the cult of heroes.

To begin with the second of these groups: the close ties between tragedy and the cult of Dionysus make it virtually certain that tragedy was rooted in ritual. In particular, the tragic chorus probably originated in a group of masked cult actors, however one pictures the details. The satyrs and maenads indicate that such groups had a central place in the cult of Dionysus: they are mythical reflections of cult groups.[3] Admittedly, these ritual origins lay in the prehistory or murky early history of tragedy. As for the fifth century, the form of the choral songs of the extant plays makes it likely that the tragic chorus was once influenced by Doric choral lyric poetry in the Peloponnesus and Magna Graecia. In those areas Arion may have been the poet who, in Corinth about 600 B.C., gave the dithyramb the form in which it was to gain importance. At all events, Herodotus reports that Arion "was, so far as we know, the first man to compose and name the dithyramb, and to supervise its production on the stage" (1.23). But since Archilochus of Paros had already mentioned the dithyramb a half-century earlier (in connection with the cult of Dionysus), this can only refer to its further development as a poetic form. Therefore, when the historian says that Arion "named" the dithyramb, he must mean that Arion gave titles to his works. These titles must have described subjects that lay beyond the narrow range of cult practice; thus, these subjects must have been mythical.

Tragedy and Choral Poetry

A glance at later archaic choral lyric poetry, of which only fragments survive, confirms this. We hear of a dithyramb of Ibycus (mid-sixth century) that told of Helen's encounter with Menelaus after the fall of Troy (fr. 296 PMG). One generation after Arion, then, dithyrambic poetry was already treating a tale from heroic myth that had nothing to do with Dionysus. Such tales in dithyrambic form may have been available to Thespis, traditionally the inventor of tragedy, in the 530s B.C. In the early fifth century, the narration of non-Dionysiac myths in the dithyrambs of Pindar and Bacchylides was a matter of course.

Myths were also narrated in the other subgenres of choral lyric poetry, from the time of Alcman, the first known choral poet, who wrote around 600 B.C. The Peripatetic Heraclides of Pontus traced the narration of myth back to the beginnings of citharodic poetry (fr. 157)—but then he went on to name, among others, Demodocus, who sang of Ares and Aphrodite and the demise of Troy, and Phemius, who sang of the return of the

Greeks from Troy—bards familiar from the *Odyssey*, not historical figures from the early history of Greek poetry. For Heraclides, choral lyric and epic poetry were of a piece, so far as their narrative themes were concerned.

The greatest teller of myths between Homer and the tragedians was Stesichorus of Himera, who was Alcman's senior by a generation. Posterity assigned to his poems such titles as *Geryoneis*, *Oresteia*, and *Sack of Troy*, which indicate that each was on a self-contained mythical theme. The fragments of the *Geryoneis* (frr. 7–87 *SLG*) indicate that it told in considerable detail the myth of the three-headed monster Geryon and included an account of the events that led up to Heracles' encounter with Geryon, a divine council, and a long main scene in which Heracles fought against and eventually slew the monster. Stesichorus's other poems, of which almost nothing survives, must have been similarly rich in detail and broad in compass; his *Oresteia* (frr. 210–19 *PMG*) reportedly comprised two books.

"Stesichorus was a source for most of the poets. Next to Homer and Hesiod, the poets agree with no one more than they do with him," an anonymous ancient scholar noted (fr. 217 *PMG*). The tragedians, in particular, were heavily indebted to Stesichorus. His treatment of the myth of Helen was notorious. Homer, of course, placed Helen in Troy, and that is where Stesichorus placed her at first—but later he recanted: "The tale that I told before is not true. . . you did not come to the citadel of Troy" (fr. 192 *PMG*). According to the new version of the myth, the woman abducted by Paris was really a phantom created by the gods; the real Helen was conveyed to Egypt, where Menelaus found her on his way home from Troy (these are the broad lines of the new version; its exact form has been unclear ever since the discovery of a papyrus that tells of not one but two palinodes). Thus, the entire Trojan War was fought for the sake of an illusion. This version of the myth was used repeatedly by Euripides, who even based an entire play on it (*Helen*). The tragedians also borrowed from Stesichorus's *Oresteia*. One Stesichorean detail, Electra's recognition of her brother by the lock placed by him on his father's tomb (fr. 217 *PMG*), was adopted by all three tragedians (Aeschylus, *Choephori* 164–204; Sophocles, *Electra* 51–53, 900–903; Euripides, *Electra* 508–31; Euripides' heroine is the first to reject the evidence of the lock). From Stesichorus (fr. 217 *PMG*) Euripides borrowed another detail, Orestes' use of Apollo's bow to defend himself against the Erinyes (*Orestes* 268–70). Stesichorus's most significant innovation, the ordering of the matricide by Apollo (fr. 217 *PMG*), was also appropriated by all three tragic poets—though toned down in Sophocles' version (Aeschylus, *Choephori* 900–903; Euripides, *Orestes* 76 and *Electra* 1245–46; Sophocles, *Elektra* 32–38).[4]

Archaic choral lyric poetry influenced not only the subject matter of tragedy but also its form, as is immediately apparent from the meter of its choral songs and from the fact that the Doric dialect was artificially used in them. Doric is the dialect of choral lyric poetry in the Peloponnesus and in Magna Graecia, and the Doric dialect of the choral songs in tragedy contrasts with the Attic dialect of tragic dialogue. Like choral lyric poems, choral songs in tragedy sometimes deal with myths. The myths told in the choral songs of tragedy often recount the events leading up to the mythical episode dramatized in the play; they may also, through comparison or contrast, interpret the action on the stage. Mythical narration is generally rare in Sophocles' choral songs. In the fourth stasimon of *Antigone* the chorus narrates three mythical paradigms as the heroine is led away to be immured. Danae, though guiltless, was once imprisoned by her father because he feared that she might one day bear a son who would kill him (even so, she was impregnated by Zeus, who came in the form of golden rain). Also imprisoned was Lycurgus, king of Thrace, for attacking Dionysus's maenads (his imprisonment brought him to his senses). After these two exempla, which offer at least a glimmer of hope, the third seems all the more dismal: Cleopatra, the daughter of Boreas, was imprisoned simply because her stepmother hated her: "But she, too, child, was assailed by the long-lived Moerae" (986–87). The chorus of Euripides' *Iphigeneia at Aulis*, in the third stasimon, draws a comparison between the feigned wedding with which Agamemnon lured his daughter to her death at Aulis and the most famous of all mythical weddings, that of Peleus and Thetis. The Muses, the chorus says, sang the wedding song to the accompaniment of flute and cithara, the gods danced, and Ganymede filled golden vessels with wine—"but as for you, Iphigeneia, the Greeks will wreathe the beautiful locks on your head... as if you were a dappled heifer, a victim without blemish" (1080–84).

The use of myth as paradigm was one of many features borrowed from choral lyric poetry. So far as we can tell, myths were not so used by Stesichorus or Ibycus, or by Pindar or Bacchylides in their paeans and dithyrambs, where the chorus's song, along with its mythical content, was performed for its own sake (the song, in the context of the festival, became a kind of offering to the god, like a votive image or statue). However, myths were so used in Alcman's Partheneion, which is the earliest more or less substantial specimen of choral lyric poetry to have come down to us, and in the victory songs of Pindar and Bacchylides.

In the victory song, which was performed in a celebration of an athletic victory, the mythical narrative served the poem's overall purpose: to praise the victor. This could be accomplished through simple comparison, as in Bacchylides' song for Hiero, a tyrant of Syracuse, on the occasion of his victory in the chariot race at the Olympic games of 468 B.C. (Bacchylides 3). Here the praise of the munificent Hiero, whose golden tripods stood in Apollo's temple in Delphi, leads, by way of an explanatory gnomic bridge—"let the god be honored with gifts, for that is the best of prosperities" (21)—to the myth of Croesus, his misfortune, and his miraculous rescue (see Chapter 6). This shows, incidentally, that choral lyric poetry, like early tragedy, took up historical themes; earlier, Ibycus had mentioned "Cyaras, the general of the Medes" (fr. 320 *PMG*). Croesus was saved by his lavish gifts to Apollo—and Hiero likewise owed his victory in the chariot race to the aid of the god to whom he had given gifts.

Yet the myth does not just apply to the time of Hiero's victory; it also explores its general validity through the person of Hiero, whose situation reflects that of all mortals, all "creatures of a day." Bacchylides refers to Croesus's defeat at the hands of the Persians as "the predetermined turning point" which "Zeus brought to fulfillment" (25–26) but also, a few lines later, as an "unexpected day" (29) in Croesus's life, without absolving him from responsibility for the defeat. This double motivation—an action has one motivation on the divine level, another on the human, but the divine predetermination of that action does not free the actor from responsibility—is characteristic of archaic Greek thought. The poet at least intimates the conclusion to be drawn from the myth: "lofty expectation clouds the thinking of creatures of a day" (75–76). That is the unwholesome kind of expectation. What is the wholesome kind? Bacchylides puts the answer in the mouth of Apollo, who once advised Admetus of Pherae to cherish two thoughts at once: that tomorrow would be his last day on earth and that his prosperity would last another fifty years (76–82). If there is a hint of doom for Hiero here, Bacchylides hastens to dispel it: "Cheer your heart through pious deeds. For this is the greatest of advantages" (83–84). Thus, Croesus, who momentarily serves as a pattern to be avoided, reverts to a pattern to be imitated.

A victory song of Pindar, written in 476 B.C. for the same Hiero on the occasion of his victory at Olympia in the single horse race, illustrates further how myth was used in choral lyric poetry (*Olympian* 1).

The song begins with praise for the Olympic victory, which is the greatest of all victories, for Hiero, and for his triumphant horse. Hiero's glory radiates over the entire Peloponnesus, the island of Pelops. The mention of Pelops forms a transition to his myth (25–96). Young Pelops, a son of Tantalus, was loved by Poseidon. While Tantalus was entertaining the gods, Poseidon seized the youth and carried him off to Olympus, "where, at another time, Ganymede also came

to Zeus for the same service" (43–45). Tantalus was honored by the gods as was no other mortal. Yet "he was not
able to digest his great prosperity" (55–56) and made
off with their nectar and ambrosia. To punish him, Zeus
suspended a huge boulder over his head. Pelops, however,
was brought back to earth, and he sought to become
famous. Oenomaus, the king of Elis (the territory surrounding Olympia), had offered his daughter in marriage
and also the land of Elis to anyone who could defeat him in
a chariot race. He would give his challenger a head start and
then shoot him in the back with an arrow. Determined to
win, Pelops prayed to Poseidon for help: "going near to the
gray sea, alone in the darkness of night, he called upon the
loud-pounding god of the splendid trident; and Poseidon
appeared close by his side" (71–74). Pelops won the race,
married the princess Hippodameia, and begat six sons; in
Pindar's day he was still honored at his tomb in Olympia.
"The victor has honey-sweet tranquillity for the rest of his
life, thanks to the games" (97–99). Thus, the narrative has,
without our realizing it, brought us back to the point of
contact between Pelops and Hiero: the glorious tomb of Pelops near the race course at Olympia, which can be seen
from a distance (93–95), is analogous to the glory of Hiero,
which shines on the island of Pelops (23–24). Pelops, the
favorite of Poseidon, whose conduct is supposed to serve as
a model for that of mortals, corresponds to the blissful
Hiero. Relying on his own strength ("Great danger does
not call upon the cowardly man," 81), he prays to the gods
for help. Just as divine providence does not annul mortal
responsibility in a catastrophe, so mortal strength alone
does not guarantee success.

Here Pindar concerns himself more exclusively with the victor
than Bacchylides does. The myth within the myth, however,
reaches beyond the victory: Tantalus, the favorite of the gods,

the fortunate man blinded by his good fortune (this is a major theme of archaic poetry), is the negative counterpart of the judicious Pelops. It is at just this point that Pindar appends the moral of the tale: "if a man expects to hide his doings from the gods, he errs" (64). Pelops's counterpart—and therefore also the counterpart of Hiero, the victor—becomes a cautionary example for everyone.[5]

A similarly cautionary function of myth is evident in a poem of Alcman (active ca. 625 B.C.), the so-called Louvre Partheneion (fr. 1 PMG), which was performed by a chorus of maidens at a religious festival, perhaps in honor of Artemis. Despite the extremely fragmentary state of the text, two myths can be distinguished in this work: the first (1–15) deals with a Spartan hero who was slain by Heracles, the second (22–35) with the punishment of wrongdoers in the afterworld. The myths are separated by a short moralizing bridge passage (16–21) and followed by a gnomic statement: "There is a vengeance from the gods" (36). Even in Alcman's day, then, a myth could be included in a song even though it made no reference to the religious festival that was its setting, because it served as an exemplum that was valid for the here and now.[6]

A mythical narrative was sometimes radically altered to suit the demands of a particular audience. For example, it was probably with a view to the civic pride of the Spartans that Stesichorus altered the myth of Helen—after all, Helen was worshiped as a goddess in Sparta. An even better example is Pindar's version of the myth of Pelops in Olympian 1, in which he expressly rejects the more familiar version, according to which Tantalus cut up, boiled, and served his own son to the gods to test their omniscience. Only Demeter, distracted with grief at the rape of her daughter, partook of the feast, eating a piece of Pelops's shoulder. Later, when the gods restored Pelops to life, the missing piece was replaced with ivory. This version of the myth, which is attested several times, exhibits certain features of ancient ritual—the theme of dismemberment and revival, and the special treatment of the shoulder blade, which has parallels in sacrificial ritual. Yet Pindar rejects this version as the malicious gossip of invidious neighbors; they made it up, he says, when the kidnapped Pelops could not be found, despite a long search. As for the partially eaten shoulder, "it is impossible for me to call any of the blessed gods gluttonous" (52). In general, "tales deceive, embellishing the talk of mortals with variegated lies beyond the true account" (28–29). This has been taken by some as a critique of the established religion, and perhaps it was a critique, to a certain extent, though not on philosophical or theological grounds. A more likely motive for the alteration of the myth is that a Pelops who is boiled, cannibalized, and later brought back to life would have made an odd model for Hiero, at whose victory festival the song was performed. The reference to the similar good fortune of Ganymede (43–45) clarifies this further. Still other details have been quietly suppressed: Pelops defeated Oenomaus by bribing his opponent's charioteer Myrtilus to sabotage the king's chariot; Oenomaus was flung to his death during the race; later, Pelops killed Myrtilus also, who, in dying, cursed him, and this curse began to work in the next generation, when his sons Atreus and Thyestes quarreled over the throne of Mycenae. Obviously, Pindar had no use for any of this material.[7]

Fifth-century tragedy clearly had much in common with archaic choral lyric poetry: the poetic form of its choral songs, its mythical subject matter, and the function of its mythical narration. However, the mythical narration of fifth-century tragedy, unlike that of archaic choral lyric poetry, was not marked by the use of tales continually modified within a purely oral tradition; instead, the tragedians tended to borrow specific poetic versions from the archaic period. They probably became acquainted with most of these versions in the form of written texts, not by attending performances of choral lyric poetry. As the oral performance was supplanted by the written text and was no longer the principal point of reference, myths began to harden into forms created once and for all time and to lose their almost limitless capacity for adaptation. This trend was in keeping with the intellectual developments of the period. At the beginning of the fifth century—the century that has been called the "tragic moment"—we find the earliest references to basic schooling (Herodotus 6.27 [ca. 494 B.C.]), the earliest representations, on vases, of people reading books,[8] and, toward the end of the century, the earliest allusion to a book market (Eupolis, fr. 327 PCG). This was accompanied by two other developments: the tradition began to lose its normative character, and the individual began to gain confidence in his own judgment (see Chapter 8).[9] To be sure, myths continued to be transmitted orally—Euripides knew of myths told by maidens working at the loom (Ion 196–97 and 506; Iphigeneia at Aulis 786–87), Plato of myths told by grandmothers and wet nurses (Republic 350e and 377c).[10] Yet if an earlier, written version of a myth was available to them, the tragic poets referred to it. At the same time, the literary versions must have exercised an increasing influence on oral performances. Thus, in the course of the fifth century, Attic vase painters tended increasingly to represent myths in the forms that had been most impressive on the stage to them and their clientele.[11]

By comparison with the narration of myth in choral lyric and in epic poetry, the dramatization of mythical events by actors on a stage was something fundamentally new. For one thing, the gods and heroes were reduced to the stature of the men who represented them—only the mask remained to express their superhumanity. In tragedy the humanization of the mythical world, which is immediately apparent even in the Homeric poems, was carried to an extreme—at least so far as the heroes are concerned. Theatrical convention distinguished between gods and heroes in at least one respect: the gods were allowed to use the crane and thus appeared to be exempt from gravity. Gods appear relatively seldom, and even more seldom is a god involved in the action as a leading character for the duration for the play, like Apollo and Athena in Aeschylus's Eumenides or

Dionysus in Euripides' *Bacchae*. Occasionally a god intervenes briefly, speaks a prologue, or untangles, as a *deus ex machina*, a plot that has gotten off course. It is significant that in the extant plays of the "pious" Sophocles, who emphasizes the distance between god and man, only two gods appear on stage—Athena in the prologue of *Ajax* and the god-hero Heracles at the end of *Philoctetes*. Gods appear most frequently in the plays of Euripides, where the nature of the divine is most at issue.

Still more significant is the fact that, in the tragic performance, the myth was transposed from the past time of the narrative into the present time of the stage production. In the mythical past, gods and heroes had immediate contact, entertained one another, and produced children together; the gods aided the heroes or destroyed them. Almost of necessity, the conversion of that past into action on the stage turned it into drama in which the relationship between gods and mortals and the operation of gods in the world became important themes—precisely because the heroes had been humanized. In fact, this is a major problem in the works of all three tragedians. Even if the gods are all but absent from the stage, as they are in Sophocles' plays, they are always in the background, influencing the action. Not until Euripides do mortals sometimes appear to be able to manage without them, as in *Medea*.

The fact that the subject matter of tragedy was almost exclusively mythical was not just a borrowing from choral lyric poetry. The traditional myths offered the most effective means of accomplishing the basic purpose of tragedy, which was to explore the human condition. But there was something new—new by comparison with older modes of narration—about the relationship between tragedy and the myths that it enacted. These myths were no longer being formed in a living, purely oral tradition; consequently, they were no longer being seamlessly adapted—even if such adaptation entailed radical renarration—to the new social and intellectual requirements of the day. Had they still belonged to such a tradition, tragedy as we know it would never have existed in the fifth century, only *Maskenspiel* (a not very serious dramatic performance by masked actors involving music and dancing). As it happened, myth had lost some of its flexibility. The long explanation with which Pindar introduces his revision of the Pelops myth is indicative of this loss; so is the invention of a story to explain what motivated Stesichorus to write his palinode (Helen, it was said, blinded him for having censured her in one of his poems, and his sight was not restored until he amended her myth). Poets could no longer alter myth at will. That is especially true of the tragedians of the democratic and increasingly enlightened polis. Instead of radically altering the traditional tales, they imbued them with values, in particular, moral values; they approached a limited number of myths from various perspectives. The cultural relevance of tragedy lay not in its myths, for they belonged to an earlier age, but in the currency of its perspectives on those myths.

The significance attached by the tragedians to the concept of justice is a case in point. Justice, a fundamental concern in any democracy, was a topic much discussed in Athens, from Solon's time to that of Plato. In Homer's *Odyssey* (3.310) there was no doubt that Orestes acted justly in murdering his mother to avenge his father. In a poem as late as Pindar's *Olympian* 1, performed in 476 B.C., Pelop's victory over Oenomaus was still described as an act of glory (admittedly, that poem omitted certain details of the myth). In tragedy, by contrast, the poet repeatedly asked how such acts were to be justified.

Not every myth lent itself to the scrutiny of values. Nor does the prestige of Homer by itself suffice to explain the prevalence of myths about Troy, Argos, and Thebes in the extant plays. These myths were selected because they revolved around war and the family—areas of conflict in which the tragedians were especially interested. For Homer, the battlefield was the place where the hero proved his worth; this assumption was never questioned, though it should be noted that the poet also concerned himself with the victims of war. Again and again, tragedy asked whether the Trojan War was just, and each time it did so from a different angle. The Ajax of Sophocles' play is a warrior whose heroism turns into madness and self-destruction; Euripides' greatest interest was in the victims of war. The other great war treated in epic poetry, that of the Seven against Thebes, held even greater potential as a medium for the scrutiny of values. Here one brother, Eteocles, defended his home city against another, Polyneices, and both of them fell. In his *Seven against Thebes*, Aeschylus fashions the tale into a conflict in which Eteocles, faced with a decision between surrendering the city that has been entrusted to him and fighting against his brother, decides for the polis. In his *Phoenician Women*, Euripides portrays him as a power-hungry politician who will stop short of nothing, not even fratricide.

The fratricide brings us to another area of conflict: the family.[12] Agamemnon murders his daughter, Clytemnestra her husband, Orestes his mother. Oedipus kills his father and marries his mother. Heracles falls in love with young Iole and commits adultery; he is destroyed by the love charm with which his wife tries to win him back. Jason opportunistically deserts Medea for another woman, and Medea retaliates by murdering her rival and even her sons. Creusa is raped by Apollo, exposes her child, and Apollo's attempt to give his sons respectable parents nearly ends in the mother's poisoning her son and husband. Phaedra falls in love with her stepson Hippolytus, and when he spurns her, she commits suicide, leaving a tablet that charges him with rape; Hippolytus's father reads the tablet and utters a curse that results in the death of his son. The examples could be multiplied. How is the prevalence of these themes to be explained? One answer is that the tragedians sought to validate the ethical norms of the polis by dramatizing the disastrous consequences of the transgression of those norms. Another is that the audience would have been keenly interested in such familial themes: in support of this argument scholars have adduced actual cases of such problems in Athenian families, preserved in forensic speeches. Both answers are correct. However, just as important is the fact that, for the Greeks, such familial crimes need not—or not exclusively—be attributed to human inadequacy and depravity; they may also indicate the operation of the gods. Nowhere is human suffering more closely experienced, nowhere is the need to explain that suffering more keenly felt, than in the family—once the family becomes, as it did in Athens, the central unit of social interaction.

The *Oresteia*

Aeschylus's *Oresteia*, a trilogy produced in 458 B.C. and the most powerful work ever staged in Athens, may serve as an example of the narration of myth in tragedy. Agamemnon, on returning from Troy, was slain by his wife Clytemnestra and her lover Aegisthus; Orestes then avenged his father by killing his mother. This tale had already been mentioned several times in the *Odyssey*, where it had served as a foil to the story of Odysseus, Penelope, and Telemachus.[13] In Homer's poem, Clytemnestra was merely Aegisthus's accomplice; the Hesiodic *Catalogue*, however, made her primarily responsible for Agamemnon's murder (fr. 23 MW). Stesichorus, in his *Oresteia*, borrowed the idea of giving Clytemnestra the dominant role. He also represented Apollo as the instigator of the subsequent matricide, and vividly portrayed its consequences: Orestes was pursued by Clytemnestra's Erinyes and protected by Apollo (frr. 217, 219 *PMG*). Such are the broad lines of the tradition from which Aeschylus took the mythical material for his trilogy.

The first play, *Agamemnon*, depicts Clytemnestra's murder of her husband Agamemnon on his return from the war at Troy. The protagonist of the play, despite its title, is the murderous wife. A tone of impending disaster is set at the outset: a watchman atop the house of the Atreidae is watching for the torch that is to indicate the fall of Troy. Even the opening line—"I ask the gods for deliverance from these toils"—is dismal, although the watchman is only referring to his nightlong surveillance. There is a note of foreboding in his reference to Clytemnestra's "expectant heart that takes counsel like a man" (11). To the Athenian audience, which was made up of men, the paradox of a woman with the will of a man signified that the natural order of the house had been perverted.

The chorus, which consists of the old Argive men left at home when the younger men went off to Troy, recounts the events that have led up to the action of the play. The campaign against Troy is just, the chorus says initially, and the Greeks are under the protection of Zeus. Agamemnon and Menelaus are likened to a pair of vultures, which, robbed of their brood, circle over their empty nest, screeching; "and on the heights some god, either Apollo or Pan or Zeus, hears the shrill cry of lamentation voiced by the birds, his fellow residents in the sky, and sends an avenging Erinys after the transgressors" (55–59). The theme of crime and punishment dominates the trilogy. Later, Clytemnestra expresses a reservation: the avengers will return home safely under the protection of the gods only if they refrain from violating the inviolable and from desecrating temples and cult statues (338–44). When the messenger from Troy reports how "the altars and shrines of the gods have vanished, and the seed of all the land has been utterly destroyed" (527–28), he is indicating that the just war has turned into a source of fresh injustice, which is certain to bring fresh disaster in its train.

The question of the justness of the campaign against Troy is raised in the second avian image of the entrance song. Two eagles, the chorus says, appeared before the Greek army as it was about to depart from Aulis; the eagles tore apart a hare, along with its unborn young. Calchas, the seer, interprets the omen to refer to the two Atreidae and the capture of Troy. He does not say that the needless atrocity will have dire consequences, but we are told that "Artemis hates the eagles' feast" (138), that she holds back the winds that the Greeks need if they are to set sail, and that, without apparent reason, she demands the sacrifice of Agamemnon's daughter Iphigeneia. (The murder of Agamemnon is also willed by divinity; Clytemnestra repeatedly describes it as the act of avenging Iphigeneia.) The chorus then lapses into a grandiose prayer to "Zeus, whoever he is" (160). Agamemnon is faced with a terrible decision: should he kill his own child or desert his allies (*symmachia*, an alliance not easily broken)? He decides against his daughter—and when the chorus describes the girl's sacrifice, the perversity of the act is apparent: the father as sacrificial priest, deaf to the pleas and cries of the girl, who is dragged bound and gagged to the altar. A recalcitrant victim bodes ill, as every Greek knows. Once Iphigeneia has been sacrificed, the winds begin to blow again. But far from averting catastrophe, the sacrifice merely postpones it. After the choral song, during which Clytemnestra is on stage, sacrificing (metaphors of sacrifice recur shortly before the murder of Agamemnon), the queen tells of Troy's fall and gives a detailed account of the chain of beacons whereby the news of the city's capture was conveyed to Argos. The chain of fire signals, which presumably was an innovation of Aeschylus, is another indication of her "heart that takes counsel like a man." The chorus regards the fall of Troy and the death of Paris as further confirmation of the operation of divine justice. It turns its thoughts from the war to the suffering in Argos, whose men have been away from home for ten years, fighting for the wife of a stranger: "dangerous is the talk of the citizens when they are angry" (456). That by itself casts a pall of gloom over Agamemnon's homecoming, and the conclusion that the chorus draws from it is even darker: "it is dangerous to be praised too much . . . may I not be a destroyer of cities" (468–72).

A herald enters to announce the arrival of Agamemnon. He praises the victor. If, in the light of the last choral song, such praise gives cause for concern, his account of the destruction of Troy is downright frightening. Angry at the Greeks for the impious acts that they committed in razing the city, the gods, he says, sent down a storm that decimated the Greek fleet as it was sailing homeward. Agamemnon's ship alone was rescued "by a god" (663)—again, catastrophe has merely been postponed.

The next choral song begins with Helen: she is compared to a lion cub that is reared in the house, but later, when it has grown up, kills its foster father's sheep. The conclusion drawn by the chorus reaches beyond Troy: pride and impious conduct engender still more impious conduct. While great prosperity does not necessarily lead to crime, justice is more likely to reside in the poor man's cottage. The simile of the lion cub—"and the house was defiled with blood, to its occupants a bane that could not be opposed" (732–33)—has a prophetic ring. Clytemnestra, after all, is Helen's sister.

Agamemnon arrives with the seeress Cassandra, Priam's daughter, whom the army commander had chosen for himself from the spoils of the fallen city. He is greeted first by the chorus and then by Clytemnestra. She has purple draperies spread out for him, and bids him tread them up to the house. He hesitates; such pomp, he says, is appropriate for gods, but it is effeminate and barbaric when rendered to mortals. Clytemnestra soon makes him change his mind, however; he removes his shoes and walks barefoot over the tapestries and into the house. Meanwhile, Clytemnestra prays: "Zeus, Zeus who fulfills, fulfill my prayers!" (973). It is worth noting that elsewhere Greek women direct their prayers not to Zeus but to Hera, as the fulfiller of the marriage bond.

Agamemnon's trampling of the purple garments was probably an Aeschylean innovation. This mode of entry is not just theatrically effective: it is also a clear demonstration of Agamemnon's downfall. Agamemnon is right, initially, to refuse an honor that is reserved for the gods. But when he tramples the draperies, he commits an act of hubris. The consequences of such hubris have been foreseen by the chorus. The mannish Clytemnestra provokes her husband. "It is not a woman's part," he protests, "to long for strife" (940). All that he can hold out to her is conventional wisdom. Ultimately, he himself becomes "effeminate," a "barbarian," a victim of the Greeks. In taking off his shoes, he celebrates his homecoming as if he were performing a religious ritual, as if he were entering a sacred space: walking barefoot is what one does when approaching a god. This is the downfall of the king—it is not surprising that the next choral song begins with an expression of inexplicable terror.

Clytemnestra wants Cassandra, too, to enter the house, but the seeress does not answer her. Eventually, the queen gives up and goes inside, whereupon Cassandra begins to sing in prophetic ecstasy, calling first on Apollo, who destroyed (*apōlesas* (1182)—an obvious pun) her, then recounting to the chorus the bloody deeds of the house of Atreus, both those of the past and those yet to come. The chorus, which recognizes her references to the past, is puzzled by her references to the future; Cassandra calms down and explains how Apollo once gave her the gift of prophecy but then, when she resisted him, caused her prophecies never to be believed. Indeed, the chorus does not believe her predictions about Agamemnon's death, even though she repeats them with ever increasing clarity; finally, certain of her death, she goes into the house. As the chorus begins to ponder whether Agamemnon will have to atone for the crimes of Atreus, his screams ring out from the house; the chorus discusses what it should do.

Clytemnestra puts an end to the chorus's indecision: she appears with the corpses of Agamemnon and Cassandra, and, in murderous ecstasy, boasts about her deed, which she describes in lurid detail.

During her lyric exchange with the chorus, Clytemnestra's frenzy gradually subsides. She seeks to justify what she has done, and finally acquiesces in the interpretation of the chorus, which maintains: "The doer must suffer. That is the law. Who could cast the seed of curses from the house?" (1564–65).

Aegisthus enters, rejoicing over the death of Agamemnon. Clytemnestra's pangs of remorse become all the more apparent when contrasted with the heartlessness of her paramour. Aegisthus says that he has avenged his father Thyestes for Atreus's crime against him—he himself played a part in the murder, but only a secondary one. The chorus rebukes him (that the old men dare to do this is quite telling of Aegisthus's—and Clytemnestra's—loss of authority). Aegisthus finds this intolerable and draws his sword. Clytemnestra is conciliatory ("Let us spill no more blood!" 1656). The chorus threatens that Orestes will have his day of vengeance. Thus, the end of the play looks ahead to *Choephori*.

This summary, though brief, shows that tragedy, *qua* drama, did not represent just any sequence of mythical events; instead, it singled out a crucial moment, a pregnant episode, in the myth. The events antecedent to the dramatic action were made known to the audience in the prologue and choral songs.

Moreover, tragedy had to be theatrically effective. Certain striking visual effects were long remembered in Athens: in the opening scene of Aeschylus's *Niobe*, the heroine was seen sitting on the stage, veiled and silent, paralyzed with pain (cf. Aristophanes, *Frogs* 911–13); in Euripides' *Telephus*, the king appeared not in royal costume but in rags (cf. Aristophanes, *Acharnians* 432–63 and *Clouds* 921–22).[14] Such innovations added to the meaning of the dramatic action (which was both visual and verbal). With his first step on the purple cloths, Agamemnon transcends human norms. The beacon of the first scene of the same play in effect throws a bridge across the sea from Agamemnon in Troy to Clytemnestra in Argos; Clytemnestra is characterized in part through her reaction to the sighting of the beacon. In the prologue of Euripides' *Electra*, the princess enters in a slave's costume, wearing a coarse garment and carrying a pot on her shorn head. Her self-abasement, openly advertised though unnecessary (as becomes clear at once), is an indication of the depth of the hatred that drives her to the murder of Aegisthus and Clytemnestra.

Above all, the playwright constantly exploited the discrepancy between the knowledge of the characters and that of the audience. In *Agamemnon*, the Trojan expedition is gradually called into question, first by Clytemnestra and then by the herald. Underlying their speeches is the question whether justice is even possible in such an endeavor. In the unending cycle of retaliation that is the mainspring of the *Oresteia*, each retaliatory act is carried out in the name of justice. Thus, Clytemnestra murders Agamemnon to avenge the murder of Iphigeneia, Aegisthus to avenge Thyestes, his father, who suffered injustice at the hands of Atreus, the father of Agamemnon. In *Choephori*, the next play of the trilogy, Orestes and Electra insist that the murder of their mother was a just act. Yet the alleged justness of that act does not keep the Erinyes from hounding Orestes. Aegisthus's justification rings hollow; Clytemnestra, too, is on uncertain ground from the start. Nor is Agamemnon free from blame; he is not simply Artemis's victim, as the chorus's review of the events antecedent to the action shows. It is true that no reason is given for Artemis's wrath. In other versions it was said that Agamemnon, while hunting, had killed a hind that was sacred to the goddess (cf. Proclus's epitome of the *Cypria* in *EGF*, p. 32; Sophocles, *Electra* 563–76; Hesiod is silent about the killing of the hind in fr. 23 MW of his *Catalogue of Women.*). Still, Agamemnon is wrong to kill his daughter—not for lack of moral principles or out of criminal ambition but because he makes a mistake in weighing the alternatives.

To be sure, it was the inexplicable wrath of Artemis that plunged him into disaster in the first place: mortals may believe that they act autonomously, but they must never disregard the gods. Thus, the chorus sees the influence of Zeus in everything. Zeus's justice required that Troy fall; he determined that Agamemnon decide against his daughter. Cassandra refers to the curse on the descendants of Atreus; Clytemnestra has recourse to this curse after she kills her husband. Yet even the family curse is no abstract mechanism. For here, too, supernatural powers—a *daimōn* ("divine power") or *alastōr* ("avenging spirit")—are at work. But this explanation comes quite late in the play: initially, we are supposed to see mortals as independent actors.

The relationship between the mortal action and divine dispensation becomes far more important in the next two plays of the Oresteian trilogy, *Choephori* and *Eumenides*.

> *Choephori* ("Libation Bearers") dramatizes the next stage of the vendetta. Orestes, having lived in exile since he was a small child, returns home, and at Agamemnon's tomb encounters his sister Electra just as she, along with her retinue, is pouring libations (*choai*) to her dead father (from this the play takes its title). Orestes takes vengeance for the murder of his father by murdering Aegisthus and Clytemnestra. The death of his mother and her paramour is seen as a just form of retribution—and that it is, so far as a son is obligated to avenge his father—until the end of the play, when it is called into doubt, as yet another consequence of the family curse. Clytemnestra's Erinyes afflict

Orestes with madness and pursue him relentlessly: the bloody punishment ordered by Apollo is itself a crime— matricide—that demands punishment. Justice, in the form of the vendetta, is hopelessly entangled in injustice.

Orestes' dilemma is even graver than that of Agamemnon at Aulis. Again the unexplained and unexplainable will of the gods has thrust mortals into a terrible predicament. Apollo makes Orestes decide between two evils: he must either avenge his father by committing matricide or be punished horribly by the Delphic god. No matter what he decides, he cannot avoid the Erinyes' frightful punishment: thus, his dilemma is more morally offensive than Agamemnon's. Artemis, as the goddess of the eerie realm that lies beyond human culture, is wild and unpredictable; Apollo, however, the god of the Delphic oracle, is supposed to be a defender of justice.

The outlines of a conflict between Apollo and the Erinyes of Clytemnestra begin to emerge in *Choephori*; in *Eumenides*, the third play of the trilogy, that conflict takes place and is resolved. It is a conflict on the divine plane; to mortals it seems irresoluble. Here, too, claims are in competition. Apollo, as the one who ordered Orestes to avenge his father's murder, admits that, if Orestes has acted wrongly, it is his fault, while from time immemorial the Erinyes have had the function of punishing matricides (and murderers generally); Apollo, they say, is encroaching on their rights. Thus, the struggle is between an older generation of gods and a younger one: "You, a young god, have ridden roughshod over us aged divinities!" the Erinyes protest (150). It soon becomes apparent that even the gods cannot resolve the conflict—not even Athena, who is called in to arbitrate. She establishes the Areopagus, a jury court made up of Athenian citizens, to decide the issue. Orestes is acquitted with a parity of votes, and the Erinyes are indignant. Athena, however, with limitless patience and rhetorical skill, conciliates the raving goddesses, persuading them to accept residence in her city as beneficent goddesses, *Eumenidai* ("Kindly Ones").

Eumenides dramatizes three etiological myths. Two of these—one explaining the foundation of the Areopagus council, another that of the cult of the Eumenides in Athens—are obvious.[15] The third *aition* concerns an external policy: after his acquittal, Orestes departs, thanking Athens and swearing an eternal alliance (*symmachia*) between Athens and Argos, which he promises to safeguard in his posthumous capacity as hero (754–77). The conflict, which has been over the question of the individual's responsibility and which has been driven forward by the evil specter of the Atreidae, is here resolved in an order that comprises the whole of Athenian society. The Eumenides are to bring prosperity to Athens; the Argives, having made a pact with Athens, are to "honor their obligation to the city of Pallas" (772–73); the council of the Areopagus, according to Athena's decree, is to be a "bulwark protecting the land and the city" (701). In the past, justice was maintained solely by retaliation on the part of the wronged—by the vendetta, the horrible cycle of crime and punishment in which every punishment was also a fresh crime. Henceforth justice is to be guaranteed by the Athenians' "pious awe and fear" (690–91) of the council and its sanctions.

Thus, the trilogy ends with allusions to contemporary politics. The pact with Argos reflects the foreign policy of the Athenians in 458 B.C., when Athens was embroiled in a power struggle with Sparta (Argos was an inveterate enemy of Sparta). In praising the Areopagus and making Athena its founder, the poet was taking a position in the debate over a constitutional reform of 462 B.C., which severely curtailed the competence of the Areopagus council. We should not simply brush aside these topical allusions, as some scholars have done, on the ground that they are insignificant by comparison with the ethical problem running through all three plays (and one that is especially prominent in

Agamemnon). This is what W. Schmid does, for example, when he writes that *"Agamemnon* and *Choephori* were composed for humanity, *Eumenides* for Athens in 458 B.C." The ethical and political levels are not so easily separated.

Quite pointedly, Aeschylus represents the conflict between Apollo and the Erinyes, which arises over Orestes' act of vengeance, as a kind of theogonic event involving two generations of gods, the very ancient Erinyes, "decrepit old girls" (69), children of the primal power Night, and the young gods Apollo and Athena. The old gods believe that they are being divested of their sphere of influence (*timē*). The conflict may be compared with the one between Zeus and the Titans (of which Aeschylus's *Prometheus Bound* represents one stage) in Hesiod's *Theogony*. That conflict ends with a new distribution of *timai* (*Theogony* 885); so does the conflict between Apollo and the Erinyes in *Eumenides*. However, the new order is not established by violent means; nor is the chain of violent acts, which began with Pelops's murder of Myrtilus, simply elevated to the divine plane and extended there by another generation. Instead, it is the votes of Athenian citizens and Athena's power of persuasion (*peithō*) that put an end to the conflict. Voting and persuasion are instruments of the democratic polis; the political order supersedes the old one, and the judges are not gods or heroes but Athenian citizens. Athens, the ideal polis, replaces and thereby redeems the heroic world.

Aeschylus the citizen, the creature of the polis (*politēs*), took stock of the old myths of epic poetry. He measured them against the norms of the democratic polis and amended them accordingly. Just how much of the etiology of *Eumenides* was Aeschylus's invention is disputed. But even if the Areopagus had already been connected with Orestes and the Eumenides before Aeschylus wrote the *Oresteia*, the interpretation of the myth as a confrontation between the old heroic order and the new polis was certainly original with him.

Born in 525/4 B.C., Aeschylus grew up during the period in

which the tyranny of the Peisistratids was supplanted by the democracy of Cleisthenes, and he took part in the battles of Marathon and Salamis, the military triumphs of the young democracy. Thus, his stance toward myth was optimistic: he believed that, with some amendments, it could continue to be useful. In this respect Aeschylus was unique among the tragedians.

Sophocles (497–406/5 B.C.) subjected his heroes, much as Aeschylus subjected Agamemnon and Orestes, to divine influence. In Sophocles' plays, however, the gods are inexorable, the heroes doomed to failure. In searching for Laeus's murderer and with him the cause of the plague in Thebes (wherein he is no less persistent than he had been in evading the oracle), Oedipus himself discovers the bewildering truth. Oedipus bears no guilt. To be sure, he insults the seer Teiresias and suspects Creon of complicity in Laeus's murder. But that does not make him guilty. The worst that may be said of him is that his character is not spotless. He is not *eu-daimōn*, that is, he does not enjoy the favor of the gods.[16] Deianeira in *Trachinian Women* may be taken to illustrate the same point. To win back her husband Heracles, she sends him a garment smeared with a fluid that she believes to be a love charm. But the fluid is actually a caustic (she received it from the centaur Nessus), and when Heracles puts on the garment, he dies a slow and intensely painful death, commanding, in the end, that he be burned alive. That does not, however, make Deianeira guilty. Yet she hangs herself. When Hyllus, helplessly indignant, protests "the great cruelty of the gods" (1266), the chorus can only reply: "all this is the work of Zeus" (1278). Thus, the play ends with the recognition that the will of the gods is beyond the ken of mortals.

Euripides, Myth, and the Gods

Euripides (ca. 480–406 B.C.) was, perhaps, the poet who wrestled most with myth and whose relationship to myth has been most baffling to scholars. In the works of no other Attic tragedian are the heroes reduced to such a low condition—low in the sense of average, often even below average. Nowhere else do we find so many skeptical statements about the gods—skeptical even to the point of denying their existence. Yet the subjects of Euripides' plays were taken, without exception, from myth. Many of his plays were written in answer to a predecessor's version of the same or similar myth. No other tragic poet concluded so many of his works with *aitia*, which offered the clearest evidence for the influence of gods and heroes on the affairs of mortals (eleven of the fifteen plays whose original endings are preserved end with such accounts; nine of these are cult *aitia*). Nowhere else do the gods appear so frequently (nine plays end with the appearance of a *deus ex machina*; in three the gods are introduced in the prologue; in *Heracles* Iris, the messenger of the gods, and Lyssa, the personification of madness, and perhaps also Athena appear in the middle of the play; finally, in *Bacchae* Dionysus is the protagonist). How does all this tally?[17]

To answer this question, we must return to the distinction between the heroic plane, which is lowered to that of ordinary mortals in Euripides' plays, and the divine plane. Euripides impugns the myths about the gods but not those about the heroes—the frequency with which his plays end in etiologies of hero cults indicates that he is trying to anchor his myths, which deal with the past, in contemporary experience. It is true that he calls into question certain details of heroic myths, but here his skepticism is restricted to things that even the likes of Hecataeus would have doubted, such as the story that Zeus visited Leda in the form of a swan (*Iphigeneia at Aulis* 793–96; *Helen* 17–21, where Helen's display of skepticism serves the characterization of her as a "sophisticated lady") or the story that the sun altered its course in disgust at Atreus's grisly banquet (*Electra* 737–45).

The Euripidean critique of myths about the gods begins with the same objection: the gods, as traditionally represented, are far too crassly anthropomorphic. This objection was not new. A century earlier, Xenophanes of Colophon had complained that

Homer and Hesiod attributed to the gods "all that is shameful
and disgraceful among men: they steal, commit adultery, and
deceive one another" (DK 21 B 11; cf. Chapter 8). "The god who
judges right and wrong for all mortals himself behaves like a vile
mortal: how can he be wise?": this is the messenger's judgment
on the Delphic murder of Neoptolemus, Achilles' son, whom
Apollo hated (*Andromache* 1161–65). "It does not befit gods to
become like mortals in their anger": thus Cadmus reproaches
the irate Dionysus (*Bacchae* 1348). On the other hand, Iris protests: "Let Heracles recognize what Hera's wrath is, let him learn
what mine is—unless the gods are powerless, and mortal affairs
will have grown too great—if this man does not pay the penalty!" (*Heracles* 840–42). The penalty, however, is undeserved:
"jealous of Zeus for a woman's sake, Hera has destroyed the
benefactor of Greece, even though he was without guilt"
(1308–10). It is hard to escape the conclusion: "Who would pray
to such a goddess?" (1307–8).

Xenophanes' position on this question was clear. Euripides,
by contrast, did not speak *in propria persona*. In his plays the
characters do the speaking, and their statements are often inconsistent or contrary to one another. At all events, the gods become
enigmatic when mortals apply to them the standard of justice
that they wish to realize in their own lives (for Aeschylus it is
the polis that guarantees justice): "Surely we are slaves and are
weak, but the gods are strong and so is the law that governs
them. For by this law we believe that the gods exist, and by it
we abide as a way of distinguishing right from wrong." So Hecuba, in an attempt to persuade Agamemnon to help her exact
vengeance on Polymestor for the murder of her little son Poly-
dorus (*Hecuba* 798–801). Here, the norm according to which
justice is determined applies to gods and men alike; indeed, it
owes its cultural relevance to the very fact that it is also applicable to the gods. But Hecuba is pleading for aid, and her optimi-
sic statement must not be understood apart from its context. Far
too often, the gods do not live up to this idea of justice; too often

they do not reward the just. In *Iphigeneia at Aulis* Clytemnestra takes heart from the notion of a justice from the gods. "If the gods exist," she says to Achilles, who has resolved to prevent the sacrifice of her daughter, "you, being a just man, will receive their benefits" (1034–35). But Iphigeneia's very dubious rescue, for which Clytemnestra longs so much, is only a partial confirmation of the existence of the gods.

Two conclusions may be drawn from such a theodicy. We may infer, with Heracles, that the gods are not just and therefore they do not deserve to be worshiped, or even that "if the gods do wrong, they are not gods" (fr. 292 Nauck). Alternatively, we may reject the tradition altogether: Artemis cannot require human sacrifice, since, as Iphigeneia says, "none of the gods is bad"; she suggests that the practice is the invention of the barbarous natives (*Iphigeneia among the Taurians* 380–91). At the end of that play, however, Athena establishes an Attic ritual to compensate for the sacrifice of Orestes: thus, it seems that the sacrifice was willed by divinity after all (1458–61). "I do not believe," Heracles declares, "that the gods engage in illicit intercourse, that they bind each other in chains, or that one god can be master of another; I have never thought it proper nor will I ever believe it. For a god, if he is truly a god, stands in need of nothing. These are the pernicious tales of singers" (*Heracles* 1341–46). Again, that sounds like Xenophanes. However, Heracles himself is a product of "illicit intercourse," and he has just finished imputing his misery to Hera's jealousy. Furthermore, his declaration follows one of the most horrifying demonstrations of divine capriciousness in the entire corpus of Greek tragedy. Heracles has returned from Hades just in time to rescue his father, wife, and children from the brazen usurper Lycus, and the chorus has struck up a song of joy, when Iris and Lyssa appear on high. At Hera's bidding, and baited by Iris, Lyssa drives the hero to take the lives of those whom he has just rescued, with the exception of his father, whom Athena saves by direct intervention. After this, can anyone really expect Heracles to believe in

morally pure gods? Or was this, as Wilamowitz thought, Euripides' own opinion, and was he trying to discredit myth?[18]

The problem is more complicated than that. To be sure, if Heracles were right, there would be no escaping the conclusion that
the myth is a lie, and Heracles along with it. But Heracles is not
Euripides. The poet has also put Iris and Lyssa before our eyes;
he has made Iris, who is Hera's mouthpiece, relate (in the passage
quoted earlier) Hera's demand for vengeance, but he has made
no effort to tell us which one of them comes closest to the truth,
Heracles or Iris. It may be that Heracles is mistaken: if so, then
the gods do not act in accordance with any ethical norms, and
we are wrong to project norms onto them. Or it may be that
what Heracles says about the gods is bound to fall short of the
mark, because the gods lie beyond the compass of human discourse.

That is just what Euripides has his choruses say. In *Helen*, for
example, the chorus describes what the Greeks and Trojans have
suffered on account of the phantom of Helen created by Hera
(Hera hated Aphrodite for having won the notorious beauty
contest by promising its arbitrator, Paris, the most beautiful
woman in the world—none other than Helen—in exchange for
his vote); then it draws the conclusion: "What god is, what is
not god, what is in between—what mortal can claim to have
discovered this, even if he should take his search to the farthest
limit, when he sees the things of the gods leaping here and there
and back again by contrary and unexpected twists of chance?"
(1137–43). Similarly, in *Hippolytus*, which was produced sixteen
years earlier (428 B.C.), the chorus says: "Greatly does the gods'
care for mortals, when it comes to my mind, relieve my pain;
though deep within me I hope to understand it, I cannot keep
up with it, as I look among the fortunes and doings of mortals.
For some things pass from one place, others from another: the
life of men is unstable, ever shifting this way and that"
(1102–10). The gods hold sway in the lives of mortals, but they
follow rules that are inscrutable to mortals. In the pathos-
charged exchange between Artemis and the dying Hippolytus

near the end of the same play, Artemis shows the vast difference between gods and mortals. Hippolytus, her favorite, lies dying before her, a victim of Aphrodite's jealousy, and yet she cannot remain at his side: "Farewell! It is not right for me to look upon the dead, or to pollute my eyes with the exhalations of the dying; and I see that you are already close to this evil" (1437–39). And with that she departs.

Is this the key to the statements about the gods in Euripides's plays—that the gods are wholly incommensurable with human thought, whether it is expressed in myth or in the philosophy of a Xenophanes? If so, then Euripides had a distinguished forerunner. "Concerning the gods I am unable to discover whether they exist or not": thus began Protagoras's *On the Gods* (DK 80 B 4), which the sophist is supposed to have read aloud at Euripides' house. Even if we take the view that Euripides is not necessarily raising doubts about the existence of the gods, we cannot escape the conclusion that, to him, myths about the gods merely show our inability to comprehend them, and that Euripidean tragedy thus represents our incommensurability with the gods and the impossibility of communication between the divine and human worlds.

Euripides also stretched heroic myth to the breaking point by making his heroes and heroines more and more similar to the men and women of his own day. That point was reached in *Orestes*, which was produced in 408 B.C.[19]

The play deals with the aftermath of the matricide. Crazed by his mother's Erinyes, Orestes lies on a sickbed at Argos, near death, tended by Electra. The assembly of the Argive people, led by partisans of Aegisthus, condemns Orestes and Electra to death by stoning, which Orestes resolves to obviate by suicide. Menelaus returns, anxiously awaited by Orestes and Electra, as well as by his wife Helen and his daughter Hermione. When Orestes and Electra appeal to him for help, he abandons them to the avengers of Aegisthus and Clytemnestra. Tyndareus, the earthly father

of Clytemnestra and Helen, makes Menelaus choose between Orestes, the murderer of his daughter Clytemnestra,
and the Spartan throne; in addition, Tyndareus hopes to
gain the throne of Argos when Orestes dies. Orestes and
Electra, supported solely by Pylades, who has been turned
out of house and succession by his father for his complicity
in the murder of Clytemnestra, now lash out in despair.
First, to avenge themselves on their treacherous uncle, they
plan to assassinate Helen (who in the meantime has already
begun to put her seal on the heirlooms in the Argive palace); Orestes imagines the posthumous fame that will be
his for having punished the woman who caused the Trojan
War. Then, to force Menelaus to help them, they take the
young, naïve, and lovable Hermione hostage. But the kid-
napping gets out of control. Orestes, Electra, and Pylades,
having failed to kill Helen, are on the point of killing Hermione before her father's eyes and setting fire to the Argive
palace when Apollo intervenes *ex machina* to restore order.

The god has every reason to do so. In *Orestes,* as in the Stesichorean and Aeschylean versions of the myth, it is Apollo who
drives Orestes to kill his mother. But in Euripides' play, for some
unknown reason, the god is slow to come to Orestes' aid. The
hero is abandoned, not only by nearly all mortals but also by the
gods. His abandonment is too obvious for one to accept Apollo's
command merely as a traditional catalyst of the action and a
feeble excuse for the matricide, too obvious for one to accept the
god's last-minute epiphany as both a traditional and a clumsy
means of steering the thoroughly perverse action back onto the
course required by the mythical tradition. At one point, Orestes
is standing on the palace roof, sword in hand, with Hermione,
his hostage, at his feet; he is flanked by Electra and Pylades, who
are brandishing torches; he asks Menelaus, at whom he has just
hurled a piece of the palace cornice, for the hand of his daughter,
whom only a moment ago he was on the point of murdering;

and Menelaus consents! The absurdity of this moment cannot be unintentional. Euripides is saying something about the absurd incalculability of divine intervention, about the problematic nature of the relationship between gods and mortals. The gods are simply not paying attention when they are needed by mortals, who consequently lapse into one atrocity after another. Nor do the gods foresee this, because they do not understand mortals or simply do not care about them.

At the same time, the mortal personae of *Orestes* are not simply bad through and through. The way in which brother and sister treat one another is touching. But they are no different from other people, and in 408 B.C. Euripides had no illusions: when cornered, man is capable of anything, and the polis is not likely to come to the aid of good people, because it, too, is dominated by lust for power and opportunism. Orestes, Electra, and Pylades illustrate those well-known pages of Thucydides (3.82), in which the historian depicts the perversion of values during the long years of the Peloponnesian War.

Thus, the gods in Euripides' plays flee upward, so to speak, into utter incomprehensibility, while the heroes flee downward into all too crass humanity, in which any trace of exemplary greatness vanishes. With that, the tragic representation of myth comes to an end. One should not be misled by *Bacchae*, Euripides' most shocking work, which was written at the end of his career and staged posthumously.[20] In it Dionysus plays a cruel cat-and-mouse game with Pentheus, the king of Thebes, who refuses to recognize the new god. Ultimately, the god has Pentheus torn to pieces by his mother, who, in an ecstatic state, triumphantly carries her son's head onto the stage. This story does not bring heroic myth back to life; instead, it demonstrates the terrible power of the god in his ritual. *Bacchae* is an enactment of Dionysiac rites in the guise of mythical narrative. The question of the meaning of mortal suffering, of the justice in that suffering, which was posed first by Aeschylus and later, again and again, by Euripides, is of no concern to the god of *Bacchae*.

CHAPTER VIII

PHILOSOPHERS, ALLEGORISTS,

AND MYTHOLOGISTS

Myth after the Fifth Century B.C.

In Greek poetry after Euripides, myths, in the narrative forms
in which they had traditionally been expressed, ceased to offer
contingently valid explanations of the universe, man, and society and to accommodate these explanations to ever-changing circumstances. In the following centuries, some Greek poets took
refuge in the aesthetic perfection of mythical narration, as Callimachus of Cyrene did in his *Hymns* and *Aetia*, whereas others
tested the limits of traditional narrative forms, as Apollonius of
Rhodes did in his *Argonautica*. Yet others freed poetry from the
constraints of myth entirely: the comedies of Menander, the
most important Greek dramatist after Euripides, dealt with
the concerns of the ordinary citizen. Similarly, Theocritus, who,
like Apollonius and Callimachus, had connections with Alexandria, wrote *Idylls* idealizing the shepherd's world. These were
utopic visions of a citydweller, in which myth played a very minor part: occasionally the *Idylls* trifled with motifs taken from
the myth of the golden age.[1]

To be sure, the treatment of myths in tragic and choral lyric
poetry did not come to an end with Euripides. Tragedies continued to be written and staged, not only in Athens but also, in-

creasingly, in other cities of the Hellenized world. The plays have vanished almost without a trace, and we would like to know more. It is true that many tragedies entered the secularized edu-cational tradition, as the practice of restaging old plays, often more than once, indicates: these plays had become "classics." But the theaters in which the plays were performed were still sanctu-aries of the god Dionysus. Moreover, tragedy probably retained, if only to a relatively slight degree, its old function, which had been to promote communal solidarity.

One form of poetry, the hymn, which was delivered at festi-vals of the gods, certainly did retain its old function. In hymns that belonged to the cult of Asclepius, which have been preserved in inscriptions,[2] the story of the god's birth continued to be told; the myth was followed by a prayer for the welfare of the entire polis. This continuity of function cannot be dismissed as tradi-tion for tradition's sake. After all, one could always use myth to justify political claims of one kind or another. That myth was exploited by religious centers for political purposes, for example, is hardly surprising. When, in A.D. 22, the emperor Tiberius re-viewed the right of Greek sanctuaries to grant asylum, most of the claims brought before him rested on documented instances in which asylum had been granted in the past. The Artemisium in Ephesus, however, justified its claim differently: the Romans and Macedonians, the Ephesians argued, were not the first to favor the sanctuary, nor were the Persians the first to recognize its sanctity; Heracles had expanded the cult during his stay in Lydia; before him, Dionysus had shown mercy to the Amazons when, during their battle with him, they took refuge at the altar of Artemis; even earlier, Apollo had fled to the same place when Zeus was angry at him for having killed the Cyclopes (Tacitus, *Annals* 3.61).

In other political spheres arguments based on the mythical tradition are not quite so self-evident. Isocrates, for example, writing in the spring of 346 B.C. to urge Philip of Macedon to undertake a war against Persia, appealed to Philip's putative de-

scent from Heracles (5.113). To take another example: an imperial inscription tells of an embassy sent to Argos by the city of
Aegae in Cilicia. The embassy's mission was to make a pact of
friendship (which entailed considerable commercial advantages).
The Cilician negotiator based his appeal for friendship on the
mythical datum according to which his city had been founded
by Perseus, the Argive hero. We learn from another source that
the same Cilician rhetor had also defended the Cretans in a legal
dispute over Crete's claim to the tomb of Zeus.[3] It would be easy
to multiply such examples.

Myth, then, understood as a form of knowledge about the distant past, retained a certain social and political significance even
after the archaic and classical periods. But its relevance in postclassical times was greatly diminished. Myths could no longer
meaningfully encompass all spheres of human experience;
Greco-Roman society had become too severely fragmented. In
many respects, philosophy was heir to myth.

Philosophical *Mythologia* and *Mythopoeia* 1: The Sophists

The philosophers were the first to question the validity of myth
fundamentally. When Presocratic thought about the universe
began to break away from the tradition, most Greeks regarded
the traditional myths as valid; indeed, at that time the poems of
Homer and Hesiod were widely accepted as the nucleus of the
Greek conception of the cosmos and of the self. But inevitably
the rift between philosophy and the religious tradition would be
discerned and the two modes of thought would come into conflict. About the end of the sixth century, for the first time, so far
as we can tell, it was stated clearly that "from the beginning all
have learned from Homer" (Xenophanes of Colophon, ca. 570–
475 B.C. [DK 21 B 10]) and that "the teacher of most is Hesiod"
(Heraclitus of Ephesus, ca. 540–480 B.C. [DK 22 B 57]). The apparent reverence was followed by criticism: "Homer and Hesiod
have attributed to the gods all that is shameful and disgraceful

among men: they steal, commit adultery, and deceive one another" (Xenophanes [DK 21 B 11]). The old myths were no longer acceptable to Xenophanes; they did not measure up to his ethically purified ideas about the gods. Indeed, they did not measure up to any of his ethical ideas: "among men he is to be praised who after drinking produces noble thoughts . . . and does not tell of the battles of the Titans or the Giants or the Centaurs, fictions of our predecessors" (DK 21 B 1 19–22). The traditional tales no longer offered explanations; on the contrary, they posed problems—and for the first time they were rejected. Heraclitus put it even more harshly: "much learning does not teach understanding. For, if it did, it would have taught Hesiod and Pythagoras" (DK 22 B 40); "Homer deserves to be expelled from the contests and thrashed, and so does Archilochus" (DK 22 B 42). For Heraclitus, the poets represented the unreflective, self-contradictory way of thinking characteristic of the general populace, which he spurned. Their depiction of the gods and heroes was probably only one among many reasons why the philosophers rejected their works.

With the sophists, the enlightened intellectuals of the fifth century, the rejection of the mythical tradition left the private sphere of philosophical polemics. The democratic polis allowed more of its members to participate in political decision making than had ever done so in the past. Increasingly, economic prosperity and trade brought Greeks into contact with unfamiliar people and unfamiliar ideas. The growing capacity to read and write also facilitated the dissemination of new ideas. Through active participation in politics, the citizen gained confidence in his own judgment, and consequently he grew more and more skeptical of the traditional tales, at least most of the time: "When a man approaches the time of his life when he begins to think about dying," says old Cephalus in Plato's *Republic* (330d), whose dramatic date is near the end of the fifth century, " . . . the stories about the underworld . . . which he once ridiculed, torment his mind."

Some sense of the sophists' attitude toward myth can be

gained from their statements about the gods. It was mentioned earlier (Chapter 7) that Protagoras admitted to being unable to speak on the subject. If he refused to speak about the gods, he probably did not believe that myths made valid statements. Other sophists were less cautious: Prodicus of Ceos (470/60– after 399 B.C.) "was of the opinion that the gods traditionally accepted by men do not exist." Early man—so Prodicus—made the forces of nature into gods: "the sun, the moon, rivers, springs, and all the things that benefit our lives" (DK 84 B 5). Later, as human culture progressed, human beings (culture heroes and benefactors of mankind) were also deified—Demeter, who invented agriculture and bread making, and Dionysus, who invented viniculture and wine pressing, were recognizable as such. The myths that tell how Demeter came to Eleusis and Dionysus to Icaria, bringing their gifts with them, were adduced to illustrate this thesis, in a historicizing vein.[4]

Whatever "early man" could do, the sophists could do at least as well. They narrated myths, too. But they did not just retell the old myths; they were professional teachers, and accordingly they forged the myths into didactic instruments. The traditional myths served as a framework for sophistic instruction—in the *Trojan Dialogue* of Hippias of Elis (DK 86 A 2), Nestor, speaking to the young son of Achilles in the destroyed city of Troy, explains how to "become a good man," that is, above all, how to be a successful statesman. This is precisely what all sophists professed to teach. Nestor became the mythical prototype of the sophistic teacher.

The sophists even invented their own myths. None other than Prodicus is credited with having invented the most influential sophistic myth, that of the "choice of Heracles" (DK 84 B 2). At an intersection of two roads Heracles encounters two godlike women, Arete and Eudaimonia, "Virtue" and "Happiness," each of whom describes to him her way of life. Heracles must choose between a pleasant but ultimately dull life and one of constant toil but with a supernatural reward. The ending was supplied by the tradition. Even if such personifications, which were frequent in poetry and in cult, were more vivid for the Greeks than they are for us, the mythical varnish remained transparent—it certainly did nothing to diminish the popularity of the story, which continued to attract readers into the modern period.[5]

In these new mythical creations the tradition was little more than a peg on which to hang the ethical message. The tradition imparted to the tale an aura of cultural relevance and poetic splendor. As a teaching aid to be used in lessons and private reading, however, the sophistic myth was isolated from the censorship of a community. Thus, the traditional figures became objects of intellectual amusement. Gorgias of Leontini, the founder of rhetoric, wrote an *Encomium on Helen* in which he absolved Helen from all responsibility for the Trojan War. He did so not by retelling the myth (as Stesichorus had done) but by means of shrewd argumentation within the framework of the tradition—an "amusement," as he himself called it (DK 82 B 11).

More closely linked to the mythical tradition is a tale told by the title figure of Plato's *Protagoras* (320c). In its main outline it probably does go back to the first and greatest of the sophists. Protagoras tells the tale to refute Socrates, who has challenged the sophistic claim that political virtue can be taught. Its first half is an interesting variation on the Prometheus theme: Epimetheus had been assigned the task of endowing all living creatures, after their creation, with the skills that they would need to survive. When he came to man, he realized that he had no more skills to dispense. Prometheus came to the aid of man, giving him, instead of horns, sharp teeth, wings, or the like, technology and fire, which he stole from the workshop of Athena and Hephaestus. For this act of stealing Prometheus was punished.

Thus far, all that has been explained is the difference between man and animal. In Hesiod's *Theogony*, the myth of Prometheus (521–616) had served the same purpose—to define the human condition; Epimetheus's thoughtless management of his resources has ethnological parallels outside antiquity, while the linearity of Protagoras's myth sets it apart from the other sophistic myths that we have considered so far. The second half of the myth also bears the marks of traditional storytelling. Man, Protagoras says, was unable to survive because he lacked the ability to form communities (Prometheus could not gain access to political knowledge, which was in Zeus's keeping). So the father of the gods sent Hermes to convey respect (*aidōs*) and justice (*dikē*) to mankind, enjoining him to distribute them equally among all. Thus, since that time, all men have possessed the ability to act politically.[6]

Zeus's role as distributor of the skills necessary for the formation of political communities and as the protector of those communities was an entirely traditional one. Even Hesiod had represented him as the father of Dike. Protagoras's tale explained a slice of Athenian reality, not unlike Aeschylus's *Eumenides*. What was new here was not so much the answer—a kind of mythical pastiche—as the question: how did man acquire political knowledge? The use of myth as the equivalent of a rational argument was also new. Protagoras leaves it to his listeners to decide whether he should give his answer to Socrates' question concerning the teachability of virtue in the form of a rational argument (*logos*) or in that of a myth. He eventually chooses the mythical form for pedagogical reasons, "as an old man speaking to his juniors" (320c). Of the two modes of explanation, myth is the more appropriate for an intellectually immature audience. With this remark Protagoras is, incidentally, only a step away from the modern thesis according to which myth belongs to the childhood of mankind.

This pedagogical function of myth became increasingly important in the following period. To be sure, this function was as old as Homer: his mythical exempla purported to demonstrate something. But the sophists seem to have been the first to reduce the functions of all myths to that of instruction. Plato followed suit: in his ideal state, myths purged of the morally offensive serve to instruct the young guardians (*Republic* 377c). Later, Plutarch would call myths, provided that they were properly interpreted, the best means of educating young people (*How the Young Man Should Study Poetry* 28e et passim [= *Moralia* 28e et passim]). This pedagogical view of myth helps to explain why Aesop's fables were so popular. The fables had always been regarded as *mythoi*. In the imperial period, the Aesopian fable was even thought to be the ideal kind of mythical narrative. For it always aimed at ethical instruction; it furnished its own moral, thereby making interpretation unnecessary (Philostratus, *The Life of Apollonius of Tyana* 5.14; *Imagines* 1.3).

Philosophical *Mythologia* and *Mythopoeia* 2: Plato

Plato (428–348 B.C.) was heir to the legacy of the sophists; he also progressed beyond sophistic doctrines. Like the sophists, Plato was a teller of myths in his own right. Much of what people thought about myths in the preceding age is to be found in his dialogues—especially criticism of myth, which was necessarily also criticism of poetry.

In the second book of the *Republic*, in which Plato speaks of the education of the military or guardian class in his ideal state, he explains why most myths are unsuitable for young people. Examples of such unsuitable myths abound in the poetry of Homer and Hesiod, the greatest tellers of myths known to him. The list of reproaches is long and little of the *Iliad* or the *Theogony* survives the attack. It is not surprising, then, that Plato bans all poets from his ideal state, though not without regret: "we are well aware that we are under their spell," he concedes (607c). However, he does not wish to exclude the narration of myths altogether: "we must admit no poetry into our state except hymns to the gods and songs in praise of good men" (607a). It is impossible to imagine a hymn to a god that does not include the narration of myth, and encomia celebrate not only "good men" but also mythical heroes. So he allows hymns and encomia with a proviso: "we must watch the mythmakers (*mytho-poioi*) closely, accepting the myths that they make well, and rejecting the ones that they do not" (377b–c).

What Plato is prescribing, then, is that the old poets be banned from the ideal state, the new ones censored. Of course, he knows other ways of dealing with the offensive qualities of myth. He rejects Homer's myths, "whether composed with underlying meanings (*en hyponoiais*) or without them" (378d): *hyponoia*, "underlying meaning," is the catchword for what was later called the allegorical interpretation of myth. The term *allēgoria*, "speaking otherwise," was not employed until the late Hellenistic period, as Plutarch observed, *Isis and Osiris* 32 (*Moralia* 363d).

Allegorical interpretation proceeds from the assumption that the poet deliberately situates his meaning not at the literal level, but at a deeper level, beneath the veil of the literal. In Plato's day, and for some time thereafter, this "true" meaning usually related to physics or natural philosophy. The so-called Derveni allegorist, a commentator on an Orphic theogony who was writing probably during Plato's lifetime (so called because his work is known from a papyrus found in a grave at Derveni in northwest Greece), fell back on the physical theories of Anaxagoras and the atomists. He believed that Uranus, for example, referred to *nous*, the fundamental intellectual and physical principle in the thought of Anaxagoras, and he took the sexual union of gods as a metaphor for the collision of atoms.[7]

In Plato's day the allegorical interpretation of myth had already been practiced for over a century. According to an ancient commentator, its first practitioner expounded, of all things, one of those theomachies that were so uncongenial to Plato, the battle of the Olympians in the twentieth book of the *Iliad*. The commentator understood this theomachy as a struggle among natural forces, namely fire (Apollo, Helius, Hephaestus), water (Poseidon, Scamander), and air (Hera). "This manner of defending Homer," the commentator wrote, "goes back to Theagenes of Rhegium, who was the first to write about Homer" (DK 8 A 2). It is not clear from the commentator's wording exactly how Theagenes interpreted Homer. He may have believed, like the Derveni commentator, that the gods were metaphors for physical forces, and that several gods could stand for the same thing. The sparse evidence for Theagenes' life indicates that he was active ca. 525 B.C. and strongly suggests that he was a rhapsode. Rhapsodes did not just recite the text of Homer; increasingly, they were required to explain it. Thus, in Plato's *Ion*, the title figure, a wandering rhapsode, claims to "have finer things to say about Homer than anyone else" (530c).[8]

In textbooks one reads that allegoresis arose as a way of "saving" Homer from his critics, the earliest of whom, so far as we know, was Xenophanes. This thesis seems to be confirmed by the fact that Theagenes chose to write about the Iliadic theomachy, which these critics found so scandalous. But neither Metrodorus of Lampsacus, the most important Homeric allegorist of the fifth century, nor the allegorist of Derveni wrote with the intention of defending Homer and Orpheus, respectively; rather, they sought to uncover their poets' true meaning. Orpheus could be said to have used an allegorical mode of expression because he was writing for a community of mystics: he deliberately made his text enigmatic, *ainigmatōdēs*, in order that the uninitiated might not be able to penetrate the literal surface of the text. The attribution of allegoresis to Homer and Hesiod must be explained differently: their prestige as the teachers of the Greeks par excellence induced the audience of a new age to see in their works hidden verities of natural science or ethics, without apologetic intention. Thus, allegorical interpretation was not necessarily a way of defending the old poets.[9]

At all events, by the late sixth century allegoresis was in the air. The theogonist and cosmogonist Pherecydes of Syros (DK 7), who seems to have been active in the middle of that century, stood on the threshold of allegoresis. According to Pherecydes, one of the primeval deities bore the name Chronus. The name, which means Time (the personification of time as a primeval power that "always existed"), is a patent etymology of the familiar Cronus. Pherecydes also recounts that Zeus wove a robe for his bride Chthonie, decorating it with Earth and Ocean, and that when Chthonie put it on, she became Gaea (Earth).[10] It is not difficult to detect physical truths beneath the veil of Pherecydes' myth. Later, in the fifth century, Empedocles would deliberately clothe his thought in enigmas (see Chapter 4). Pherecydes is believed to have been Pythagoras's teacher, and Empedocles was a Pythagorean. There is additional evidence to suggest that the Pythagoreans made use of allegoresis. The Pythagoreans reportedly construed the *akousmata*, old sayings (mostly religious taboos) ascribed to Pythagoras, as moral precepts (DK 58 C 6). The master himself was said to have employed mythical allegory to describe physical phenomena. Aristotle reports the Pythagorean doctrine that "the sea is Cronus's tear, and the Bears [i.e., the constellations Ursa Major and Ursa Minor] are Rhea's hands" (fr. 196). Although its antiquity is impossible to determine, the doctrine is another example of allegoresis without apologetic intention. Thus, even if allegoresis did arise as a way of defending Homer, its potential as a way of explaining myth—that is, as a way of adapting the meaning of myth to radically new modes of thought—was very soon appreciated.[11]

The Pythagorean interpretation of the *akousmata* aimed at ethical, not physical, truths. This use of allegoresis was apparently the achievement of the Pythagoreans. At all events, the first myth to be understood as a vehicle of ethical truth may have originated in a Pythagorean milieu. According to this myth, which is found in Plato's *Gorgias* (493a–b), in the afterlife the souls of the uninitiated (*amyētoi*) must pour water into a leaky jar (*pithos*). The point of the myth, as "its narrator, an ingenious man, perhaps a Sicilian or Italian," explained, is that the part of the soul in which the appetites are situated and which is both persuasive (*peistikon*, a derivation of the verb *peithein*) and persuadable (*pithanon*) can never be satisfied if the soul belongs to one of those who lack understanding (*anoētoi*). The teller of the myth was obviously working with similarly sounding words, "etymologies." His provenance (Sicily or Italy) and his interest in the doctrine of the soul point to Pythagoreanism; the community of mystics, to whom the myth belongs, has been sought in the same area.

To be sure, Anaxagoras, not Pythagoras, is supposed to have been "the first to show that Homer's poetry speaks of good and bad" (DK 59 A 1). However, this statement does not necessarily refer to allegoresis. A sharp distinction is to be drawn between the allegorical use of myth, which presupposes that myth is an enigmatic mode of expressing ethical doctrine, and the use of myth as an example for moral instruction. It is to the latter use that myth owed its reputation as a didactic instrument—a reputation that remained undiminished throughout antiquity.

It was not just in his criticism of myth that Plato was dependent on earlier thinkers. From the sophists he borrowed the practice of combining the narration of myth with philosophy. However, he put the result of this combination, the philosophical myth, to fundamentally new uses. Plato's most important myths express what is inexpressible in dialectical, argumentative discourse (*logos*). Whereas *mythos* and *logos* are interchangeable in Protagoras's vocabulary, they are not so in Plato's. His major myths deal either with the fate of the soul after it has been separated from the body or with the sensible world that is characterized by "coming-into-being" or "becoming." In Platonic ontology a sharp distinction is drawn between the world of being, which is immutable and can only be apprehended by the intellect, and that of becoming, which is mutable and can be perceived by the senses. Truth belongs exclusively to the world of being. While the world of being can be comprehended dialectically, only opinions are possible concerning the world of becoming. "Don't be surprised, Socrates, if we are unable to give entirely self-consistent and accurate reports [*logoi*] about many matters concerning the gods and the origins of the universe . . . concerning these things you should accept a plausible story [*eoikōs mythos*] and not seek anything more than that." Thus the title figure of the *Timaeus* begins his long cosmogonic narrative, in which he represents the divine creator of the universe at work (29c). In the *Critias*, the incomplete continuation of the *Timaeus*, is told the tale, adumbrated in the *Timaeus*, of the ideal state of Atlantis, its conflict with prehistoric Greece, and its ultimate decline. The tale of Atlantis is, like the cosmogonic account in the *Timaeus*, a myth about the world of becoming, set in a vaguely delineated past and replete with an elaborate pedigree that makes its origins so remote in time and space as to be beyond recovery. Plato disclaims responsibility for the wording of the story; it is a mental experiment, a dynamization of the model of the state set forth in the *Republic*: Socrates says that he wishes to see that ideal state in motion, just as one wishes to see the splendidly painted image of an animal come to life (*Timaeus* 19b; cf. 27a). Of course, this clear statement of intention has never discouraged anyone from looking for the remains of Atlantis at the bottom of the Atlantic or the Mediterranean.[12]

Similarly, only in myth was Plato able to speak of the destiny of the soul after the death of the body. All that could be demonstrated by means of dialectic was its immortality: "To tell what kind of thing it is would require an entirely divine and lengthy discourse, but what it resembles [*eoiken*] can be told by human beings and in less time" (*Phaedrus* 246a): thus Socrates introduces one of the four eschatological myths found in the Platonic corpus, an *eoikōs mythos*, to use the language of the *Timaeus*.

In Plato's four eschatological myths, which are told in the *Gorgias, Phaedo, Phaedrus,* and *Republic*, it is impossible to discern a set of shared features; nor can these myths be combined to produce a larger picture. Although they exhibit thematic affinities, each of them stands alone: myth cannot capture the truth, only hover about it. The most famous, perhaps, is the one told at the end of the *Republic*. Socrates introduces it "not as a tale for Alcinous [i.e., a tall tale such as Odysseus told Alcinous] but as a tale of a brave [*alkimos*] man, Er, the son of Armenias, a Pamphylian" (614b). The tongue-in-cheek connection, in which there is much wordplay, between the myth that follows and Odysseus's tale at the court of Alcinous, the king of the Phaeacians, acts as a disclaimer: one ought not to take the story too literally. Socrates often dismisses myths as lies, and he refers, at the very beginning of the *Republic*, to an ambivalent attitude toward, of all things, myths about the afterlife (in the passage [330 D] cited earlier). There he says that old Cephalus, who once ridiculed such tales, began, as he approached death, to ask himself whether there was something to them after all.

Er, the Pamphylian, had been wounded in battle and, taken for dead, placed on the pyre, whereupon he regained consciousness. In the meantime, his soul had traveled into the beyond, as every soul does once it has departed from the body. Er's soul was admitted in order that it might tell mortal men about the afterworld. The myth (as Socrates explicitly calls it at the end of the tale) serves the primary purpose of the *Republic*, which is to ascertain what justice is and how it can be realized on this earth. The creation of the model state has indeed fulfilled this purpose, and the myth purports to indicate how this earthly order fits into a greater one. After death the soul is judged, and punishments and rewards are meted out in accordance with the degree to which one has acted justly during one's life. Beyond the place of judgment, there is a forked road, leading either down to Tartarus, an eternal prison where the depraved are punished, or up to the sky, where the just are rewarded.

Even if the entire myth is a Platonic invention, its general structure and many of its details make it seem far more traditional than any known sophistic myth. The image of Ananke, a transparent personification ("Necessity"), sitting at the center of the afterworld and holding in her lap a thinly veiled model of the cosmos is admittedly innovative. Yet the myth abounds in traditional motifs: the three Moerae, who assign to each soul its lot before it reoccupies a body; the Sirens, to whose song, performed during the revolution of the cosmos, is ascribed the harmony of the spheres; Tartarus, as the afterworldly prison; and encounters with epic heroes—Orpheus, for example, or Agamemnon. The theme of the journey of the soul through the next world has analogues outside Greece, but it is also found in the thought of Parmenides (see Chapter 4). In the case of Plato, as in that of Parmenides, the theme can be traced back to Pythagorean traditions; the transmigration of the soul and the harmony of the spheres point in the same direction. The ultimate source of the theme was the ritual experience of the shamanistic journey of the soul and, along with it, the ritual schema of the rite of passage: these thematic and structural echoes contributed greatly to the success of the Platonic myth.

Plato had still other myths in store. Elsewhere in the *Republic* (415a) Socrates creates his own *mythos*, in which he explains the political role of myth in the ideal state. His purpose in inventing this myth is twofold: on the one hand, to induce the citizens of his state to respect one another as brothers and to love and defend the earth as their common mother; on the other, to compel the fathers to observe their sons carefully from birth in order that each may be assigned to his proper caste. Socrates wants to have it proclaimed that all inhabitants of the state were once created beneath the earth's surface; that to the future rulers the divine creator added gold, to the guardians silver, to the handworkers and farmers copper and iron; that the added metals are not necessarily passed down from father to son. Although the myth is, as Socrates says, fictional, having a clear social function, it makes use of old beliefs. That original inhabitants were children of the earth was a belief held by the Athenians, who themselves claimed to be autochthonous. The hierarchy of the elements can be traced back to Hesiod's myth of the ages and came originally from the Orient (very much to our surprise, Socrates says that the myth is "not at all new but borrowed from the Phoenicians," 414c).[13]

To be sure, Socrates' interlocutor has his reservations. It is hardly likely that the new inhabitants of the ideal state would believe the myth; after all, they would remember how they were born. Only the children of later generations, having been raised apart from their parents, could accept it. Implicit in Socrates' myth is a theory of the origin of myth. Just as Socrates invents a myth for the first generations of citizens in his state, so, in the early days of mankind, some imaginative mind created the myths for the moral guidance of the people; with the passage of generations, people began to believe the myths. Such a theory is well known: "At that time a clever and wise man invented fear of the gods for mortals, in order that there might be a way of frightening the wicked, even if they did, said, or thought something in secret" (DK 88 B 25 = *TrGF* vol. 1, 43 F 19). The statement may have been made by the author, sophist, and tyrant Critias of Athens: Critias was Plato's uncle.[14]

Although the influence of Platonism outlasted that of any other philosophical school, Plato's invention of myths to express that which he felt could not be expressed otherwise had no sequel. Aristotle introduced logic as the foundation of philosophical inquiry and with it the requirement that every philosophical statement be intelligible to others in accordance with certain laws. They left little room for myth as a mode of philosophical expression. Moreover, Aristotle, who had an evolutionistic view of the history of philosophy, regarded myth not as a complement to philosophy but as an earlier form of thought that prepared the ground for it, a relic of the philosophy of an earlier phase in human history (*Metaphysics* 8.1074a–b14).[15] After Plato the treatment of myth went in different directions. Those directions were euhemerism, mythography, and allegoresis.

Euhemerus

Mythography, in the narrow sense, refers to the treatment of myth by grammarians and philologists. In the broad sense, the term is also applied to the many Hellenistic works, "novels" in which myths were retold for the purpose of entertainment and in which details, even whole stories, were often invented. These "novelists" had no qualms about inventing ancient authors, whose works they claimed to have copied. Myth, to the mythographical mind, was poetic narrative: the older the poet, the more authoritative the myth. Euhemerus of Messene, whose name is associated with the historicizing interpretation of myths about the gods (euhemerism), went a step farther. His *Sacred Document (Hiera Anagraphē)*, written not long after 300 B.C. (*FGrH* 63), purports to contain an inscription tracing the history of the gods from the time of Uranus. According to the inscription, the gods were originally great rulers; Uranus was an astronomer who introduced the cult of the constellations; Zeus was an ouster of tyrants; in gratitude for their benefactions, later generations deified these rulers along with their families. Euhemerus's account of the history of the gods shows the influence of the ideal of the deified Hellenistic ruler; it also shows the influence of the theology of Prodicus, with his division of the development of religion into an early phase, in which man worshiped the constellations, and a later one, in which he deified human benefactors. The inscription is set within the framework of a travel narrative. Euhemerus claims to have found it while in the service of King Cassander of Macedon, in the temple of Zeus in Panchaea, an island located far away in the Indian Ocean and inhabited by extremely pious people—an insular utopia modeled after Plato's Atlantis, which was "modernized," that is, adapted to current conditions, much as was the utopia described by Thomas More, of which another voyager, Raphael Hythlodaeus, reports. Like More's *Utopia*, Euhemerus's book met with a strong response. As late as the third century, it was still being imitated—by Dionysius Scytobrachion, among others. A century later, it was translated into Latin by Ennius. A century after that, Diodorus of Sicily, who wrote a world history, took both Euhemerus and Scytobrachion at face value. That Christian apologists plunged into Euhemerus is hardly surprising.[16]

Mythographers

Mythography, in the narrow sense defined earlier, originated in the scholarly paraphrase of poetic subject matter. The first work of this kind bore the title *Subjects of Tragedy* (*Tragōidoumena*). Composed in the fourth century by Asclepiades of Tragilus (*FGrH* 12), it retold tragedies, embellishing its summaries with variants from other poetic works. Later, the library at Alexandria, with its vast holdings, afforded access to nonpoetic myths from recondite local chronicles. Grammarians and poets drew inspiration from these fresh sources. Callimachus, for example, made use of such myths in his *Aetia*, which retold local tales of an etiological character. Even if the poet was not also a scholar, as Callimachus was, he might collaborate with one. Chance has preserved for us a small collection of erotic myths taken from local stories. The author, Parthenius of Nicaea, an erudite poet, dedicated it to his friend Cornelius Gallus, the Roman politician, poet, and friend of Vergil, as raw material "for epics and elegies."

Of all the results of this intense activity, only one substantial work has come down to us, and even it has not been preserved in its entirety: the *Library* of a certain Apollodorus, who may have lived in the first century of the imperial period. In this work[17] the myths of the Greeks are told in more or less narrative chronological order, beginning with the creation of the gods and the universe. For the most part, it combines the works of the old poets, which by that time had acquired classic status. The author did not necessarily know them all from his own reading; often his knowledge came from earlier compilations.

This holds true, generally, for the mythographers: none of them collected myths through field work, conducting interviews like the Grimm brothers or modern anthropologists, although many myths were certainly still being circulated orally. Rather, mythographers were grammarians, literati, who collected and systematized the traditional tales of classical Greek literature.

The name of the author of the *Library*, Apollodorus, poses a quandary. Most editors of the work refer to its author as Pseudo-

Apollodorus. They question the attribution to the eminent grammarian Apollodorus of Athens, who was active in Alexandria around the middle of the second century B.C., pointing out that Apollodorus is a name that occurs frequently. Although the attribution is admittedly somewhat incautious, it would, should it prove to be correct, confirm the prestige of that Apollodorus who is not to be ranked among the mythographers in the broad sense, but whose work, *On the Gods (Peri Theōn)*, written when he was an old man, was of cardinal importance for those ancients who concerned themselves with myths and gods, right down to the Christian polemicists. The work has been lost, but citations by later authors give us some idea of what it was like. It was a philological investigation that aimed at explaining the names and epithets of the gods, in particular of Homer's gods. This its author did with a sound grasp of Greek religion and by invoking the entire mythical and poetic tradition—for this reason it became a nearly inexhaustible source for later generations.[18]

Allegorists

Allegoresis was alien to this sober and strictly scientific philology. Among the grammarians, only those at Pergamum cultivated it. Pergamum had a library that was second only to that of Alexandria. The founder of that library, Crates of Mallos (second century B.C.) was a Stoic; he took allegoresis from the Stoics, who had been practicing it since the time of the school's founder, Zeno of Citium (ca. 333–262 B.C.). The Stoics regarded the cosmos as a structure formed and guided by reason (*logos*). Accordingly, they thought, it must be amenable to reason. Taken literally, myths often seemed less than rational, and yet one could not simply dismiss them, because they had the authority of the time-honored poets. So the Stoics understood them allegorically. Thus, they rationalized the mythical tradition; at the same time, they could claim that the foundations of their philosophical doctrine had been laid by none other than Homer.

Stoic allegoresis was concerned primarily with the physical universe. Zeus was identified with *aithēr*, the fiery air located at the outer limits of the cosmos. This is what Homer meant, the Stoics held, when he said that the god lived on Mount Olympus, the highest point on earth. Hera was identified with *aer*, the lower air. This interpretation of the goddess resulted from the transposition of two letters in the Greek name, ΗΡΑ, to ΑΗΡ; it was known even to Empedocles and Plato, and it may have originated in a reading of an intriguing Homeric verse (*Iliad* 21.6). One could explain the totality of the Homeric corpus in this fashion. When Zeus threatens Hera in *Iliad* 15.18, reminding her how he once suspended her from a golden chain, with two anvils attached to her feet—"you hung in the upper air (*aithēr*) and in the clouds"—the poet, it was argued, is not depicting a divine act of torture. Rather, "in these verses the creation of the universe has been attributed to the deity, and the arrangement of these verses reflects that of the four unceasingly celebrated elements . . . : first the upper air, then the lower air, followed by water and, lastly, earth." The *aithēr* is named by Homer: the *aēr* is Hera, while the heavy elements water and earth are signified by the two anvils. The golden chain from which Hera is suspended signifies the zone where the two layers of air coalesce and where the fiery air warms up the cold into golden rays. So wrote the Stoic Heraclitus in his *Homeric Allegories* (40), a short book from the imperial period that was inspired by much that preceded it.[19]

Besides physical allegoresis, the Stoics also practiced moral allegoresis. In so doing they paid little attention to systematization, as another passage from Heraclitus's work illustrates. Hera, for Heraclitus, was not just the air in the physical sense; she was also "the cloud of unknowing" in the moral sense. "When Homer portrayed the wounding of Hera by Heracles (*Iliad* 5.392–94)," Heraclitus wrote, "he wished to show that Heracles, by using divine reason [*logos*], was the first to perceive the thick air that obscures our thought. For with his many admonitions he wounded the ignorance of every human being" (*Homeric Allegories* 34.2). While the moral interpretation of Hera presupposed the old physical one (the latter is in fact older than the former), the hero Heracles was understood, in an historicizing vein, as a great man—indeed, as the first Stoic philosopher (*Homeric Allegories* 33.1).

Still other ways of understanding myths allegorically were devised by the Neoplatonists. Neoplatonism, which arose in the third century A.D., revived the teachings of the Academy and developed the ontological, eschatological, and mystical sides of Platonism. The Neoplatonists carried the devaluation of the sensible world, which had been a feature of Plato's thought, to extremes. Above this world they constructed a multilayered ontological and theological system, at the apex of which the absolute One sat enthroned as the supreme deity. The soul alone had a share in this hierarchy of being and could move within it. The philosopher, in his mystical ascent, strove to reach the supreme deity, if only for a moment.

The Neoplatonists interpreted myth philosophically: myth was to be understood theologically (*theologikon*) or psychologically (*psychikon*), to use the language of a late synthesis written for a broad readership, the little book *Concerning the Gods* by Sallustius, who was active during the reign of the emperor Julian.[20] By way of illustration, Sallustius (4.1) offered an allegorical explanation of a tale that must have been a thorn in the side of every philosopher—and one that Plato condemned (*Republic* 378a): the tale according to which Cronus swallowed his children. Understood theologically, Cronus represented the supreme deity, whom Sallustius equated with the intellect (*nous*; the equation had been made earlier by the allegorist of the Derveni papyrus [col. 10]). Being perfect, the supreme god was necessarily self-contained (if he had not been so, he would have stood in need of something outside himself, and therefore he would not have been perfect). Thus, the myth "expresses enigmatically the essence of the god," as Sallustius wrote. Understood psychologically, the myth dealt with human thought: "the thoughts of our souls remain where they were created even when we let them migrate to others."

Thus, in late antiquity the interpreter had at his disposal a large arsenal of hermeneutic instruments with which he could save myth from being rejected for its apparent scandalousness. Indeed, the task of discovering the meaning hidden enigmatically beneath the scandalous exterior of myth was regarded as a challenge to the sage. For the Christians, the discovery of hidden meaning was not just a way of explaining difficult passages in the Holy Scripture; it was also a way of making it easier for believers to accept the heathen myths in unaltered form. For even in the Christian period the works of the great Greek and Roman authors soon became much-read classics and school textbooks. Moreover, every species of allegoresis continued to flourish, right down to the threshold of modernity (and beyond). The species varied with the times. Thus, physical allegoresis was in demand during the Renaissance of the twelfth century in the Latin West, which saw renewed interest in the natural sciences. By contrast, Florentine Neoplatonists, with their mystical outlook, stressed theological and psychological allegoresis.[21] There were some, it is true, who rejected allegoresis completely: "It is certain that those who composed the fables were not in a position to understand ethics and physics, let alone to discover the art of disguising such knowledge under borrowed images," wrote Bernard de Fontenelle (it is well to remember that Fontenelle assigned the creation of myths to an early phase of human history). But this argument bore little fruit. In the nineteenth century, Max Müller and the other nature mythologists in his circle were still practicing physical allegoresis, and Friedrich Creuzer was still elaborating the theological allegoresis of the Neoplatonists. Even in this century, the *Odyssey* has been read as an allegory of the soul's journey.

All this was foreseen by Fontenelle. "Can this," he wrote in the same connection, "hold back those who are hopelessly in love with antiquity? They imagine that beneath the fables are hidden the secrets of the natural and moral worlds." His remark may be apt for some modern allegorists, but it hardly suffices to explain what motivated ancient allegorists. The latter were not attempting to "save" Homer and the other time-honored tellers of myth simply because they loved them; instead, their intention was to maintain the cultural relevance of myth as a valid statement about the world and man's place in it, as a culturally relevant model whereby one could explain the whole of human experience. They sought to do this at a time when their world was undergoing changes so radical and intense that it became impossible for the collective and traditional manifestations of myth to be adapted to new requirements through continual re-telling. Ossified in grand and discrete poetic forms, myth had lost its flexibility. Instead of melting it down and pouring it into new molds, the allegorists flocked around its hardened form and read their own thinking into it.

ABBREVIATIONS AND SOURCES

Abbreviations

The following abbreviations are used in citations of collections of fragments:

ANET Pritchard, J. B., ed., *Ancient Near Eastern Texts Relating to the Old Testament*, 3rd ed. (Princeton, 1969).

DK Diels, H., ed., *Die Fragmente der Vorsokratiker*, 5th ed., rev. W. Kranz (Berlin, 1934–37; later editions are enlarged reprints).

EGF Davies, M., ed., *Epicorum Graecorum Fragmenta* (Göttingen, 1988).

FGrH Jacoby, F., ed., *Die Fragmente der griechischen Historiker* (Berlin, 1927–58).

MW Merkelbach, R., and M. L. West, eds., *Fragmenta Hesiodea* (Oxford, 1967).

Nauck Nauck, A., ed., *Tragicorum Graecorum Fragmenta*, 2nd ed. (Leipzig, 1889).

PCG Kassel, R., and C. Austin, eds., *Poetae Comici Graeci* (Berlin, 1983–).

PMG Page, D. L., ed., *Poetae Melici Graeci* (Oxford, 1962).

SLG Page, D. L., ed., *Supplementum Lyricis Graecis* (Oxford, 1974).

Snell Snell, B., ed., *Pindari Carmina cum Fragmentis*, 8th ed., rev. H. Maehler, 2 vols. (Leipzig, 1987–88).

TrGF   Snell, B., R. Kannicht, and S. Radt, eds., *Tragicorum Graec-orum Fragmenta* (Göttingen, 1977–).
Wehrli   Wehrli, F., ed., *Die Schule des Aristoteles*, 2nd ed., 10 vols. (Basel, 1967).

Literary Sources

Mythical narration plays a part in nearly every genre of Greek litera-ture. Limitations of space preclude listing every literary source for Greek myth: the reader is advised to consult a history of Greek litera-ture. The extant mythographical texts are:

Apollodorus, *The Library*, ed. J. G. Frazer (London, 1921).
Antoninus Liberalis, *Les métamorphoses*, ed. M. Papathomopoulos (Paris, 1968).
Hyginus, *Hygini Fabulae*, ed. H. J. Rose (Leiden, 1933).

Visual Sources

In addition to the written sources, we possess mythical representations in visual media dating from the geometric period onward. In the course of the archaic period these representations gain in scope and signifi-cance, culminating in the mythological scenes on Attic red-figure vases of the fifth century. Visual representations of myth are important for two reasons. On the one hand, many Greek myths are attested on vases earlier than in literary sources. Thus, of the twelve labors of Heracles, only the Cerberus adventure occurs for the first time in a literary text (Homer, *Iliad* 8.366–69). In some cases, the first known representation of a myth in geometric art predates its first known representation in late archaic poetry by several centuries. On the other hand, visual sources sometimes represent myths or mythical episodes that are not attested in any extant literary source. Such cases pose problems of interpreta-tion. For one thing, language is the privileged mode of mythical expres-sion; illustrations that have no corresponding texts are often difficult to interpret, even if the artist labeled his figures. In some cases, to be sure, such labels are helpful. For example, those vase paintings which show Heracles overawing an emaciated figure identified by an inscription as Geras (Old Age; fig. 10) present no difficulties: the scene is a variant of

Heracles' struggle with Thanatos (Death), which Euripides used in his *Alcestis*. But inscriptions cannot solve every mystery, as the tondo of a cup by Douris, now in Munich, shows. A lifeless figure, identified by an inscription as Jason, droops from the maw of a monstrous serpent, before which stands Athena. It was once supposed that the scene refers to a myth that ends with the swallowing of the Argonaut Jason by the serpent that guards the golden fleece. However, by examining its details more closely (Jason's eyes are open) and comparing it with both Greek and non-Greek analogues, scholars have arrived at another interpretation: Jason, with Athena's help, has climbed into the throat of the serpent in order to kill it from within (fig. 11).

A scene that does not correspond exactly to any of the extant written sources is not necessarily a new variant. The language of visual representations is governed by its own laws and conventions. These laws and conventions do not apply just to the geometric and early archaic periods, and even the iconography of these periods is difficult to interpret.[1] A painter may add "filler figures" in order to attain symmetry; he may combine persons or things separated in time and space in a single scene; he may be restricted by his medium—as when, for example, in a representation of the blinding of Polyphemus, convention requires that he depict the monster in profile, thus making it impossible for him to show that the monster has only one eye. Finally, not every representation need refer to myth; the world of men, it is well to remember, is not always differentiated iconographically from that of heroes. Not every boar hunt is the Calydonian one; not every parting warrior is Hector. In such cases, caution dictates that we regard as mythical only those scenes which are easily recognizable as such through attributes or inscriptions.

The student of mythical scenes in Greek art will find the following works useful:

Brommer, F., *Vasenlisten zur griechischen Heldensage,* 3rd ed. (Marburg, 1973).
———, *Denkmälerlisten zur griechischen Heldensage* (Marburg, 1971–76),
Carpenter, T. H., *Art and Myth in Ancient Greece: A Handbook* (London, 1991).
Enciclopedia dell'arte antica classica e orientale (Rome, 1958–66)
Gantz, T., *Early Greek Myth: A Guide to Literary and Artistic Sources* (Baltimore, 1993).
Lexicon Iconographicum Mythologiae Classicae (Zurich, 1981—).

Schefold, K., *Frühgriechische Sagenbilder* (Munich, 1964).
———, *Götter- und Heldensagen der Griechen in der spätarchaischen Kunst* (Munich, 1978).
———, *Die Göttersage in der klassischen und hellenistischen Kunst* (Munich, 1981).

NOTES

Introduction: A Provisional Definition

1. See esp. G. S. Kirk, *Myth: Its Meaning and Functions in Ancient and Other Cultures* (Berkeley, 1970); W. Burkert, *Structure and History in Greek Mythology and Ritual* (Berkeley, 1979).

2. The opposition between *mythos* and *logos* appears first in Pindar, *Olympian Odes* 1.28–29 (476 B.C.).

3. M. Detienne, *The Creation of Mythology*, trans. M. Cook (Chicago, 1986; orig. 1981) 36–37, offers an illustrative example from Africa.

4. Rhetorical theorists from Cicero (*De inventione* 1.27) to Isidore of Seville (*Etymologiae* 1.44.5), however, defined myth (*fabula*) as a tale that was neither true nor plausible.

5. See B. Gentili, *Poetry and Its Public in Ancient Greece: From Homer to the Fifth Century*, trans. A. T. Cole (Baltimore, 1988; orig. 1985).

6. R. Chase, *Quest for Myth* (Baton Rouge, 1949) 73.

7. V. Propp, *Morphology of the Folktale*, trans. L. Scott, rev. L. A. Wagner (Austin, Tex., 1968).

8. See D. Fehling, *Amor und Psyche: Die Schöpfung des Apuleius und ihre Einwirkung auf das Märchen* (Wiesbaden, 1977).

9. On the ways in which myths may be transformed into fairy tales or folktales, see W. G. Doty, *Mythography: The Study of Myths and Rituals* (Tuscaloosa, Ala., 1986) 228–32.

10. See also Theon, *Progymnasmata* 3, and Philostratus, *Imagines* 1.3 on Aesop and *mythoi*.

Chapter 1: The Rise of the Scientific Study of Myth

1. On Heyne's life, see F. Klingner, *Studien zur griechischen und römischen Literatur* (Zurich, 1964) 701–18; on his theories, see C. Hartlich and W. Sachs, *Der Ursprung des Mythosbegriffes in der modernen Bibelwissenschaft* (Tübingen, 1952); E.-A. Horstmann, "Der Mythosbegriff bei Christian Gottlob Heyne," *Archiv für Begriffsgeschichte* 16 (1972) 60–85; M. M. Sassi, "La freddezza dello storico: Christian Gottlob Heyne," *Annali della Scuola Normale Superiore di Pisa* 16 (1986) 105–26; F. Graf, "Die Entstehung des Mythosbegriffs bei Christian Gottlob Heyne," in *Mythen in mythenloser Gesellschaft: Das Paradeigma Roms,* ed. F. Graf (Stuttgart, 1993).

2. C. G. Heyne, "Quaestio de caussis fabularum seu mythorum veterum physicis" (1764), in *Opuscula Academica Collecta et Animadversionibus Locupletata,* vol. 1 (Göttingen, 1785) 184–206.

3. C. G. Heyne, "Sermonis mythici seu symbolici interpretatio ad caussas et rationes ductasque inde regulas revocata" (1807), in *Commentationes Societatis Regiae Scientiarum Gottingensis* 16 (1807) 285–323.

4. C. G. Heyne, "Vita antiquissimorum hominum, Graeciae maxime, ex ferorum et barbarorum populorum comparatione illustrata" (1779), in *Opuscula Academica Collecta et Animadversionibus Locupletata,* vol. 3 (Göttingen, 1788) 1–38.

5. Cf. V. Verra, *Mito, rivelazione e filosofia in J. G. Herder e nel suo tempo* (Milan, 1966); Hartlich and Sachs, *Ursprung des Mythosbegriffes.*

6. J. G. Herder, *Journal meiner Reise im Jahre 1769,* in *Sämtliche Werke,* ed. B. Suphan, vol. 4 (Berlin, 1878) 343–486.

7. Robert Lowth, *De sacra poesi Hebraeorum* (Göttingen, 1753).

8. See M. T. Hodgen, *Early Anthropology in the Sixteenth and Seventeenth Centuries* (Philadelphia, 1964); R. Cabrini and G. Viscuso, *Preistoria delle teorie etnologiche* (Bologna, 1978). On the eighteenth century, see F. E. Manuel, *The Eighteenth Century Confronts the Gods* (Cambridge, Mass., 1959).

9. Bernard de Fontenelle, *De l'origine des fables,* in *Oeuvres complètes,* ed. Alain Niderst, vol. 3 (Paris, 1989) 187–202.

10. A. Lang, *Myth, Ritual, and Religion* (London, 1906); L. Lévy-Bruhl, *Primitive Mentality,* trans. L. A. Clare (Boston, 1966; orig. 1923); see Chapter 2.

11. On Lafitau, see A. Pagden, *The Fall of Natural Man: The*

American Indian and the Origins of Comparative Ethnology (Cambridge, 1982).

12. On Euhemerus, see Chapter 8; on euhemerism in the eighteenth century, see Manuel, *Eighteenth Century Confronts the Gods.*

13. E. Rohde, *Psyche: Seelenkult und Unsterblichkeitsglaube der Griechen,* 2nd ed. (Tübingen, 1897) 1:1–102; see P. McGinty, *Interpretation and Dionysos: Method in the Study of a God* (The Hague, 1978) chap. 2.

14. G. B. Vico, *Opere,* ed. F. Nicolini (Bari, 1928); a good (abridged) translation is that of T. A. Bergin and M. H. Fisch, *The New Science of Giambattista Vico* (Ithaca, N.Y., 1961).

15. Cf. M. Boulby, *Karl Philipp Moritz: At the Fringes of Genius* (Toronto, 1979).

16. Cf. A. Henrichs, "Welckers Götterlehre," in *Friedrich Gottlieb Welcker: Werk und Wirkung,* ed. W. M. Calder III, A. Köhnken, W. Kullmann, and G. Pflug (Stuttgart, 1986) 179–229. On Wilamowitz, see A. Henrichs, "'Der Glaube der Hellenen': Religionsgeschichte als Glaubensbekenntnis und Kulturkritik," in *Wilamowitz nach 50 Jahren,* ed. W. M. Calder III, H. Flashar, and T. Lindken (Darmstadt, 1985) 263–305.

17. Cf. H. Gockel, *Mythos und Poesie: Zum Mythosbegriff in Aufklärung und Frühromantik* (Frankfurt, 1981); H. Anton, "Romantische Deutung griechischer Mythologie," in *Die deutsche Romantik,* ed. H. Steffen (Göttingen, 1967) 277–88.

18. See E. Howald, *Der Kampf um Creuzers Symbolik: Eine Auswahl von Dokumenten* (Tübingen, 1926); N. H. Münch, *La "symbolique" de Friedrich Creuzer* (Paris, 1973).

19. See Maurice Olender, *Les langues du paradis. Aryens et Sémites: Un couple providentiel* (Paris, 1989).

20. See A. Momigliano, "K. O. Müller's *Prolegomena zu einer wissenschaftlichen Mythologie* and the Meaning of 'Myth,'" in *Settimo contributo alla storia degli studi classici e del mondo antico* (Rome, 1984) 271–86. There is a reprint of the *Prolegomena* (Darmstadt, 1970) edited, with an introduction, by K. Kerényi.

21. Vol. 1, *Orchomenos und die Minyer* (Breslau, 1820; 2nd ed., 1844); vols. 2–3, *Die Dorier* (Breslau, 1824; 2nd ed., 1844).

22. K. O. Müller, *Geschichte der griechischen Literatur bis auf Alexander,* 2nd ed. (Breslau, 1857) chap. 2.

23. For an explanation of the same myth as an outgrowth of ritual, see H. D. Müller, *Mythologie der griechischen Stämme,* vol. 1 (Göttingen, 1857) 111–12.

24. Max Müller, *Deutsche Liebe* (Leipzig, 1857), often translated. There is a short bibliography in W. Burkert, *Entretiens sur l'antiquité classique* 29 (Geneva, 1980) 166 n. 2; see also H. Lloyd-Jones, *Blood for the Ghosts* (London, 1982) 155–64.

25. On Usener, see H. J. Mette, "Nekrolog einer Epoche: Hermann Usener und seine Schule," *Lustrum* 22 (1979–80) 5–106; *Aspetti di Hermann Usener, filologo della religione*, ed. G. Arrighetti, et al. with a preface by A. Momigliano (Pisa, 1982).

26. The literature on Frazer is even more copious than his own writings. See esp. John B. Vickery, *The Literary Impact of* The Golden Bough, (Princeton, 1973); R. Ackerman, *J. G. Frazer: His Life and Work* (Cambridge, 1987); R. Ackerman, *The Myth and Ritual School: J. G. Frazer and the Cambridge Ritualists* (New York, 1991); R. Fraser, *The Making of* The Golden Bough: *The Origins and Growth of an Argument* (London, 1990); William M. Calder III, ed., *The Cambridge Ritualists Reconsidered* (Atlanta, 1991). See also B. Malinowski, *Sir James Frazer: A Biographical Appreciation* (New York, 1942).

27. See H.-J. Braun, H. Holzhey, and E. W. Orth, eds., *Über Ernst Cassirers Philosophie der symbolischen Formen* (Frankfurt, 1988).

28. See F. Schachermeyr, *Poseidon und die Entstehung des griechischen Götterglaubens* (Bern, 1950) 189–203, and again in *Die griechische Rückerinnerung im Lichte neuer Forschungen* (Vienna, 1983) 291–92.

29. See H. Freier, *Die Rückkehr der Götter: Von der ästhetischen Überschreitung der Wissensgrenze zur Mythologie der Moderne* (Stuttgart, 1976); L. Processi Xella, "Ipotesi sulla mitologia nel tardo romanticismo tedesco: La Schellinghiana introduzione storico-critica alla filosofia della mythologia," *Studi Storico-Religiosi* 6 (1982) 253–85.

30. On W. F. Otto and K. Kerényi, see A. Magris, *Carlo Kerényi e la ricerca fenomenologica della religione* (Milan, 1975); on W. F. Otto, see also H. Cancik, "Die Götter Griechenlands 1929: W. F. Otto als Religionswissenschaftler und Theologe am Ende der Weimarer Republik," *Der altsprachliche Unterricht* 27 (1984) 151–76; H. Cancik, "Dionysos 1933: W. F. Otto, ein Religionswissenschaftler und Theologe zum Ende der Weimarer Republik," in *Die Restauration der Götter: Antike Religion und Neo-Paganismus*, ed. R. Faber and R. Schlesier (Würzburg, 1985) 105–23; K. Kerényi, "Walter Friedrich Otto: Erinnerung und Rechenschaft" (1959) in *Wege und Weggenossen*, Werke in Einzelausgaben, vol. 5, pt. 2 (Munich, 1988) 251–64.

31. See Hans-Georg Kippenberg and Brigitte Luchesi, eds., *Religionswissenschaft und Kulturkritik: Beiträge zur Konferenz "The His-*

tory of Religion and Critique of Culture in the Days of Gerardus van der Leuuw (1890–1950)" (Marburg, 1991).

Chapter II: New Approaches to the Interpretation of Myth in the Twentieth Century

1. On Oedipus, see J. N. Bremmer, "Oedipus and the Greek Oedipus Complex," in *Interpretations of Greek Mythology,.* ed. J. N. Bremmer (London, 1987) 41–59; L. Edmunds, *Oedipus: The Ancient Legend and Its Later Analogues* (Baltimore, 1985); W. Burkert, *Oedipus, Oracles, and Meaning: From Sophocles to Umberto Eco* (Toronto, 1991).

2. K. Abraham, *Dreams and Myths: A Study of Race Psychology,* trans. W. A. White (New York, 1913; orig. 1909). Another important pupil of Freud was Otto Rank; see his *The Myth of the Birth of the Hero: A Psychological Interpretation of Mythology,* trans. F. Robbins and S. E. Jelliffe (New York, 1952; orig. 1909).

3. G. Roheim, *Psychoanalysis and Anthropology* (New York, 1950).

4. See G. Baierle, "Le mythe dans la psychologie de C. G. Jung," *Cahiers Internationaux de Symbolisme* 35–36 (1978) 151–62.

5. C. G. Jung and M. L. von Franz, eds., *Man and His Symbols* (London, 1964).

6. C. G. Jung and K. Kerényi, *Essays on a Science of Mythology: The Myth of the Divine Child and the Mysteries of Eleusis,* trans. R. F. C. Hull (Princeton, 1963; orig. 1941). See further P. Radin, *The Trickster: A Study in American Indian Mythology,* with commentaries by C. G. Jung and K. Kerényi (New York, 1956).

7. G. Murray, cited in J. E. Harrison, *Themis,* 2nd ed. (London, 1927) 532 n.2.

8. See J. Stuart, *Jane Ellen Harrison: A Portrait from Letters* (London, 1959); S. J. Peacock, *Jane Ellen Harrison: The Mask and the Self* (New Haven, Conn., 1988); see the contributions of T. W. Africa, W. M. Calder III, S. J. Peacock, and especially R. Schlesier in *The Cambridge Ritualists Reconsidered,* W. M. Calder III, ed. (Atlanta, 1991).

9. See S. Lukes, *Émile Durkheim: His Life and Work* (London, 1973).

10. B. Malinowski, *Myth in Primitive Psychology* (New York, 1926). A good introduction is R. Métraux, "Bronislaw Malinowski," in *International Encyclopedia of Social Sciences,* ed. D. L. Sills, vol. 9 (1968) 541–49.

11. See P. Smith and D. Sperber, "Mythologiques de Georges Du-

mézil," *Annales: Economies, Sociétés, Civilisations* 26 (1971) 559–86; C. S. Littleton, *The New Comparative Mythology: An Anthropological Assessment of the Theories of Georges Dumézil* (Berkeley, 1982); W. W. Belier, *Decayed Gods: Origins and Development of Georges Dumézil's "ideologie tripartite"* (Leiden, 1991). Dumézil himself offers a short list of the most likely traces of trifunctionalism in Greece in *Hommages Lucien Febvre* (Paris, 1953) 2:25–32; see also J. Puhvel, "The Indo-European Strain in Greek Myth," in *Panhellenica: Essays in Ancient History and Historiography in Honor of Truesdell S. Brown*, ed. S. M. Burstein and L. A. Okin (Lawrence, Kans., 1980) 25–30.

12. C. Lévi-Strauss, *Structural Anthropology*, vol. 1, trans. C. Jacobson and B. G. Schoepf (New York, 1963; orig. 1958) chap. 11.

13. Ibid., vol. 2, trans. M. Layton (New York, 1976; orig. 1973) chap. 9.

14. C. Lévi-Strauss, *The Elementary Structures of Kinship*, trans. J. H. Bell, J. R. von Sturmer, and R. Needham, rev. R. Needham (Boston, 1969; orig. 1949); and *The Savage Mind* (Chicago, 1966; orig. 1962).

15. Among the most important critiques of Lévi-Strauss's work are: B. Nathorst, *Formal or Structural Studies of Tales* (Stockholm, 1968); R. Makarius and L. Makarius, *Structuralisme ou éthnologie? Pour une critique radicale de l'anthropologie de Lévi-Strauss* (Paris, 1973); L. L. Thomas, J. Z. Kronenfeld, and D. B. Kronenfeld, "Asdiwal Crumbles: A Critique of Lévi-Straussian Myth Analysis," *American Ethnologist* 3 (1976) 147–73; M. Detienne, *The Creation of Mythology*, trans. M. Cook (Chicago, 1986; orig. 1981); G. Ferraro, *Il linguaggio del mito* (Milan, 1979); D. Mandelbaum, "Myth and Mythmakers: Some Anthropological Appraisals of the Mythological Studies of Lévi-Strauss," *Ethnology* 26 (1987) 31–36.

16. G. S. Kirk, *Myth: Its Meaning and Functions in Ancient and Other Cultures* (Cambridge, 1970) 162–71.

17. R. L. Gordon, ed., *Myth, Religion, and Society: Structuralist Essays by M. Detienne, L. Gernet, J.-P. Vernant and P. Vidal-Naquet* (Cambridge, 1981).

18. V. Propp, *Morphology of the Folktale*, 2nd ed., trans. L. Scott, rev. L. A. Wagner, introd. A. Dundes (Austin, Tex., 1968; orig. 1928); see C. Lévi-Strauss, "La structure et la forme," *International Journal of Slavic Linguistics and Poetics* 3 (1960) 122–49.

19. W. Burkert, *Structure and History in Greek Mythology and Ritual* (Berkeley, 1979) 5–14.

20. The most important (and rewarding) critiques of the myth-and-ritual theory are J. Fontenrose, *The Ritual Theory of Myth* (Berke-

ley, 1966), and H. S. Versnel, "What's Sauce for the Goose Is Sauce for the Gander: Myth and Ritual, Old and New," in *Approaches to Greek Myth*, ed. L. Edmunds (Baltimore, 1990) 23–30.

21. H. Jeanmaire, *Couroi et courètes: Essai sur l'éducation spartiate et sur les rites d'adolescence dans l'antiquité hellénique* (Lille, 1939) 228–383.

22. On the method of Brelich and his school in Rome, see his "La metodologia della scuola di Roma," in *Il mito greco*, ed. B. Gentili and G. Paioni (Rome, 1977) 3–29; on Brelich himself, see especially his *Storia delle religioni — perché?* (Naples, 1979).

23. For English translations, see *Mythologies*, trans. A. Lavers (New York, 1974), and *The Eiffel Tower and Other Mythologies*, trans. R. Howard (New York, 1979). See also W. G. Doty, *Mythography: The Study of Myths and Rituals* (Tuscaloosa, Ala., 1986) 216–23.

24. Significantly, a volume of *Arethusa* in honor of J.-P. Vernant (containing a useful bibliography) was published in 1972, to which Charles Segal wrote a laudatory afterword.

25. See, among other writings, C. Calame, *Le récit en Grèce ancienne: Énonciations et représentations de poètes* (Paris, 1986) and *Illusions de la mythologie* (Limoges, 1990). His earlier analyses were much more formalistic; see, for example, "Mythe grec et structures narratives: Le mythe des Cyclopes dans l'*Odyssée*," in *Il mito greco*, ed. B. Gentili and G. Paioni (Rome, 1977) 369–87.

26. C. Segal, "Greek Myth as a Semiotic and Structural System and the Problem of Tragedy," *Arethusa* 16 (1983) 173–98, reprinted in *Interpreting Greek Tragedy: Myth, Poetry, Text* (Ithaca, N.Y., 1986) 48–74.

27. C. Calame, "'Mythe' et 'rite' en Grèce: des catégories indigènes?" *Kernos* 4 (1991) 179–204; F. Graf, "Il mito tra menzogna e Ur-wahrheit," in *Atti del Covegno sul Mito del'IRSSAE dell'Umbria* (Perugia, 1993) 43–56 and "Der Mythosbegriff bei C. G. Heyne," in *Mythos in mythenloser Gesellschaft: Das Paradeigma Roms*, ed. F. Graf (Stuttgart, 1993).

Chapter III: Myth and Epic Poetry

1. Aristotle remarked that the *Iliad* could be made into as many as three tragedies (*Poetics* 23, 1459b2).

2. The major source for the Trojan part is the *Chrestomathy* of Proclus. See W. Kullmann, *Die Quellen der Ilias* (Wiesbaden, 1960).

3. See W. Kullmann, "Vergangenheit und Zukunft in der Ilias," *Poetica* 2 (1969) 15–37.

4. See G. M. Calhoun, "Homer's Gods: Myth and Märchen," *American Journal of Philology* 60 (1939) 1–28.

5. See C. M. Bowra, *Heroic Poetry* (London, 1952) chap. 3.

6. See M. M. Willcock, "Mythological Paradeigma in the *Iliad*," *Classical Quarterly* 14 (1964) 141–54.

7. See J. T. Kakridis, *Homeric Researches* (Lund, 1949) 11–64; K. E. Petzold, "Die Meleagros-Geschichte der Ilias," *Historia* 25 (1976) 146–69; J. R. March, *The Creative Poet: Studies in the Treatment of Myths in Greek Poetry* (London, 1987) 27–46; J. N. Bremmer, "La plasticité du mythe: Méléagre dans la poésie homérique," in *Métamorphoses du mythe en Grèce antique*, ed. C. Calame (Geneva, 1988) 37–56.

8. H. Lloyd-Jones and P. J. Parsons, eds., *Supplementum Hellenisticum* (Berlin, 1983) no. 903 A; see H. Lloyd-Jones "The *Meropis* (SH 903 A)" (1984), reprinted in *Greek Epic, Lyric and Tragedy: The Academic Papers of Sir Hugh Lloyd-Jones* (Oxford, 1990) 21–29.

9. See E. A. Havelock, *Preface to Plato* (Cambridge, Mass., 1963) 44–45.

10. See F. Hampl, "Die Ilias ist kein Geschichtsbuch," in *Geschichte als kritische Wissenschaft*, vol. 2 (Darmstadt, 1975) 51–99; E. Meyer, "Gab es ein Troja?" *Grazer Beiträge* 4 (1975) 155–69.

11. U. von Wilamowitz-Moellendorff, "Über die ionische Wanderung," *Sitzungsberichte der Deutschen Akademie der Wissenschaften zu Berlin: Klasse für Sprachen, Literatur und Kunst* (1906) 60, reprinted in his *Kleine Schriften*, vol. 5, pt. 1 (Berlin, 1937) 152–53. Later, he changed his mind. "Heroic saga," he wrote, "is primarily the memory of historical deeds and historical persons. The kernel of the *Mahabharata* is the battle between Kuru and Pandu; the memory of Ermanarich, Theoderich, Attila, and the Burgundian princes was perpetuated in the heroic epic poetry of the Germans. Similarly, the Ionians in Asia celebrated, in their poetry, the memory of the Peloponnesians' campaign against Thebes and the battle of the Curetes of Pleuron against Calydon; to this list the Trojan War has been added" (the last clause indicates his change of position): "Die griechische Heldensage," *Sitzungsberichte der Deutschen Akademie der Wissenschaften zu Berlin: Klasse für Sprachen, Literatur und Kunst* (1925) 58, reprinted in *Kleine Schriften*, vol. 5, pt. 2 (Berlin, 1937) 79.

12. M. I. Finley, J. L. Caskey, G. S. Kirk, and D. L. Page, "The Trojan War," *Journal of Hellenic Studies* 84 (1964) 1–20. But the discussion continues; see M. J. Mellink, ed., *Troy and the Trojan War: A Symposium held at Bryn Mawr College, October, 1984* (Bryn Mawr, Pa.,

1986), and K. A. Raaflaub, "Homer und die Geschichte des 8. Jh.s v. Chr.," in *Zweihundert Jahre Homer-Forschung: Rückblick und Ausblick*, ed. J. Latacz (Stuttgart, 1991) 205–56, esp. 207–15.

13. See J. N. Bremmer, "Heroes, Rituals, and the Trojan War," *Studi Storico-Religiosi* 2 (1978) 5–38.

14. On Helen, see M. L. West, *Immortal Helen* (London, 1975); L. L. Clader, *Helen: The Evolution from Divine to Heroic in Greek Epic Tradition* (Leiden, 1976). On Odysseus, see A. Heubeck, in A. Heubeck, S. West, and J. B. Hainsworth, *A Commentary on Homer's* Odyssey, vol. 1 (Oxford, 1988) 19–20. On Achilles, see H. Hommel, *Der Gott Achilleus* (Heidelberg, 1980); K. C. King, *Achilles: Paradigms of the War Hero from Homer to the Middle Ages* (Berkeley, 1987).

15. See Bremmer, "Heroes, Rituals."

16. At *Iliad* 11.746–48 Nestor says that he "captured fifty chariots." I assume that in doing so Nestor acquired a chariot for himself, which made up for the horses for which his father had not yet thought him fit (*Iliad* 11.718); the Pylian acclamation of "Zeus among gods and Nestor among men" (*Iliad* 11.761) shows that Nestor has attained a new status as an adult warrior. The combination of capturing a chariot in battle and being acclaimed on one's return is echoed in a Cretan initiatory practice reported by Strabo (10.4.21).

17. See F. Bader, "Rhapsodies homériques et irlandaises," in *Recherches sur les religions de l'antiquité classique*, ed. R. Bloch (Paris, 1980) 9–83.

18. See V. J. Abaev, "Le cheval de Troie: Parallèles caucasiennes," *Annales: Economies, Sociétés, Civilisations* 18 (1963) 1041–70.

19. See G. Nagy, *Comparative Studies in Greek and Indian Metre* (Cambridge, 1974) 231–55.

20. See M. Durante, *Sulla preistoria della tradizione poetica greca*, 2 vols. (Rome, 1971–76).

21. See the discussion between G. S. Kirk, *Homer and the Oral Tradition* (Cambridge, 1976) 19–40, and A. Hoekstra, *Epic Verse before Homer* (Amsterdam, 1981).

22. See M. Gérard-Rousseau, *Les mentions religeuses dans les tablettes mycéniennes* (Rome, 1968); G. Neumann, "i-pi-me-de-ja, eine mykenische Gottheit," *Münchner Studien zur Sprachwissenschaft* 46 (1985) 165–71.

23. See V. Karageorghis, "Myth and Epic in Mycenaean Vase Painting," *American Journal of Archaeology* 62 (1958) 383–87; E. T. Vermeule, "Mythology in Mycenaean Art," *Classical Journal* 54 (1958) 97–108.

24. See J. N. Coldstream, *Geometric Greece* (London, 1977); O.

Murray, *Early Greece* (Brighton, Sussex, 1980); R. Hägg, ed., *The Greek Renaissance of the Eighth Century B.C.* (Stockholm, 1983). For important qualifications, see P. Blome, "Die dunklen Jahrhunderte—aufgehellt," in Latacz, *Zweihundert Jahre Homer-Forschung,* 45–60 and Raaflaub, "Homer und die Geschichte," 215–22.

Chapter IV: The Origin of the World and the Gods

1. See C. O. Pavese, *Tradizioni e generi poetici della Grecia arcaica* (Rome, 1972); P. Mureddu, *Formula e tradizione nella poesia di Esiodo* (Rome, 1983); H. S. Versnel, "Greek Myth and Ritual: The Case of Kronos," in *Interpretations of Greek Mythology,* ed. J. N. Bremmer (London, 1987) 121–52.

2. See W. Staudacher, *Die Trennung von Himmel und Erde* (Tübingen, 1942).

3. See B. Gatz, *Weltalter, goldene Zeit und sinnverwandte Vorstellungen* (Hildesheim, 1967).

4. See F. Graf, *Nordionische Kulte* (Rome, 1985) 360.

5. On the myth of Prometheus, see J.-P. Vernant, "The Myth of Prometheus in Hesiod," in *Myth and Society in Ancient Greece,* trans. J. Lloyd (Sussex, 1980; orig. 1974) 183–201; J. Rudhart, "Le mythe hésiodique des races et celui de Prométhée," in *Du mythe, de la religion grecque et de la compréhension d'autrui* (Geneva, 1981) 245–81.

6. Because it is easily accessible, I usually refer to *ANET*. New (and often better) translations may be found in H. A. Hoffner, *Hittite Myths,* ed. G. M. Beckman (Atlanta, 1990) and S. Dalley, *Myths from Mesopotamia: Creation, the Flood, Gilgamesh, and Others* (Oxford, 1989).

7. See W. Burkert, "Von Ullikummi zum Kaukasus: Die Felsgeburt des Unholds," *Würzburger Jahrbücher für die Altertumswissenschaft* 5 (1979) 253–61.

8. See J. Siegelová, *Appu-Märchen und Hedammu-Mythus* (Wiesbaden, 1971).

9. Eudemus fr. 150 Wehrli; see W. Burkert, *The Orientalizing Revolution: Near Eastern Influence on Greek Culture in the Early Archaic Age,* trans. W. Burkert and M. E. Pinder (Cambridge, Mass., 1992) 92–93.

10. For the Babylonian flood myth, see W. G. Lambert and A. R. Millard, *Atrahasis: The Babylonian Story of the Flood* (Oxford, 1969); Dalley, *Myths from Mesopotamia,* 1–38.

11. See J. Trumpf, "Stadtgründung und Drachenkampf," *Hermes*

86 (1958) 129–57; J. Fontenrose, *Python: A Study of Delphic Myth and Its Origins* (Berkeley, 1959).

12. See W. G. Lambert and P. Walcot, "A New Babylonian Theogony and Hesiod," *Kadmos* 4 (1965) 64–72, and esp. Dalley, *Myths from Mesopotamia*, 278–84 (I wish to thank Jerrold Cooper for arousing my interest in this text, too often overshadowed by *Enuma Elish*).

13. See H. S. Versnel, "Greek Myth and Ritual: The Case of Kronos," in *Interpretations of Greek Mythology*, ed. J. N. Bremmer (London, 1987) 121–52; F. Graf, "Römische Aitia und ihre Mythen: Das Beispiel von Saturnalia und Parilia," *Museum Helveticum* 49 (1992) 13–25.

14. For a synthesis, see W. Helck, *Die Beziehungen Ägyptens und Vorderasiens zur Ägäis bis ins 7. Jahrhundert v. Chr.* (Darmstadt, 1979); for the literature, see the monograph of Burkert, *Orientalizing Revolution*.

15. I am aware that the existence and extent of Mesopotamian oral traditions has been a matter of debate among specialists: see, for example, A. L. Oppenheim, *Ancient Mesopotamia* (Chicago, 1964) 258–59 versus Dalley, *Myths from Mesopotamia*, whose acute observations confirm my position. For the current state of the controversy, see M. E. Vogelzang and H. L. J. Vantisphout, *Mesopotamian Epic Literature: Oral or Aural?* (Lewiston, N. Y., 1992).

16. See C. Wilcke, "Die Anfänge der akkadischen Epen," *Zeitschrift für Assyriologie* 67 (1977) 153–216, esp. 153–55, 214–16.

17. See J. Boardman, *The Greeks Overseas*, 3rd ed. (London, 1980) chap. 3.

18. Ibid., p. 68.

19 The most important work on the subject is M. L. West, *The Orphic Poems* (Oxford, 1983).

20. On Thales and the Near East, see U. Hölscher, "Anaximander und die Anfänge der Philosophie," *Hermes* 81 (1953) 385–91; M. L. West, *Early Greek Philosophy and the Orient* (Oxford, 1971).

21. See esp. W. Jaeger, *The Theology of the Early Greek Philosophers* (Oxford, 1947).

22. R. Meiggs and D. Lewis, eds., *A Selection of Greek Historical Inscriptions to the End of the Fifth Century B.C.* (Oxford, 1969) no. 8.

23. See W. Burkert, "Das Proömium des Parmenides und die Katabasis des Pythagoras," *Phronesis* 14 (1969) 1–30; A. P. Mourelatos, *The Route of Parmenides* (New Haven, Conn., 1970); B. Feyerabend, "Zur Wegmetaphorik beim Goldblättchen aus Hipponion und dem Proömium des Parmenides," *Rheinisches Museum* 127 (1984) 1–22.

24. The fragments (with translation and commentary) are collected in M. R. Wright, *Empedocles: The Extant Fragments* (New Haven, Conn., 1981); see also D. Furley, *The Greek Cosmologists*, vol. 1 (Cambridge, 1987) 79–104.

Chapter V: Myth, Sanctuary, and Festival

1. M. Eliade, *Myth and Reality*, trans. W. R. Trask (New York, 1963; orig. 1963) 158: "The 'classic' Greek myths already represent the triumph of the literary *work* over religious *belief*. Not a single Greek myth has come down to us in its cultic context."

2. See F. Cassola, ed., *Inni omerici* (Milan, 1975) 79–151 and 485–516; W. Burkert, "Kynaithos, Polycrates, and the Homeric *Hymn to Apollo*," in *Arktouros: Hellenic Studies Presented to Bernard M. W. Knox*, ed. G. W. Bowersock, W. Burkert, and M. C. J. Putnam (Berlin, 1979); A. Aloni, *L'aede e i tiranni: Ricerche sull'Inno omerico a Apollo* (Rome, 1989).

3. See M. L. West, ed., *Hesiod: Theogony* (Oxford, 1966) ad loc.

4. The texts are collected in H. Gallet de Santerre, *Délos primitive et archaïque* (Paris, 1958) 188–92, and P. Bruneau, *Recherches sur les cultes de Délos à l'époque hellénistique et à l'époque impériale* (Paris, 1970) 19–35. On Theseus and Delos, see also C. Calame, *Thésée et l'imaginaire athénien: Légende et culte en Grèce antique* (Lausanne, 1990), esp. 116–21.

5. The texts are collected in Bruneau, *Cultes de Délos*, 38–48. See W. Sale, "The Hyperborean Maidens on Delos," *Harvard Theological Review* 54 (1961) 75–89.

6. On the hair offerings, see F. Graf, *Nordionische Kulte* (Rome, 1985) 219–20. On the collection ritual, see N. Robertson, "Greek Ritual Begging in Aid of Women's Fertility and Childbirth," *Transactions of the American Philological Association* 113 (1983) 143–69 (Robertson collects the material but does not offer a convincing analysis); for an interesting analytical approach see D. Baudy, "Heischegang und Segenszweig. Antike und neuzeitliche Riten des sozialen Ausgleichs: Eine Studie über die Sakralisierung von Symbolen," *Saeculum* 37 (1986) 212–27.

7. The texts are collected in Bruneau, *Cultes de Délos*, 413–30.

8. On the sacrifice of dogs, see Graf, *Nordionische Kulte*, 422 n.112.

9. Ovid shares the story of the transformation of the maidens into doves with Lycophron 580: here the background of Hellenistic poetry is still discernible.

10. See C. Sourvinou-Inwood, "The Myth of the First Temples at Delphi" (1979), reprinted in *"Reading" Greek Culture: Texts and Images, Rituals and Myths* (Oxford, 1991) 192–216.

11. For thatched huts at the Athenian Thesmophoria, see Aristophanes, *Women at the Thesmophoria* 624 and 658; for the Thesmophoria as an imitation of archaic life, see Diodorus Siculus 5.4.7; M. P. Nilsson, *Griechische Feste von religiöser Bedeutung* (Leipzig, 1906) 319.

12. For the details, see Graf, *Nordionische Kulte*, 81–96.

13. See F. Graf, "Apollon Delphinios," *Museum Helveticum* 36 (1979) 2–22.

14. See A. Henrichs, "Human Sacrifice in Greek Religion: Three Case Studies," in *Le sacrifice dans l'antiquité,* Entretiens sur l'antiquité classique 27 (Geneva, 1981) 195–235; D. D. Hughes, *Human Sacrifice in Ancient Greece* (London, 1991). On the Spartan ritual, see Graf, *Nordionische Kulte,* 86–89.

15. See F. Cassola, ed., *Inni omerici* (Milan, 1975) 23–77 and 466–85.

16. See F. Graf, "Das Götterbild aus dem Taurerland," *Antike Welt* 10, pt. 4 (1979) 33–41.

17. See A. Brelich, *Paides e parthenoi* (Rome, 1969); on the rites of the maidens, see also C. Calame, *Les choeurs des jeunes filles en Grèce archaïque* (Rome, 1977).

18. The anonymous author of *On the Sublime* (13.3) calls him "the most Homeric" of the lyric poets.

19. See W. Burkert, *Greek Religion,* trans. J. Raffan (Cambridge, Mass., 1985; orig. 1977) 92–95.

Chapter VI: Myth as History

1. See P. Vidal-Naquet, "Divine Time and Human Time" (1960), reprinted in *The Black Hunter: Forms of Thought and Forms of Society in the Greek World,* trans. A. Szegedy-Maszak (Baltimore, 1986) 39–60.

2. Eratosthenes appears to have been an exception. See H. Strasburger, "Homer und die Geschichtsschreibung," in *Studien zur alten Geschichte* (Hildesheim, 1982) 1057–97.

3. F. Schachermeyr, *Die griechische Rückerinnerung im Lichte neuer Forschungen* (Vienna, 1983) 14.

4. See M. L. West, *The Hesiodic Catalogue of Women* (Oxford, 1985).

5. See P. Smith, "Aineidai as Patrons of *Iliad* XX and of the Hom-

eric *Hymn to Aphrodite*," *Harvard Studies in Classical Philology* 85 (1981) 17–59.

6. Schachermeyr, *Griechische Rückerinnerung*, 72 with fig. 3 (Heropythus of Chios).

7. See P. Cartledge, *Sparta and Lakonia* (London, 1979) 341–46; M. Clauss, *Sparta: Eine Einführung in seine Geschichte und Zivilisation* (Munich, 1983) 117–26.

8. See A. M. Snodgrass, *The Dark Age of Greece* (Edinburgh, 1971); F. Cassola, *La Ionia nel mondo miceneo* (Naples, 1957); M. B. Sakellariou, *La migration grecque en Ionie* (Athens, 1958). On the myths, see F. Prinz, *Gründungsmythen und Sagenchronologie* (Munich, 1979) 314–69.

9. For opposing views, see Cartledge, *Sparta and Lakonia*, 75–101, and J. T. Hooker, *The Ancient Spartans* (London, 1980) 25–46.

10. See esp. Prinz, *Gründungsmythen*, 206–13. The main texts are Diodorus Siculus 4.57–58 and Apollodorus, *Library* 2.167–80.

11. See W. Burkert, "Das Ende des Kroisos," in *Catalepton: Festschrift Bernhard Wyss*, ed. C. Schäublin, (Basel, 1985) 4–15.

12. See C. Ampolo and M. Manfredini, eds., *Plutarcho: Le vite di Teseo e di Romolo* (Milan, 1988); C. Calame, *Thésée et l'imaginaire athénien: Légende et culte en Grèce antique* (Lausanne, 1990); for the iconography see F. Brommer, *Theseus: Die Taten des griechischen Helden in der antiken Kunst und Literatur* (Darmstadt, 1982).

13. See H. A. Shapiro, *Art and Cult under the Tyrants in Athens* (Mainz, 1989) 143–49.

14. See L. Deubner, *Attische Feste* (Berlin, 1932) 36–38; H. W. Parke, *Festivals of the Athenians* (London, 1977) 31–32; E. Simon, *Festivals of Attica: An Archaeological Commentary* (Madison, Wis., 1983) 50.

15. H. Herter, "Theseus der Ionier," *Rheinisches Museum* 85 (1936) 182.

16. G. S. Kirk, *Myth: Its Meaning and Functions in Ancient and Other Cultures* (Berkeley, 1970); B. Vickers, *Towards Greek Tragedy* (London, 1973).

Chapter VII: Myth, Choral Song, and Tragedy

1. On Dionysus, W. F. Otto, *Dionysus: Myth and Cult*, trans. R. B. Palmer (Bloomington, Ind., 1965; orig. 1933), is still one of the best works. On the marginality of the festival, *communitas*, and the theater, see V. Turner, *The Ritual Process: Structure and Anti-Structure*, 2nd

ed. (Chicago, 1970) 81–154, and *From Ritual to Theater: The Human Seriousness of Play* (New York, 1982).

2. On the theory, see H. Patzer, *Die Anfänge der griechischen Tragödie* (Wiesbaden, 1962), and A. Lesky, *Die tragische Dichtung der Hellenen*, 3rd ed. (Göttingen, 1972). On the non-Aristotelian tradition and the ritualist interpretation, see W. Burkert, "Greek Tragedy and Sacrificial Ritual," *Greek, Roman and Byzantine Studies* 7 (1966) 87–121.

3. See esp., on the male participants, G. M. Hedreen, *Silens in Attic Black-figure Vase-painting: Myth and Performance* (Ann Arbor, Mich., 1992); on the female participants, J. N. Bremmer, "Greek Maenadism Reconsidered," *Zeitschrift für Papyrologie und Epigraphik* 55 (1984) 267–86.

4. See K. von Fritz, "Die Orestesage bei den drei großen griechischen Tragikern," in *Antike und moderne Tragödie* (Berlin, 1962) 113–59.

5. See A. Köhnken, *Die Funktion des Mythos bei Pindar* (Berlin, 1971); P. Angeli Bernardini, *Mito e attualità nelle odi di Pindaro* (Rome, 1983); E. Krummen, *Pyrsos Hymnon: Festliche Gegenwart und mythisch-rituelle Tradition bei Pindar* (Berlin, 1990) 155–211.

6. See C. Calame, ed., *Alcman: Fragmenta* (Rome, 1983) ad locc. (Fr. 1 *PMG* = fr. 3 Calame).

7. On Stesichorus, see M. L. Bowra, *Greek Lyric Poetry*, 2nd ed. (Oxford, 1967) 111–12. On Pindar, see A. Köhnken, "Pindar as Innovator: Poseidon Hippios and the Relevance of the Pelops Story in *Olympian 1*," *Classical Quarterly* 24 (1974) 199–206; N. J. Richardson, "Pindar and Later Literary Criticism in Antiquity," *Papers of the Leeds Latin Seminar* 5 (1985) 383–401; Krummen, *Pyrsos Hymnon*, 205–11. On the ritualistic features of the myth, see W. Burkert, *Homo Necans* (Berlin, 1972) 114–16.

8. See H. R. Immerwahr, "Book Rolls on Attic Vases," in *Classical, Mediaeval and Renaissance Studies in Honor of Berthold Louis Ullman*, ed. C. Henderson (Rome, 1964) 1:17–48.

9. See E. A. Havelock, *The Literature Revolution in Greece and Its Cultural Consequences* (Princeton, 1982) 27–28.

10. On the role of grandmothers as narrators in traditional rural societies, see P. Connerton, *How Societies Remember* (Cambridge, 1989) 39.

11. See A. D. Trendall and T. B. L. Webster, *Illustrations of Greek Drama* (London, 1971).

12. See B. Vickers, *Towards Greek Tragedy* (London, 1973) 210–67; B. Knox, "Myth in Attic Tragedy," in *Word and Action* (Baltimore, 1979) 3–24.

13. See J. R. March, *The Creative Poet: Studies in the Treatment of Myths in Greek Poetry* (London, 1987) 79–118.

14. See O. Taplin, *Greek Tragedy in Action* (London, 1978), and K. Reinhardt, *Aeschylus als Regisseur und Theologe* (Bern, 1949).

15. On the etiology, see E. R. Dodds, "Morals and Politics in the *Oresteia*," in *The Ancient Concept of Progress* (Oxford, 1973) 45–63; J. Fontenrose, "Gods and Men in the *Oresteia*," *Transactions of the American Philological Association* 102 (1971) 71–109; A. L. Brown, "The Erinyes in the *Oresteia*: Real Life, the Supernatural, and the Stage," *Journal of Hellenic Studies* 103 (1983) 13–34.

16. On the *daimōn*, see R. P. Winnington-Ingram, "Tragedy and Greek Archaic Thought," in *Classical Drama and Its Influence: Studies Presented to H. D. F. Kitto*, ed. M. J. Anderson, (New York, 1965) 32–35.

17. Much has been written on Euripides' use of myth; see esp. J. Kamerbeek, "Mythe et réalité dans l'oeuvre d'Euripide," *Entretiens sur l'antiquité classique* 6 (Geneva, 1960) 3–25; W. Steidle, *Studien zum antiken Drama* (Munich, 1968); R. Eisner, "Euripides' Use of Myth," *Arethusa* 12 (1979) 153–74; R. Schlesier, " 'Heracles' et la critique des dieux chez Euripide," *Annuario della Scuola Normale Superiore di Pisa* 15 (1985) 7–40; M. Lefkowitz, "Impiety and Atheism in Euripides' Tragedies," *Classical Quarterly* 39 (1989) 70–83.

18. U. von Wilamowitz-Moellendorff, *Euripides: Herakles*, 2nd ed. (Darmstadt, 1959) 2:130.

19. See Steidle, *Studien zum antiken Drama*, pp. 96–117; W. Burkert, "Die Absurdität der Gewalt und das Ende der Tragödie: Euripides' Orestes," *Antike und Abendland* 20 (1974) 97–109.

20. See C. P. Segal, *Dionysiac Poetics and Euripides' Bacchae* (Princeton, 1982); on Euripides' innovations, see J. R. March, "Euripides' *Bacchae*: A Reconsideration in the Light of Vase Painting," *Bulletin of the Institute of Classical Studies* 36 (1988) 33–65.

CHAPTER VIII: Philosophers, Allegorists, and Mythologists

1. For a general introduction, see G. O. Hutchinson, *Hellenistic Poetry* (Oxford, 1988); on single points see G. W. Müller, *Erysichthon: Der Mythos als narrative Metapher im Demeterhymnos des Kallimachos* (Mainz, 1987); R. Hunter, " 'Short on Heroics': Jason in the *Argonautica*," *Classical Quarterly* 38 (1988) 436–53; C. Segal, *Poetry and Myth in Ancient Pastoral: Essays on Theocritus and Virgil* (Princeton, 1981).

2. The hymns are collected in I. U. Powell, ed., *Collectanea Alex-*

andrina (Oxford, 1925) 132–40, and W. Peek, "Inschriften aus dem Asklepeion von Epidauros," *Abhandlungen der philologisch-historischen Klasse der Sächsischen Akademie der Wissenschaften zu Leipzig* 60, pt. 2 (1969) 45–52.

3. The person in question is P. Anteius Antiochus, on whom see Philostratus, *Lives of the Sophists* 2.4; L. Robert, "Documents d'Asie Mineure," *Bulletin de Correspondance Hellénique* 101 (1977) 121–24.

4. See A. Henrichs, "The Sophists and Hellenistic Religion," *Harvard Studies in Classical Philology* 88 (1984) 139–58.

5. See E. Panofsky, *Hercules am Scheideweg und andere antike Bildstoffe in neuerer Kunst* (Leipzig, 1930).

6. For the goddess Dike see Hesiod, *Theogony* 902–3; *Works and Days* 256–62. See Hugh Lloyd-Jones, *The Justice of Zeus*, 2nd ed. (Berkeley, 1983).

7. R. Merkelbach has published a version of the Derveni papyrus in an appendix (1–12) of *Zeitschrift für Papyrologie und Epigraphik* 47 (1982). On the Derveni allegorist, see J. S. Rusten, "Interim Notes on the Papyrus from Derveni," *Harvard Studies in Classical Philology* 89 (1985) 121–40; W. Burkert, "Der Autor von Derveni: Stesimbrotos *Peri Teleton?*" *Zeitschrift für Papyrologie und Epigraphik* 62 (1986) 1–5.

8. R. Pfeiffer, *History of Classical Scholarship* (Oxford, 1968) 1:10.

9. See J. Tate, "On the History of Allegorism," *Classical Quarterly* 18 (1934) 105–14.

10. See G. S. Kirk, J. E. Raven, and M. Schofield, *The Presocratic Philosophers*, 2nd ed. (Cambridge, 1983) 50–71.

11. See W. Burkert, *Lore and Science in Ancient Pythagoreanism* (Cambridge, Mass., 1972) 170–75.

12. See J. V. Luce, *The End of Atlantis* (London, 1969)—to cite only one well-known attempt.

13. On the theme of autochthony, see N. Loraux, *L'invention d'Athènes* (Paris, 1981). On the myth of the age of metal, see M. L. West, ed., *Hesiod: Works and Days* (Oxford, 1978) 174–77.

14. See M. Davies, "Sisyphus and the Invention of Religion ('Critias' *TrGF* 1 43 F 19 = B 25 DK)," *Bulletin of the Institute of Classical Studies* 36 (1989) 16–32; A. Dihle, "Das Satyrspiel 'Sisyphos,'" *Hermes* 105 (1977) 28–42, defends the ancient attribution to Euripides.

15. See J. Bollack, "Mythische Deutung und Deutung des Mythos," in *Terror und Spiel*, ed. H. Fuhrmann, (Munich, 1971) 67–92.

16. On Euhemerus, see G. Vallauri, ed., *Evemero di Messene* (Torino, 1956). A history of euhemerism from antiquity through the

modern period does not exist. In the meantime, see, for antiquity, J. S. Rusten, *Dionysius Scytobrachion* (Opladen, 1982).

17. Two translations, with useful notes, are K. Aldrich, trans., *Apollodorus: The Library of Greek Mythology* (Lawrence, Kans., 1975), and M. Simpson, trans., *Gods and Heroes of the Greeks: The "Library" of Apollodorus* (Amherst, Mass., 1976).

18. On the author of the *Library,* see M. van der Valk, "On Apollodori Bibliotheca," *Revue des Études Grecques* 71 (1958) 100–68. On the author of the *Peri Theon,* see A. Henrichs, "Philodems De Pietate als mythographische Quelle," *Cronache Ercolanesi* 5 (1975) 5–38.

19. On Heraclitus the allegorist, see F. Buffière, ed., *Héraclite: Allégories d'Homère* (Paris, 1962), whose introduction is useful.

20. The edition with the best commentary is that of A. D. Nock, ed., *Sallustius Concerning the Gods and the Universe* (Cambridge, 1920); see also G. Rochefort, ed., *Salloustios: Des dieux et du monde* (Paris, 1960).

21. On the Christians, see H. Rahner, *Griechische Mythen in christlicher Deutung,* 3rd ed. (Zurich, 1957); D. Bush, *Pagan Myth and the Christian Tradition* (Philadelphia, 1968); see also, on the reception of Greek myth in Christian art, K. Weitzmann, *Greek Mythology in Byzantine Art* (Princeton, 1952). On the Middle Ages, see B. Stock, *Myth and Science in the Twelfth Century: A Study of Bernard Sylvester* (Princeton, 1972). On Florentine Neoplatonism, see E. Wind, *Pagan Mysteries in the Renaissance* (London, 1958); see also J. Seznec, *The Survival of the Ancient Gods: The Mythological Tradition and Its Place in Renaissance Humanism and Art,* trans. B. F. Sessions (New York, 1953; orig. 1940).

Abbreviations and Sources

1. Archaeologists have begun to develop their own method of interpreting visual representations. The new method departs from the traditional "philological" one, which consists in comparing visual with textual representations of myth; see C. Robert's still very readable *Archäologische Hermeneutik* (Berlin, 1919). The proponents of the new method argue that visual representations have their own "language"; that this language can be deciphered through comparison of similar (or dissimilar) visual representations with one another; and that within this language "semantic fields"—patterns of meaning—can be discerned. The method has yielded convincing results, but these have been limited, in the main, to those visual representations which can be construed

seriatim. Not surprisingly, the method has been applied most fruitfully in studies of the rich inventory of Attic vase painting. See C. Sourvinou-Inwood, *"Reading" Greek Culture: Texts and Images, Rituals and Myths* (Oxford, 1991), esp. chap. 1, and "Theseus and Medea as a Case Study," in *Approaches to Greek Myth*, ed. L. Edmunds, (Baltimore, 1990) 393–445.

SUGGESTIONS FOR FURTHER READING

Lexica and Handbooks

Bonnefoy, Y., ed., *Mythologies*, trans. under the direction of W. Doniger, 2 vols. (Chicago, 1991; orig. 1981).

Hunger, H., *Lexikon der griechischen und römischen Mythologie*, 8th ed. (Vienna, 1969).

Kerényi, K., *Die Mythologie der Griechen*, 2 vols. (Zurich, 1951–58).

Pfister, F., *Götter- und Heldensagen der Griechen* (Heidelberg, 1956).

Preller, L., *Griechische Mythologie*, rev. C. Robert, 4th ed. (Berlin, 1894–1921): the most comprehensive and scholarly paraphrastic compendium.

Roscher, W. H., ed., *Ausführliches Lexikon der griechischen und römischen Mythologie* (Leipzig, 1884–1937): still indispensable for the scholarly study of the ancient myths.

Rose, H. J., *A Handbook of Greek Mythology*, 6th ed. (London, 1958).

Tölle, R., *Genealogische Stammtafel der griechischen Mythologie* (Hamburg, 1967).

Tripp, E., ed., *The Meridian Handbook of Classical Mythology* (New York, 1974).

General Introductions and Readers

Bremmer, J. N., ed., *Interpretations of Greek Mythology* (London, 1987).

Burkert, W., "Mythos und Mythologie," in *Propyläen Geschichte der Literatur*. Vol. 1: *Die Welt der Antike* (Berlin, 1981) 11–35.

———, "Mythos: Begriff, Struktur, Funktionen," in *Mythen in my-*

thenloser Gesellschaft: Das Paradeigma Roms, ed. F. Graf (Stuttgart, 1993).

Detienne, M., *The Creation of Mythology,* trans. M. Cook (Chicago, 1986; orig. 1981).

Dowden, K., *The Uses of Greek Mythology* (London, 1992).

Edmunds, L., ed., *Approaches to Greek Myth* (Baltimore, 1990).

Kirk, G. S., *Myth: Its Meaning and Function in Ancient and Other Cultures* (Berkeley, 1970).

————, *The Nature of Greek Myths* (Harmondsworth, 1974).

Nagy, G., *Greek Mythology and Poetics* (Ithaca, N.Y., 1990).

Radermacher, L., *Mythos und Sage bei den Griechen* (Baden bei Wien, 1938).

Introduction

Burkert, W., "Mythisches Denken: Versuch einer Definition an Hand des griechischen Befundes," in *Philosophie und Mythos: Ein Kolloquium,* ed. H. Poser (Berlin, 1979) 16–39.

Burkert, W., and A. Horstmann, "Mythos, Mythologie," in *Historisches Wörterbuch der Philosophie,* vol. 6 (Basel, 1984) 282–318.

Calame, C., "'Mythe' et 'rite' en Grèce: Des catégories indigènes?" *Kernos* 4 (1991) 179–204.

Dundes, A., ed., *Sacred Narrative: Readings in the Theory of Myth* (Berkeley, 1984).

Finnegan, R., *Oral Poetry: Its Nature, Significance, and Social Context* (Cambridge, 1977).

Hampl, F., "Mythos–Sage–Märchen," in *Geschichte als kritische Wissenschaft,* vol. 2 (Darmstadt, 1975) 1–50.

Okpewho, I., *Myth in Africa: A Study of Its Aesthetic and Cultural Relevance* (Cambridge, 1983).

Röhrich, L., "Märchen–Mythos–Sage," in *Antiker Mythos in unseren Märchen,* ed. W. Siegmund (Kassel, 1984) 11–35.

Chapters I and II

Burkert, W., "Griechische Mythologie und die Geistesgeschichte der Moderne," in *Les études classiques au XIXe et XXe siècles: Leur place dans l'histoire des idées,* Entretiens sur l'antiquité classique 26 (Geneva, 1980).

Cohen, P. S., "Theories of Myth," *Man* 4 (1969) 337–53.

Engell, J., "The Modern Revival of Myth: Its Eighteenth-Century Origins," *Harvard English Studies* 9 (1981) 245–72.

Feldman, B., and R. D. Richardson, *The Rise of Modern Mythology, 1680–1860* (Bloomington, Ind., 1972).

Gruppe, O., *Geschichte der klassischen Mythologie und Religionsgeschichte während des Mittelalters im Abendland und während der Neuzeit* (Leipzig, 1921).

Humphreys, S. C., *Anthropology and the Greeks* (London, 1978).

Jamme, C., *Einführung in die Philosophie des Mythos*. Vol. 2: *Neuzeit und Gegenwart* (Darmstadt, 1991).

Kerényi, K., ed., *Die Eröffnung des Zugangs zum Mythos: Ein Lesebuch* (Darmstadt, 1967).

Segal, R. A., "In Defense of Mythology: The History of Modern Theories of Myth," *Annals of Scholarship* 1 (1980) 3–49.

Starobinsky, J., "La mythologie au XVIIIᵉ siècle," *Critique* 366 (1977) 975–97.

Vernant, J.-P., "The Reason of Myth," in *Myth and Society in Ancient Greece*, trans. J. Lloyd (Sussex, 1980; orig. 1974) 203–60.

Vries, J. de, *Forschungsgeschichte der Mythologie* (Freiburg 1961).

Chapter III

Bader, F., "Rhapsodies homériques et irlandaises," in *Recherches sur les religions de l'antiquité classique*, ed. R. Bloch (Paris, 1980) 9–83.

Bremmer, J. N., "Heroes, Rituals, and the Trojan War," *Studi Storico-Religiosi* 2 (1978) 5–38.

Cobet, J., "Gab es den Trojanischen Krieg?" *Antike Welt* 14, pt. 4 (1983) 39–58.

Codino, F., *Introduzione a Omero* (Turin, 1965).

Dihle, A., *Homer-Probleme* (Opladen, 1970).

Durante, M., *Sulla preistoria della tradizione poetica greca*, 2 vols. (Rome, 1971–76).

Finley, M. I., J. L. Caskey, G. S. Kirk, and D. L. Page, "The Trojan War," *Journal of Hellenic Studies* 84 (1964) 1–20.

Graf, F., "Religion und Mythologie im Zusammenhang mit Homer: Forschung und Ausblick," in *Zweihundert Jahre Homer-Forschung*, ed. J. Latacz (Stuttgart, 1991) 331–62.

Hampl, F., "Die Ilias ist kein Geschichtsbuch," in *Geschichte als kritische Wissenschaft*, vol. 2 (Darmstadt, 1975) 51–99.

Heubeck, A., *Die homerische Frage: Ein Bericht über die Forschung der letzten Jahrzehnte* (Darmstadt, 1974); continued in *Gymnasium* 89 (1982) 385–447.

Hölscher, U., "The Transformation from Folk-Tale to Epic," in *Homer: Tradition and Invention*, ed. B. Fenik (Leiden, 1978) 51–67.

Kirk, G. S., *The Songs of Homer* (Cambridge, 1962); abridged paperback version, *Homer and the Epic* (Cambridge, 1965).

Kullmann, W., *Die Quellen der Ilias* (Wiesbaden, 1960).

Latacz, J., *Homer: Der erste Dichter des Abendlands*, 2nd ed. (Zurich, 1989).

Nilsson, M. P., *The Mycenaean Origin of Greek Mythology* (Berkeley, 1932).

Otto, W. F., *The Homeric Gods: The Spiritual Significance of Greek Religion*, trans. M. Hadas (London, 1954; orig. 1934).

Siciliano, I., *Les chansons de geste et l'épopée: Mythes–histoire–poèmes* (Turin, 1968).

Snodgrass, A., *Archaic Greece: The Age of Experiment* (Berkeley, 1980).

Vermeule, E. T., "Mythology in Mycenaean Art," *Classical Journal* 54 (1958–59) 97–108.

Chapter IV

Burkert, W., "Orpheus und die Vorsokratiker," *Antike und Abendland* 14 (1968) 93–114.

Kirk, G. S., J. E. Raven, and M. Schofield, *The Presocratic Philosophers*, 2nd ed. (Cambridge, 1983).

Lamberton, R., *Hesiod* (New Haven, Conn., 1988).

Philippson, P., *Genealogie als mythische Form: Studien zur Theogonie des Hesiod* (Oslo, 1936).

Rudhardt, J., "Le mythe hésiodique des races et celui de Prométhée," in *Du mythe, de la religion grecque et de la compréhension d'autrui* (Geneva, 1981) 245–81.

Schwabl, H., "Weltschöpfung," in *Paulys Realenzyklopädie der classischen Altertumswissenschaft*, ed. G. Wissowa et al., suppl. 9 (Stuttgart, 1962) 1433–1582.

Vernant, J.-P., "The Myth of Prometheus in Hesiod," in *Myth and Society in Ancient Greece*, trans. J. Lloyd (Sussex, 1980; orig. 1974) 183–201.

West, M. L., *Hesiod: Theogony* (Oxford, 1966).

————, *The Orphic Poems* (Oxford, 1983).

The Orient

Burkert, W., *The Orientalizing Revolution: Near Eastern Influence on Greek Culture in the Early Archaic Age,* trans. W. Burkert and M. E. Pinder (Cambridge, Mass., 1992), esp. chap. 3.

Dalley, S., *Myths from Mesopotamia: Creation, the Flood, Gilgamesh, and Others* (Oxford, 1989).

Haas, V., *Hethitische Berggötter und hurritische Steindämonen* (Mainz, 1982).

Hoffner, H. A., *Hittite Myths,* ed. G. M. Beckman (Atlanta, 1990).

Mondi, R., "Greek Mythic Thought in the Light of the Near East," in *Approaches to Greek Myth,* ed. L. Edmunds (Baltimore, 1990) 141–98.

Pritchard, J. B., ed., *Ancient Near Eastern Texts Relating to the Old Testament,* 3rd ed. (Princeton, 1969).

Siegelová, J., *Appu-Märchen und Hedammu-Mythos* (Wiesbaden, 1971).

Walcot, P., *Hesiod and the Near East* (Cardiff, 1966).

Chapter V

Burkert, W., *Greek Religion,* trans. J. Raffan (Cambridge, Mass, 1985; orig. 1977).

Bruneau, P., *Recherches sur les cultes de Délos à l'époque hellénistique et à l'époque impériale* (Paris, 1970).

Cassola, F., ed., *Inni omerici* (Milan, 1975).

Gallet de Santerre, H., *Délos primitive et archaïque* (Paris, 1958).

Sourvinou-Inwood, C., "The Myth of the First Temples at Delphi," *Classical Quarterly* 29 (1979) 231–51; reprinted in *"Reading" Greek Culture: Texts and Images, Rituals and Myths* (Oxford, 1991) 192–216.

Rites

Deubner, L., *Attische Feste* (Berlin, 1932).

Nilsson, M. P., *Griechische Feste von religiöser Bedeutung mit Ausschluβ der attischen* (Leipzig, 1906).

Parke, H. W., *Festivals of the Athenians* (London, 1977).

Tyrrell, W. B., and F. S. Brown, *Athenian Myths and Institutions: Words in Action* (Oxford, 1991).

Method
Graf, F., *Nordionische Kulte: Religionsgeschichtliche und epigraphische Untersuchungen zu den Kulten von Chios, Erythrai, Klazomenai und Phokaia* (Rome, 1985).

Chapter VI

Calame, C., *Thésée et l'imaginaire athénien: Légende et culte en Grèce antique* (Lausanne, 1990).
Cartledge, P., *Sparta and Lakonia: A Regional History, 1300–362 B.C.* (London, 1979).
Feeney, D. C., *The Gods in Epic: Poets and Critics of the Classical Tradition* (Oxford, 1991).
Finley, M. I., "Myth, Memory, and History" (1965), reprinted in *The Use and Abuse of History* (London, 1975) 11–33.
Fritz, K. von, *Die griechische Geschichtsschreibung* (Berlin, 1967).
Henige, D. P., *The Chronology of Oral Tradition: Quest for a Chimera* (Oxford, 1974).
Hill, J. D., ed., *Rethinking History and Myth: Indigenous South American Perspectives on the Past* (Urbana, Ill., 1988).
Lasserre, F., "L'historiographie grecque à l'époque archaïque," *Quaderni di storia* 2, pt. 4 (1976) 113–42.
Piérart, M., "L'historien ancien face aux mythes et aux légendes," *Studi Classici* 51 (1983) 47–62.
Prinz, F., *Gründungsmythen und Sagenchronologie* (Munich, 1979).
Strasburger, H., *Homer und die Geschichtsschreibung* (Heidelberg, 1972).
Vansina, J., *Oral Tradition as History* (Madison, 1985).
Wardman, A. E., "Myth in Greek Historiography," *Historia* 9 (1960) 403–13.
West, M. L., *The Hesiodic Catalogue of Women* (Oxford, 1985).

Chapter VII

Burkert, W., "Greek Tragedy and Sacrificial Ritual," *Greek, Roman and Byzantine Studies* 7 (1966) 87–121.
———, "Die Absurdität der Gewalt und das Ende der Tragödie: Euripides' Orestes," *Antike und Abendland* 20 (1974) 97–109.
Euripide. Entretiens sur l'antiquité classique 6 (Geneva, 1960).
Fritz, K. von, "Die Orestessage bei den drei großen griechischen Tra-

gikern," in *Antike und moderne Tragödie: Neun Abhandlungen* (Berlin, 1962) 113–59.

Herington, J., *Poetry into Drama: Early Tragedy and the Greek Poetic Tradition* (Berkeley, 1985).

Köhnken, A., *Die Funktion des Mythos bei Pindar: Interpretationen zu sechs Pindargedichten* (Berlin, 1971).

Lesky, A., *Greek Tragic Poetry*, trans. M. Dillon (New Haven, Conn., 1983; orig. 1972).

March, J. R., *The Creative Poet: Studies in the Treatment of Myths in Greek Poetry* (London, 1987).

Reinhardt, K., "Die Sinneskrise bei Euripides" (1953), reprinted in *Tradition und Geist* (Göttingen, 1960), 227–56, in *Die Krise des Helden* (Munich, 1962) 19–52, and in *Euripides*, ed. E. R. Schwinge (Darmstadt, 1968) 507–42.

Segal, C., "Greek Myth as a Semiotic and Structural System and the Problem of Tragedy," in *Interpreting Greek Tragedy: Myth, Poetry, Text* (Ithaca, N.Y., 1986) 48–74.

Snell, B., "Myth and Reality in Greek Tragedy" (1944), reprinted in *The Discovery of the Mind: The Greek Origins of European Thought*, trans. T. G. Rosenmeyer (Cambridge, Mass., 1953) 90–112.

Trendall, A. D., and T. B. L. Webster, *Illustrations of Greek Drama* (London, 1971).

Vickers, B., *Towards Greek Tragedy* (London, 1973).

Chapter VIII

Brisson, L., *Platon: Les mots et les mythes* (Paris, 1982).

Buffière, F., *Les mythes d'Homère et la pensée grecque* (Paris, 1956).

Carrière, J.-C. and B. Massonie, eds., *La "Bibliothèque" d'Apollodore traduite, annotée et commentée* (Paris, 1991).

Dörrie, H., *Der Mythos und seine Funktion in der antiken Philosophie* (Innsbruck, 1972).

Frutiger, P., *Les mythes de Platon* (Paris, 1930).

Henrichs, A., "Three Approaches to Greek Mythography," in *Interpretations of Greek Mythology*, ed. J. N. Bremmer (London, 1987) 242–77.

Kerferd, G.-B., *The Sophistic Movement* (Cambridge, 1981).

Lamberton, R., *Homer the Theologian: Neoplatonist Allegorical Reading and the Growth of the Epic Tradition* (Berkeley, 1986).

Lévêque, P., *Aurea catena Homeri: Une étude d'allégorie grecque* (Paris, 1959).

Pépin, J., *Mythe et allégorie: Les origines grecques et les contestations judéo-chrétiennes* (Paris, 1958).

Rahner, H., *Griechische Mythen in christlicher Deutung* (Zurich, 1957).

Rusten, J. S., *Dionysius Scytobrachion* (Opladen, 1982).

Valk, M. van der, "On *Apollodori Bibliotheca*," *Revue des Études Grecques* 71 (1958) 100–68.

Whitman, J., *Allegory: The Dynamics of an Ancient and Medieval Technique* (Oxford, 1987).

Recent Additions (1995)

Handbooks

Reid, J. D., *The Oxford Guide to Classical Mythology in the Arts: 1300–1990s* (Oxford, 1993).

Parada, C., *Genealogical Guide to Greek Mythology* (Jonsered, 1993).

Introduction

Bremmer, J. N., *Greek Religion* (Oxford, 1994), chap. 5.

Buxton, R., *Imaginary Greece: The Contexts of Mythology* (Cambridge, 1994).

Saïd, S., *Approches de la mythologie grecque* (Paris 1993).

Chapter V

Robertson, N., *Festivals and Legends: The Formation of Greek Cities in the Light of Public Ritual* (Toronto, 1992).

Chapter VI

Scheer, T. S., *Mythische Vorväter: Zur Bedeutung griechischer Heroenmythen im Selbstverständnis kleinasiatischer Städte* (Munich, 1993).

Chapter VIII

Feeney, D. C., *The Gods in Epic: Poets and Critics of the Classical Tradition* (Oxford, 1991).

INDEX

abduction of women, 121–22, 136–37

Abraham, Karl, 37

Achilles: anger of, 57, 59, 60, 62, 65, 74; death of, 68; as mythical, not historical, figure, 73; as reflecting ephebe, 74, 77, 125, 141, 171

Aegae, in Cilicia, embassy from, 178

Aeneas, 109; genealogy of, 125–26, 127, 129

Aeschylus, 10, 92, 142, 147, 153; *Seven against Thebes,* 156; *Niobe,* 162; *Prometheus Bound,* 167; attitude of, toward myth, 167–68

—*Oresteia,* 157–67; sources of, 157; gods and mortals in, 164–67; *aitia* in, 166–67, 182; contemporary politics in, 166–67, 182; innovation in, 167. *See also* justice

Aesop, 8, 183

Aethiopis, 60

Africa, tales of, 3, 13

agalma, 119, 148

Agamemnon, 2, 60, 69, 73, 109, 127–28, 131, 134, 148, 156, 157–62, 163–64, 165, 168, 170, 190

Agathon, 142

agriculture, 23, 26, 27, 28, 29, 91, 180. *See also* fertility; seasons

ainos, 7

aition. See etiology

akousmata, 186

Alcman, 96, 145, 148, 151

Alexandria, 176, 193, 194

allēgoria, 184

allegory/allegoresis, 4, 16, 21; as prevailing approach to myth before Heyne and Herder, 13, 25; aversion of Enlightenment thinkers to, 13–14; Moritz's reasons for rejecting, 19; rise of, to time of Plato, 100, 121, 184–87; as means of defending Homer, 185, 186; as key to an author's true meaning, 185–86, 198; as distinguished from moral instruction, 187; after Plato, 191, 194–98; as apology in late antiquity, 197. *See also allēgoria;* Christians; Crates; Creuzer; Derveni commentator; Florentine Neoplatonists; Heraclitus (Stoic allegorist); Hesiod; Homer; Metrodorus; nature mythology; Neoplatonic allegorists; Orpheus; Pythagoras; rhapsodes; Sallustius; Stoics; Zeno

America, tales of, 13, 15

Anaxagoras, 184, 187

Anaximander, 98

Anaximenes, 98

Anius, 108–9

anthropology, 26, 28, 29, 35, 37, 42, 44, 193

anthropomorphism: of Greek myth, 141; of gods, 169–71

aoidos (epic bard), 61–62; as collector and systematizer of myths, 76, 126
Aphrodite, 59–60, 81, 145, 172, 173; statue of, 106, 109, 111–13
Apollo, 39, 60, 68, 73; cult of, 102–8; birth of, as central myth of Homeric *Hymn to Apollo*, 102–5, 109, 110, 115–16; Delphinius, 113–14, 118, 119, 120, 133, 135, 147, 148, 149, 153, 156, 157, 158, 161, 165–67, 170, 174, 177, 189
Apollodorus, 92, 193–94
Apollonius, 176
Apuleius, 7
Arcadia, 6
archetypes, 38–39, 53
Archilochus, 5, 145, 179
Areopagus, 165–66
Argonauts, 66, 76
Argos, 50, 69, 111, 127, 155, 159, 163, 166, 173, 174, 178
Arion, 145
Aristotle: on origin of tragedy, 144; on myth, 191
Artemis, 50, 64–65, 102, 104, 105, 107, 118, 119, 128, 136, 151, 159, 163–64, 165, 171, 172–73, 177; statue of, 111–12, 116–17
Artemisium, 107, 177
Asclepiades, 193
Athena, 31, 48, 59, 66, 67; birth of, 83, 111, 153, 154, 165, 166, 167, 169, 171, 181, 201; statue of, 111–12
Athens, 95, 104, 106, 107, 122, 132, 134, 136–40, 144, 155, 156–57, 166–67, 190
Atlantis, 2, 188, 192
Atthidographers, 138
autochthony, 46, 190

Babylonia, tales of, 90–91
Bacchylides, 119; on Croesus, 135–36, 145, 148–49, 150
Barthes, Roland, 53–54
Bayle, Pierre, 14
Bellerophon, 76, 83
Bible. *See* Old Testament
Boeotian epic poetry, 79–80
book titles, 123
Brelich, Angelo, 53

Brosses, Président de, 11
Bruehl, Count Heinrich von, 9
Burkert, Walter, 29, 50, 52–53

Calame, Claude, 55
Callimachus, 104, 105, 176, 193
Calydon, 64, 65, 67–68
Calydonian boar hunt, 64–65
Cambridge school, 30, 35, 40–42
Canaanite myths, 95
carnival, 84, 143–44
Cassirer, Ernst, 28
castration. *See* mutilation
Catalogue of Women. *See* Hesiod
cheese-stealing competition, 115
childbirth, 103, 107, 108
"childhood of mankind," childlike mentality of prehistoric man, 10, 18, 22, 33, 37, 38, 182
choral lyric poetry, 2, 4, 119, 144–52, 176. *See also* Alcman; Bacchylides; Ibycus; Pindar; Stesichorus
Christians, 6, 101, 192, 194, 197
codes, 45, 46, 47
collective: creation myth as, 20, 198; dreaming, 37; unconscious, 39; as transcendent power, 41
colonization, 69, 78, 99
comparative method, 13, 16, 25, 30, 39, 43
cosmogony/cosmogonic myths. *See* creation
crane dance. *See geranos*
Crates, 194
creation: of gods, 80–84, 96–97, 185–86, 192; of mankind, 85, 90; of world, 91, 96–98
Crete, 69, 81, 106, 117, 118, 178, 211 n.16
Creuzer, Friedrich, 20–22, 32, 33, 38, 197
Critias, 191
criticism of myth: by Presocratics, 178–79; conditions fostering, 179; by sophists, 179–80; by Plato, 183–84
Croesus, 122, 135, 148–49
Cronia, 84
Cronus, 17, 63, 80, 83–84, 87, 88–89; as Chronus, 185–86; as understood by Neoplatonic allegorists, 196–97

Cû Chulainn, 74, 75
culinary triangle, 47
cult. *See* religion
cultural relevance/cultural centrality, 3–6, 7, 43, 61–62, 99; of gods and heroes, 143, 155, 170, 176, 178, 181, 198
cultural specificity, "national" character of myth, 11–12, 13, 17, 20, 23, 24, 55
Cupid and Psyche, 7
Cyclops/Cyclopes, 44, 77, 80, 81
Cypria, 59, 61, 78, 109

Damascius, 93, 94
Daphne, 39
"dark age," 70, 72, 73, 77, 95
dawn, 25–26
Deliades, 103, 118–19
Delos, 102–10, as neutral space, 105
Delphi, 102, 110–11
Demeter, 23, 108, 113, 116, 151, 180
Derveni commentator, 184
Detienne, Marcel, 47, 48, 49, 55
deus ex machina, 154, 169
Dieterich, Albrecht, 29
Diodorus, 192
Dionysia, 4, 143–44
Dionysius Scytobrachion, 192
Dionysus, 4, 17, 97, 108, 109, 136, 143–45, 147, 154, 169, 170, 175, 177, 180; statue of, 112
"disease of language," 25–26, 124
dithyramb, 144, 145
divinity/the divine, 11, 17, 19, 31–32, 33, 38
dogs, 108, 109
Dorian migration, 131–32
Dorian invasion, 133
double motivation, 149
dreams, 36, 37, 38
Dumézil, Georges, 22, 43
Durkheim, Émile, 40–41, 43, 48

earthquake, 30–31
Edda, 12, 20
Eileithyia, 103, 104, 107
elements, as gods, 100
Eliade, Mircea, 101
Empedocles, 99–100, 186
empirical explanation, 14–15

Enlightenment, 13, 24, 37, 56
Ennius, 192
Enuma Elish, 90–92
eoikōs mythos, 188
ephebe, 51, 53, 54, 74, 112, 113–15
Epic Cycle, 59–60, 61
Epic of Gilgamesh, 8, 71
epic poetry: recitation of, at set occasions, 4–5; 57–86, 119; themes of, 57, 67, 87, 119, 134; oral, 58–59, 61, 66, 72–73, 87; cultural relevance of, 61–62; Pylian, 63; poetic and non-poetic forms of, 66–68; local, 67; prehistory of Homeric, 68–78; heroic, 68–76; and ritual, 72; Indo-European, 74–75; Mycenaean, 75–76; posing as history, 76–78; cosmogonic and theogonic myths in, 79–97; Boeotian, 79–80; Boeotian, 80; as vehicle of heroic myth, 87, 140; as vehicle of philosophy, 99–100; mythical narration in, through genealogy, 125–28; with political purpose, 138–39; as source for tragedy, 142, 167. *See also* Epic Cycle; Hesiod; Homer; Homeric *Hymns*
—Homeric myths in: about Trojan War, 59–61; about gods and heroes, 62–64, 86–87; not about Trojan War, 64–66
—non-Homeric myths in: about Trojan War, 59–60; about gods and heroes, 63–64; not about Trojan War, 64–68
eponyms, 126, 127
epos, 1
Er, 188–90
esprit humain, 38, 48. *See also* Lévi-Strauss
ethnology, 1, 27–30, 35, 36, 41, 48, 54, 55
etiology (*aitia*), 11, 39–40, 42, 52; Delian myths as examples of, 102–10; as explaining significant features of objects or rituals, 110–18; as explaining more than ritual, 113–16; as expressing mood of ancient ritual, 115–16; as explaining entirety of ritual, 116; as migratory from cult to cult, 116–17; as old feature

etiology *(continued)*
  of Greek cult, 120; in Aeschylus's
  Eumenides, 166–67; in plays of Euripides, 169; in poems of Callimachus, 193
etymology: of myth, 22; and myth,
  26, 186, 187
Eudemus, 93
Euhemerus/euhemerism, 16, 17, 21,
  23, 121, 191–92. *See also* history
Euripides, 5; *Iphigeneia at Aulis*, 148,
  171; *Medea*, 154; *Phoenician
  Women*, 156; *Telephus*, 163; *Electra*, 163, 168–75; and heroes as ordinary people, 168–69, 173–75;
  skepticism about divine myths,
  169–73; *aitia* in plays of, 169; frequency of appearance of gods in
  plays of, 169; uncritical acceptance
  of heroic myths, 169; gods and
  mortals in plays of, 169–75; *Hecuba*, 170; *Heracles*, 171–72; *Helen*,
  172; *Hippolytus*, 172–73; *Orestes*,
  173–74; as last narrator of culturally relevant myth in tragedy, 175;
  Bacchae, 175
evolution, 27, 29, 42, 114, 140, 191
exemplum, 64–65, 147–51

fable, 6, 7–8, 183
fable/fabula, 10, 14, 203n.4
fantastic, elements of, 49, 77,
  140–41
farming. *See* agriculture
Farnell, Lewis Richard, 26
fear, as impulse to mythopoesis, 10,
  12, 17, 18, 19
fertility, 23, 28–29, 35, 40
festival, 6, 74, 102–6 *passim*, 112–13;
  115–16, 118–20, relevance of
  myths at, 119, 148, 151. *See also*
  Cronia; Dionysia; hymns; Synoecia; Tonaea
fetishism, 11
Finley, Moses I., 71
fire, 82, 85–86, 181
fire ritual, 65
flogging ritual, 112, 114–15
Florentine Neoplatonists, 197
folktale/folktale motifs, 6–7, 24–25,
  36, 38, 49, 52, 69

Fontenelle, Bernard de, 14, 15, 16, 18,
  31, 32, 124, 197–98
formulas, 58–59
foundation, 103, 106, 108–9, 110,
  120, 126, 138, 166, 178
Frazer, Sir James George, 16, 27–30,
  32, 40, 42, 43. *See also* Cambridge
  school
Fréret, Nicolas, 16–17, 18
Freud, Sigmund, 36–37, 38
functionalism, 36, 42–43

Gaea, 17, 39, 59, 80–85 *passim*, 89,
  186
games, 62, 78, 106, 109, 120
genealogy, 71; as interpretive mode,
  89; as means of organizing myths,
  125–31; as ethnic and political
  "map," 127; as mainspring of
  myth, 127; and curses, 127–28; as
  enhancing personal status, 129;
  and chronology, 129–30; as political history, 130–31
geranos, 106, 109
Germany, tales of, 24–25
Gernet, Louis, 48
gifts, collection of, as rite, 107–8
gods, myths about, 68, 121. *See also*
  creation; religion
Goerres, Johann Joseph von, 20–21
Goethe, Johann Wolfgang von, 19, 85
golden age, 84, 111, 176
Gorgias, 181
Greimas, Algirdas Julien, 55
Grimm, Jacob, 6, 24, 26
Grimm, Wilhelm, 7, 24–25
Gruppe, Otto, 19

hair offering, 106–8, 109, 113
Harrison, Jane Ellen, 30, 40, 43, 50,
  51
Hecataeus, 5, 30, 123–24; rational ap-
  proach of, 124; ancestry of, 129
Hedammu, 89
Hegel, Georg Wilhelm Friedrich, 31
Helen, 60, 73, 122, 136–37, 145; and
  Stesichorus, 146, 155; and Sparta,
  151, 160, 169, 172, 173–74, 181
helmet, of boar's tusk, 69–70
Hera, 50, 59, 65–66, 87, 89, 87, 100,
  103, 104, 105, 116, 124, 161, 170,

171–72; statue of, 111–12; as *aēr*, 195; as "cloud of unknowing," 195–96
Heracles, 63, 66–67, 81, 83, 116, 120, 122; and Cerberus, 124, 141, 130, 137, 146, 151, 154, 156, 168, 171–72, 177, 178, 180–81, 195–96, 200–201. *See also* Heraclids
Heraclides, 145–46
Heraclids, return of, 31, 132–35; as legitimizing settlement of Peloponnesus, 134–35
Heraclitus (Presocratic), 178–79
Heraclitus (Stoic allegorist), 195
Herder, Johann Gottfried, 11–13, 16, 17, 18–19, 20, 21, 22, 23, 24, 31
Herodotus, 2; on abduction of women as cause of Persian Wars, 121–22; on Minos, 123; as rationalist, 124–25; on Croesus, 135–36
heroes: myths of, 57–58 *passim*, esp. 62–78; cult of, 73, 78, 101, 169
Hesiod, 5, 17, 48, 63, 68, 76, 79–80; *Works and Days*, 79, 86, 101; *Catalogue of Women*, 83, 126–27, 128, 157; normative views of, 178; criticism of, 178–79; as allegorist, 185, 190
—*Theogony*, 79–86; in relation to Near Eastern tales, 88–94, 89, 91–92; genealogy in, 126, 127, 167, 181
Heyne, Christian Gottlob, 9–11, 12, 16, 18–19, 21, 22, 23, 26, 31, 40, 55
Hippias, 180
hippota, 63
history: myth as, 5, 121–41; as impulse to mythopoesis, 10, 21, 23, 30–31, 33, 35; as distinguished from myth, 123; as myth, 135–36. *See also* Euhemerus; myth
Hittite tales, 88–90
Homer, 23, 79; as "author," 58; myth and, 57–68, 101, 102; and genealogy, 125–26; as father of tragedy, 142; normative views of, 178; criticism of, 178–79; as allegorist, 185. *See also* epic poetry
—poems of: genesis of, 58–59; as sources for mythography, 66; realism in, 140; *Odyssey*, 2, 12, 48, 57–68 *passim*, 79, 80, 157, 197; *Iliad*, 30, 57–68 *passim*, 79, 80
Homeric *Hymns*, 119; *Hymn to Apollo*, 102–6, 118–19, 120; *Hymn to Demeter*, 116
Horned Altar, 105–6, 109
horses, 30–31, 73, 77. *See also* Trojan horse
Humboldt, Wilhelm von, 19
Hume, David, 16, 17, 18, 27
hunting, 29, 50, 52, 67, 105
hymns, 6, 102, 107, 119, 177, 183–84
Hyperborean girls, 107–8, 109, 113
hyponoia, 184

Ibycus, 8, 145, 148–49
"ideal" and "real," 23, 31–32
Iliad. See Homer
Iliupersis, 60
imagination, mythopoeic, 17, 19, 23, 31, 44
India, tales of, 20, 21, 22, 25, 43, 75
Indo-European, 22, 25, 26, 34, 43; poetic tradtion, 74–75; myths, 75
initiation, 41, 51–53, 74, 106–7; rituals and myths, synchronic and diachronic dimensions of, 117; as transformation, 117–18; 211n.16
Io, myth of, as example of "girl's tragedy," 50, 116, 121, 123, 124
Iphimedeia, 76

Jason, 156, 201
Jeanmaire, Henri, 52
Jung, Carl Gustav, 38–39, 53
justice: in tragedy, 155–56; in Aeschylus's *Oresteia*, 163–64, 166, 170, 175; in Euripides' plays, 170–71

Kalevala, 71
Kerényi, Karl, 32, 35, 38
Kingship in Heaven, 88–89
Kirk, Geoffrey Stephen, 48, 141
klea andrōn, 62, 75
Kuhn, Adalbert, 25, 26, 43
kykeōn, 116

labor, 86, 89, 91
Lafitau, François Joseph, 15–16
Lang, Andrew, 14, 27, 28

language: of prehistoric man, 10, 12, 21, 25–26, 33; myth as, 21; as communicative medium analogous to myth, 44–45, 47, 53–54. *See also* metalanguage

langue, 44

legend, 6

"lesser" myths, 4, 5–6, 7, 153

Lessing, Gotthold Ephraim, 8, 20

Lévi-Bruhl, Lucien, 14

Lévi-Strauss, Claude, 3, 38, 44–48, 49, 52, 53–54, 55

Linear B, 69

literacy: in Mesopotamia, 94–95; in Greece, 153, 179

log motif, 65, 68, 77

logos, 1, 2; from *mythos* to, 98, 187–88; Stoic, 194, 203n.2

Lowth, Robert, 12

Lycurgus (Spartan lawgiver), 114–15

Lycurgus (Thracian king), 17, 147

Macpherson, James, 12

magic, 28, 40. *See also* fantastic, elements of

Malinowski, Bronislaw, 42

mankind: creation of, 85, 90, 97; definition of, 85–86, 91, 97

Mannhardt, Johann Wilhelm Emanuel, 26, 27, 28, 29

Märchen. See folktale

marriage, 46, 82, 83, 86, 91, 93, 107–8. *See also* premarital ritual

Meleager, 59, 64–66, 67–68, 76

Menander, 176

Meropes, 66–67

Meropis, 67

Mesopotamia, 88, 94–95, 97

Metrodorus, 185

Meuli, Karl, 29

Miltiades, ancestry of, 129

Minos, 51, 122–23

Minotaur, 51, 136, 137, 138, 141

monsters, 7, 74, 77, 88, 89, 90, 137, 141, 146

Moritz, Karl Philipp, 19–20, 33

motifeme. See Propp

Müller, Friedrich Max, 22, 25, 26, 40, 43, 124, 197

Müller, Karl Otfried, 21, 22–24, 26, 30

Murray, Gilbert, 40

Musaeus, 96

Muses, 62, 72, 78, 79

mutilation, 80, 88, 93

Mycenaean period, 68–70, 71–72, 73, 75–76, 78; epic poetry of, 75–76; receptivity of, to oriental inuence, 95–96

Myth: origins of modern notion of, 1, 57; definition of, 1–6, 101; adaptation of, 3, 66, 72–73, 80, 86, 104, 110, 136, 151–53, 154–55, 176, 198; as subject to group control, 4–5, 61–62, 181; rationalization of, 5, 77, 124–25, 126, 138–40, 194; distinct characteristics, 6–8; national character of, 11–12, 13, 17, 20, 23, 24, 55; as charter, 42, 43; as metalanguage, 47, 54; universality of, 55–56; local, 67, 93–94, 96, 118, 120; historicity of, 68–73, 121–41, 178; as nonfiction, 73–74; chronology of, 76, 77, 121–41 *passim*, 193; separation of heaven and earth, 80–81, 86, 88, 89, 90; and genealogy, 125–31; eschatological, 179, 186, 188–90. *See also* criticism of myth; gods; history, *mythos*; poetry; politics; religion; transmission; visual representations of myth; written vs. oral myth

myth-and-ritual theory, 35, 39–42, 44, 113

mythemes, 45, 46

mythōdes, to, 2, 123

mythography: as scholarly retelling of myth, 191, 193–94; as Hellenistic novel-like literature, 191–92

mythologos, 1–2

mythology, as preserve of classicists, 1, 35

mythos, 1–2, 14, 18, 55, 123, 187–88, 203n.2

mythus, as coinage of Heyne, 10, 55

narration, suprapersonal, 79, 98, 99

narrative analysis, 30, 35, 36, 42, 47, 49–50, 54, 55

narrative patterns: quest, 49, 50, 52, 53; "girl's tragedy," 50, 52, 53; crime and punishment, 50, 52; animal hunt, 52, 59; as migratory, 116

"national" character of myth. *See* cultural specificity
nature mythology, 18, 25–26, 27, 29, 30, 31, 32
nature, as impulse to mythopoesis, 10, 14–15, 18, 21, 23, 25–26, 28, 31, 33; vs. culture, 48; deification of, in Prodicus's view, 180
Near East: study of, 41; Greeks in, 95–96, 97
Near Eastern myths, 76, 88–96, 97; as written versions of oral works, 94–95; 190. *See also* transmission
Neo-Hittites, 95–96
Neoplatonic allegorists, 196–97
Nestor, 63, 66, 67, 69, 74, 125; as prototype of sophistic teacher, 180, 211n.16
Nibelungenlied, 71, 77
Nilsson, Martin Peer, 29, 68–70, 71
Nostoi, 60

Odysseus, 58, 59, 69, 73, 77
Odyssey. See Homer
Oedipus, 7, 36, 40, 41, 45, 156, 168
"Oedipus complex," 36
Old Testament, 12, 34
Olen, 107–8, 118
On the Gods (Apollodorus), 194
ontology, 99, 187, 196
oral poetry: as vehicle of myth, 2–3; traditional nature of, 58–59; particular performance of, 61; as entertainment, 61, 62; lost, evidence for, 63, 66; subject to adaptation, 72–73, 80
oral vs. written tradition of mythical narration: in Mesopotamia, 94–95; in Greece, 152–53
Orestes, 2, 116–17, 146–47. *See also* Aeschlyus, *Oresteia*
Orpheus/Orphism, 96–97, 185, 190
Ossian, 12, 20
Otto, Walter Friedrich, 32, 35, 38
Ouraniones, 87
Ovid, 104

Panathenaea, 5, 62
Pandora, 82, 85
Panionion, 105
Panyassis, 66
paradigm. *See* exemplum

Paris, 59–60, 122, 146, 159; judgment of, 43, 60, 73, 172
Parmenides, 99, 190
parole, 44
Parthenius, 193
pedagogy, myth and, 180–83
Peloponnesus, 31; settlement of, 131–34
Pelops, 24, 149–51, 151–52
Persephone, Kore, 23, 97, 116, 136
Perseus, 83, 178
personification, 7, 98, 181
phallus, 80, 88, 89
Pherecydes (of Athens), 129
Pherecydes (of Syros), 185–86
Philip, 177–78
Philo, 92–93
philological historical method, 9, 11, 12, 22, 22–23, 116
Philostratus, 8
Phrynichus, 142
Piaget, Jean, 37
Pindar, 10, 119, 148–49; revision of myth of Pelops by, 151–52, 155
Plato, 2, 183–84, 187–91; use of myth by, 4, 187; eschatological myths of, 188–90; myth of metals in *Republic*, 190–91
Plutarch, 124, 183
poetry, as related to myth, 10, 12, 13, 18, 19. *See also* choral lyric poetry; epic poetry; oral poetry
polis, 4, 98, 179
politics, and myth, 23, 31, 127, 130, 131, 134, 135, 138–40, 166–67, 177–78, 181–82, 190
Polycrates, 102
Poseidon, 30–31, 59, 63, 87
premarital ritual, 107–8, 113, 118
Presocratics, 96, 97–100, 178–82
primitive mentality, of prehistoric man, 10, 14–15, 18, 25, 27, 31, 33
Prodicus, 180–81; as choice of Heracles, 180–81; 192
program of action, 52–53. *See also* narrative patterns
Prometheus, 8, 37, 48, 81–82, 85, 86, 110, 113; and Epimetheus, 127, 181–82
Propp, Vladimir, 7, 50, 53, 59; on function, 49, 52
prose vs. poetry, 67, 98

Protagoras, 173, 180, 181
psychoanalytic interpretation, 35, 36–39
Pylos, epic poetry of, 63, 69, 74
Pythagoras/Pythagoreans, 186–87, 190

"quarrel of the ancients and moderns," 13

rational thought, 3, 97–100; conditions fostering development of, 98, 153, 179
rationalization of myths. See myths
reduction/reductionism, 19, 29, 30–31, 32, 33, 41
religion, 10, 12, 18, 24, 28, 85; myth as related to, 4–5, 101–20. See also divinity
Rhapsodes, 80, 185
Rhea, 17, 81, 83–84, 87
ritual, 26, 27, 28, 29, 40–42, 50–53, 65, 72, 74; as stable compared with myth, 102, 106–7, 108, 113–18; and myth, as autonomous phenomena, 116. See also cheese-stealing competition; fire; flogging; premarital
Rohde, Erwin, 17
Roheim, Géza, 37–38
romantics, 19–22, 24, 31–32

sacral kingship, 40
sacrifice, 82, 84, 85, 86, 91; human, 112, 114–15, 118, 171
sacrificial animal, division of, 82, 86, 113
saga, 6
Sallustius, 196–97
sanctuaries, 102–5, 107, 114; relevance of myths told at, 119–20, 143, 177
satyr drama, 144
Saussure, Ferdinand de, 44, 53
"savages," 10, 12, 13, 14, 15, 18, 26, 46, 86
Schachermeyr, Fritz, 24
Schelling, Friedrich Wilhelm Joseph von, 31–32, 35, 38
Schlegel, August Wilhelm von, 20
Schlegel, Friedrich von, 20, 21, 22, 24

Schliemann, Heinrich, 30, 69, 70
Schmid, W., 167
Schwab, Gustav, 6
"science of myth," 22
seasons, cycle of, 23, 27, 40, 44
Segal, Charles, 55
semiotics, 53–56
sickle, 80, 88
sign. See semiotics
Smith, William Robertson, 40
snake/dragon, 8, 89, 91
Socrates. See Plato
Song of Roland, 71, 77
Song of Ullikummi, 88–89
sophists, invention by myths by, 180–81; and use of myth for pedagogical purposes, 180–82
Sophocles, 8, 36; Antigone, 147–48; Ajax, 156; gods and mortals in plays of, 168; Trachinian Women, 168
Sparta, 60, 69, 111, 112, 114–15, 117, 130–31, 132, 133, 134, 151, 166, 174
statues, 102, 120; special powers of, 112; and ritual, 112–13
Stesichorus, 2, 119, 146–47, 148–49, 151; on Helen, 155, 157
Stoics, as allegorists, 194–96; natural allegoresis of, 195; moral allegoresis of, 195–96
stone/rock, 81, 88
structure/structuralism, 19–20, 36, 42, 43–50, 53, 54
succession/succession myth, 83–84, 87, 88–89, 90–94
surface structure, 35; vs. deep structure, 45, 47, 49
"survivals," 27, 28
symbol/symbolism, 12, 21, 32, 38, 47–48
sympathetic interpretation, 12, 18
Synoecia, 139
synoecism, 139
Syria, 76, 88, 92, 95

Tantalus, house of, 127–28
technology, 85, 151
Telemachus, 58
temenos, 104
temple, 78, 102; of Apollo at Delphi,

100–111; of Apollo on Delos, 103–4, 109; of Apollo of Athens, 113–14; of Zeus at Olympia, 119–20
Tethys, with Oceanus, as *genesis* of the gods, 87, 90–91
Thales, 97–98
Theagenes, 100, 185
Theban myths, 66, 76, 143, 155, 156
Theocritus, 176
Theogony of Dunnu, 93
Theogony. See Hesiod
theogony. See creation
Theon, 4
Theseid, 138
Theseus, 51, 53, 54; myths of, on Delos, 106, as *aitia*, 109; and ritual, 117; "raising the ox," 113–14; and Heraclids, 134; as Attic hero, 136–40; as civilizing agent, 137; as political innovator, 139–40
Thespis, 145
Thucydides, 2, 122–23; on Minos, 122; as "modern" compared with "naive" Herodotus, 122
thunder/thunderstorm/thunderbolt, 25, 81, 82, 83, 87, 92, 97
timai, 83, 84, 167
Titans, 63, 80; expelled by Zeus, 81–82, 85, 87, 89; soot of, as origin of mankind, 97, 167
tomb, 78, 107, 108, 109, 130, 147, 150, 164, 178
Tonaea, 112
totemism, 27
tradition/traditional nature of myth, 1, 2, 3, 61. *See also* oral poetry
tragedy, 2, 4, 61, 142–75; rare nonmythical themes of, 142; influenced by epic poetry, 142; definition of, 142–43; and cult of Dionysus, 143–45; origin of, 144–45; themes borrowed from choral lyric poetry, 145–52; form of, influenced by choral lyric poetry, 147; myths in choral songs of, 147; paradigmatic function of myths in, 147–48, 152; use of literary versions of myths in, 153; and humanization of mythical world, 153–54; gods and mortals in, 153–

54 (*see also* Aeschylus, *Oresteia*; Euripides; Sophocles); limited adaptation of myths in, 154–55; cultural relevance of, in scrutiny of values, 155–57; war in, 155–56; family in, 155, 156–57; as dramatizing single mythical episode, 162; stage action in, 162–63; dramatic irony in, 163; after Euripides, 176–77
transmission: of myths, 23–24, 26, 34; of dreams, 38; of archetypes, 38–39; of Near Eastern tales, 94–96; of narrative patterns, 94
trifonctionnalité, 43
Trojan horse, 30–31, 60, 73, 112
Trojan War, myths of, 57, 59–61, 78, 143, 155; historicity of, 70–73; and Helen, 146, 174, 181; justness of, 155–56
Troy, 30, 70–72, 73; mythical predecessors of, 126
Tylor, Edward Burnett, 27
Typhoeus/Typhon, 82–83, 84, 87, 89, 91–92, 141
typical scene, 59, 116

universality of myths. *See* myths
Uranus, 17, 80–81, 83, 87, 88, 89
Usener, Hermann, 27, 28, 44

values, 62; scrutiny of, 155–57; perversion of 175
vase painting, 76, 136, 141, 153, 200–201, 220n.1
Ventris, Michael, 69
Vernant, Jean-Pierre, 48, 55
Vickers, Brian, 141
Vico, Giambattista, 16, 17–18, 19, 33
victory song, 148–51
visual representations of myth, 119–20, 200–201; "language" and conventions of, 201, 220n.1
votive offering, as vehicle of myth, 120

wanax, 69–70
Welcker, Friedrich Gottlieb, 19
Wilamowitz-Moellendorff, Ulrich von, 19, 70, 210n.11
Winckelmann, Johann Joachim, 9

winds, 83, 84, 90, 92
woman, 82, 86
Works and Days. See Hesiod
written vs. oral myth, 3–4, 152–53, 154–55, 198
wuot, 74

Xenophanes, 169–70, 178–79

Zeno, 194

Zeus, 8, 17, 25, 50; plan of, 59, 62–63, 73, 78, 81–87 *passim;* marriages of, 83, 89, 91–92, 97, 100, 102, 103, 104, 126; statue of, 112; temple of, at Olympia, 119–20, 127, 135–36, 147, 149, 150, 158, 159, 160–61, 164, 167, 168, 169, 170, 177; tomb of, 178, 182, 186, 192; as *aithēr*, 195